AF316571

A Journey
with Charlotte

A Journey with Charlotte

The World of Multidisciplinary Artist Charlotte De Cock

LANNOO

Introduction

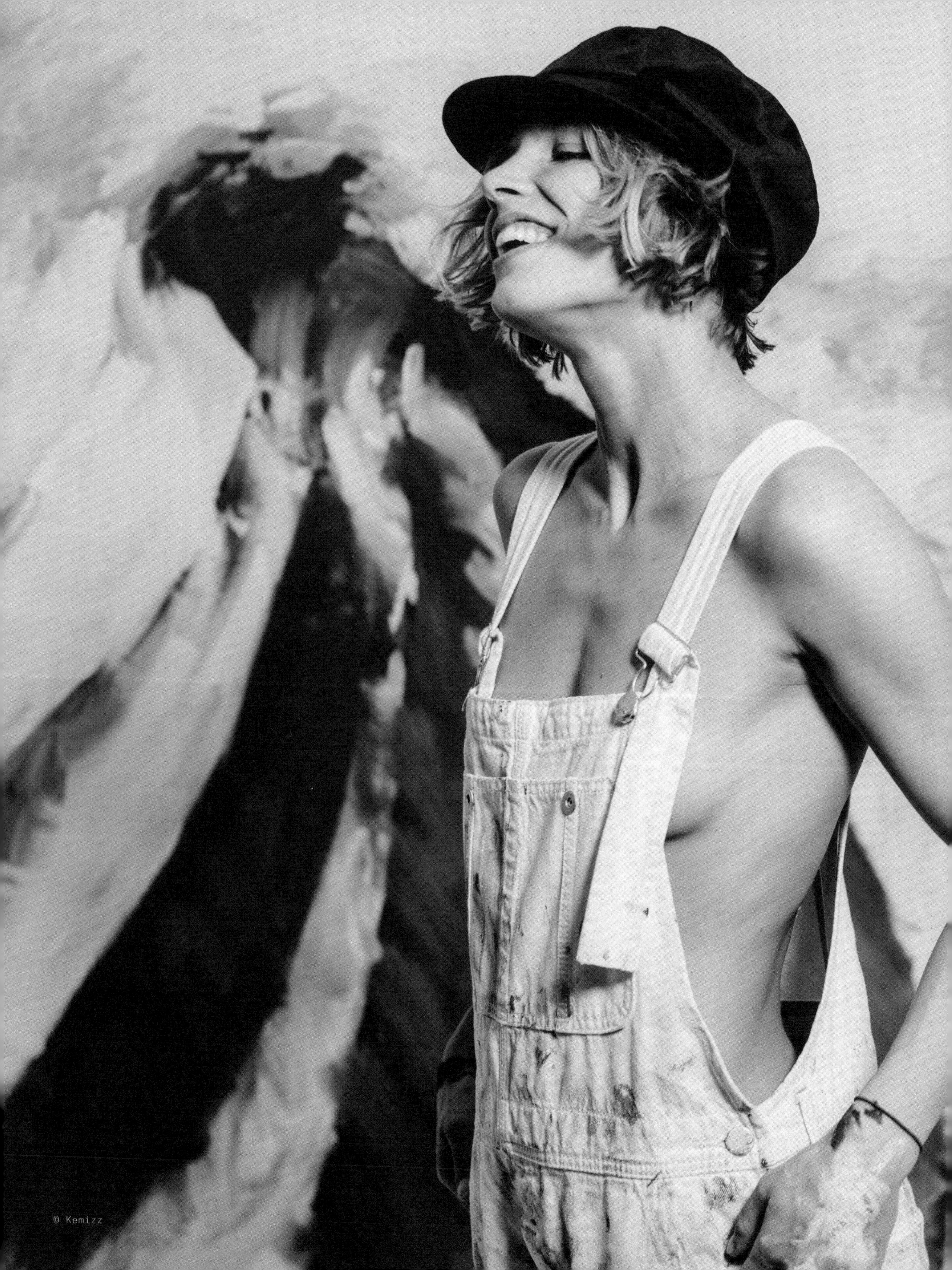
© Kemizz

Foreword

Stefan Ashkenazy

In a time when multi-hyphenated careers are commonplace and avant-garde movements have been smoothly co-opted by a process of commodification and commercialization, it is difficult to separate or tease out the actual threads of true creativity and grit. Where much of the art, music and entertainment worlds have combined and coalesced into a throbbing, teeming mass of pop culture, marketing, over-stimulation and over-consumption, Charlotte De Cock—painter, photographer, filmmaker, DJ and event producer —is a breath of fresh air.

Charlotte reminds me of an archaeologist. For starters, she documents a journey, a time and place, in nature. Using multiple media, she maps out a specific terrain, then painstakingly excavates it inch by inch, over years if necessary, obsessing over capturing a fleeting emotion, a spirit, for what it might reveal about our humanity. A second reason is simply that there is a great deal of dust and dirt in her work. Granted, her murals and portraiture are certainly not so dusty, but as a multi-hyphenated talent, one can be allowed some inconsistency.

In the current climate where social media reigns supreme, Charlotte's work raises questions about its place in the larger artistic world. When viewing both her body of work and her social media pages, one cannot help but to see them as commentary on the impact of our video age.

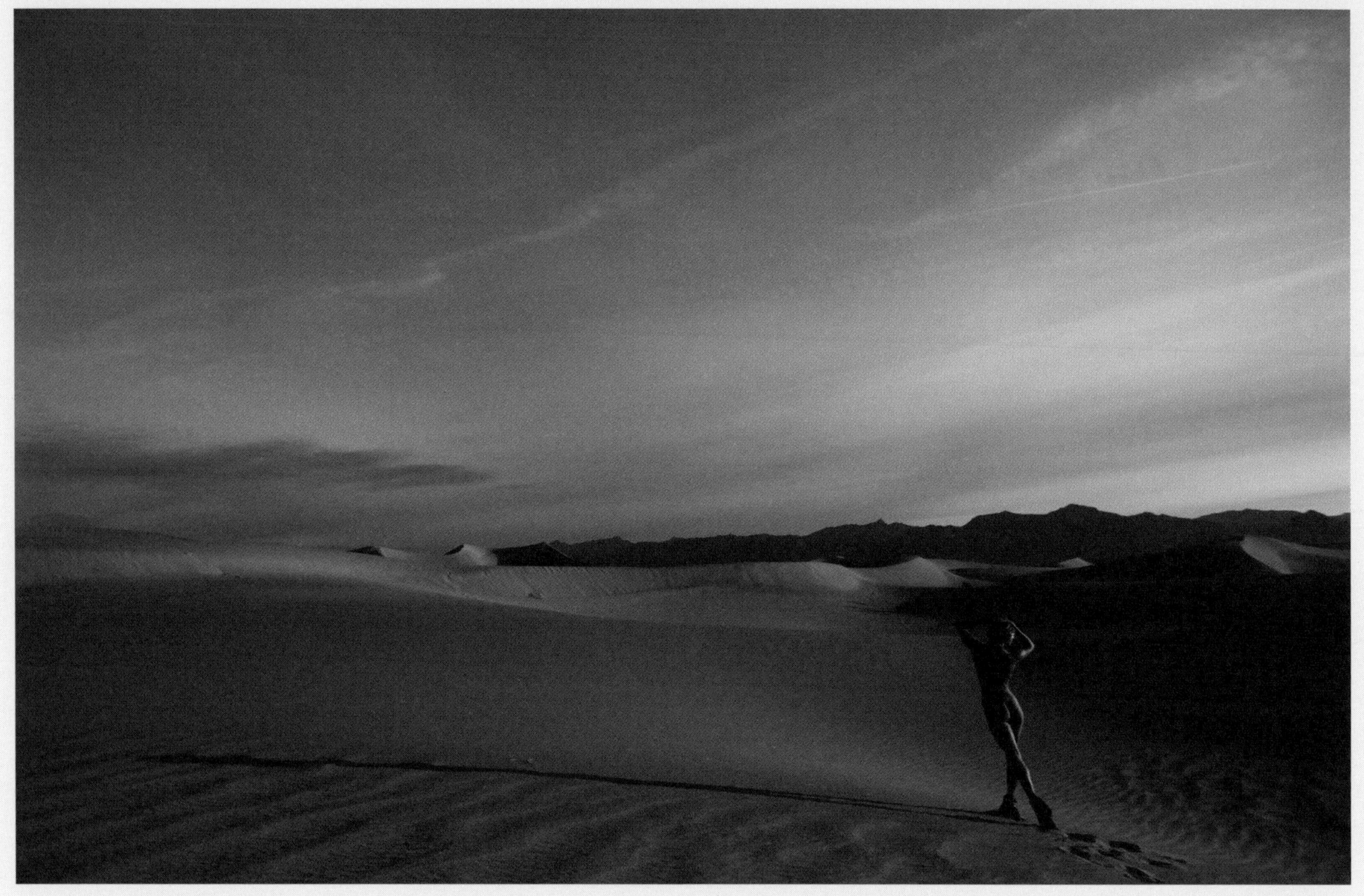

© Kris Lathouwers

 INTRODUCTION STEFAN ASHKENAZY

It is tempting to think of Charlotte as a contemporary shaman, opening a portal to our hazily remembered primal motivations; or to view her work as a testament to art's mystical power pitted against the combined forces of electronic media and mass consumption.

Either way, it is important to retain a sense of critical perspective. After the inevitable PR tour and shout from the proverbial social-media roof top, it is not necessary to exaggerate the value of the work in order to bestow upon it the quality of a miracle. One aspect of De Cock's content exists in particularly telling relation to her style and situation. This can be seen with her more recent visual work, in her self-studies, and also in her music and event producing.

At the 2016 Bombay Beach Biennale, a clandestine renegade art festival located in its namesake, I met Charlotte De Cock. She was making her wayacross California, documenting her journey through the deserts of the American West for part 2 of her *My California* series, and she just happened to stumble upon our event. I was immediately taken by how eager she was to get involved, and when we met again several months later, and I learned more about her multi-faceted approach to life and art, I was even more impressed that such a young person could be so driven and multi-talented.

Charlotte is a woman who has forged her own path for her whole life. As someone who started expressing herself creatively from as young an age as she can remember, Charlotte is one of those rare humans compelled to create in any possible form available to her. From her initial opulent, yet uninhibited, *Marie Antoinette* series inspired by director Sofia Coppola to her *La Chasse* series of lush landscapes and nostalgic hunting iconography to her *The Thirteen Masters*, which features portraits of Antwerp icons, her scope is both broad and nuanced.

Self-expression is key to Charlotte, who also models for her own portraits, yet she likewise uses her beauty and presence as a form of self-expression in itself. The painting aspect of this can be seen in both her *Self-Portraits* and *Feathers* series, and her physical being is also used through the media of photography and filmmaking, both in short and documentary form.

For her aforementioned *My California* series, which highlights her affinity for American literary iconoclasts from the Beat generation to the Gonzo journalism movement, she paints images based upon photographs she took during her journey across the American West. Many of those pictures are of off-the-grid people living in desert areas where they are free to live as they so desire. They do not exist within the normal societal structures—and yet Charlotte's work is still a vision of privileged access. She is an outsider whose gift is none other than observation. She observes the desert. She observes her subjects. There is, inevitably, some poignancy about the way her paintings convey a time and a place as a result of her photographic work.

This observational gift and power also shine through in Charlotte's music project: DAOUD. Much like her personal odyssey through the California deserts, DAOUD explores new experiences and places with an air of universal longing. Her music speaks to the awakened generation and enlightens the spirit.

In addition to visual arts and music, Charlotte is an organizer of the Barefoot Festival in Antwerp, which has grown exponentially in the last few years. It is a festival focusing upon music, self-expression and love, and it is a positive gathering of people that uses the event platform as a catalyst for social change. As a fellow artist who creates experiences and communities for a living, it is refreshing and vital to see this environmentally and spiritually conscious approach to the event world in practice.

It is an inspiration to see an artist generating such interesting and high-calibre content across so many forms of media. Hopefully this book showcases at least some of the vast talent of this remarkably fearless, thoughtful, and vibrant artist, whom I know we shall see, hear, and experience a great deal more from in years to come.

Stefan Ashkenazy is owner of the Petit Ermitage Hotel in Hollywood, founder of the Cirque Gitane Member's club, a private community comprised of dreamers from all over the globe who create for a living and who support the creative arts, and is co-founder of the Bombay Beach Biennale.

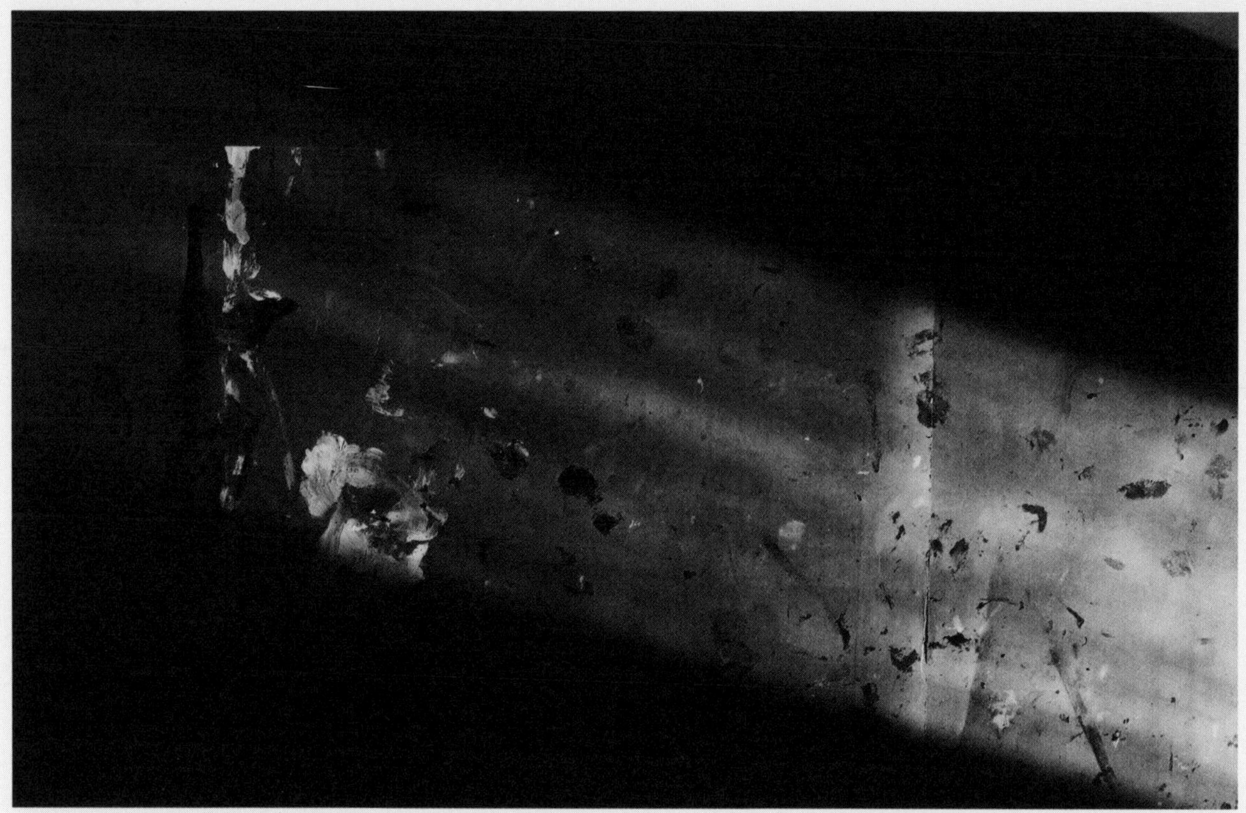

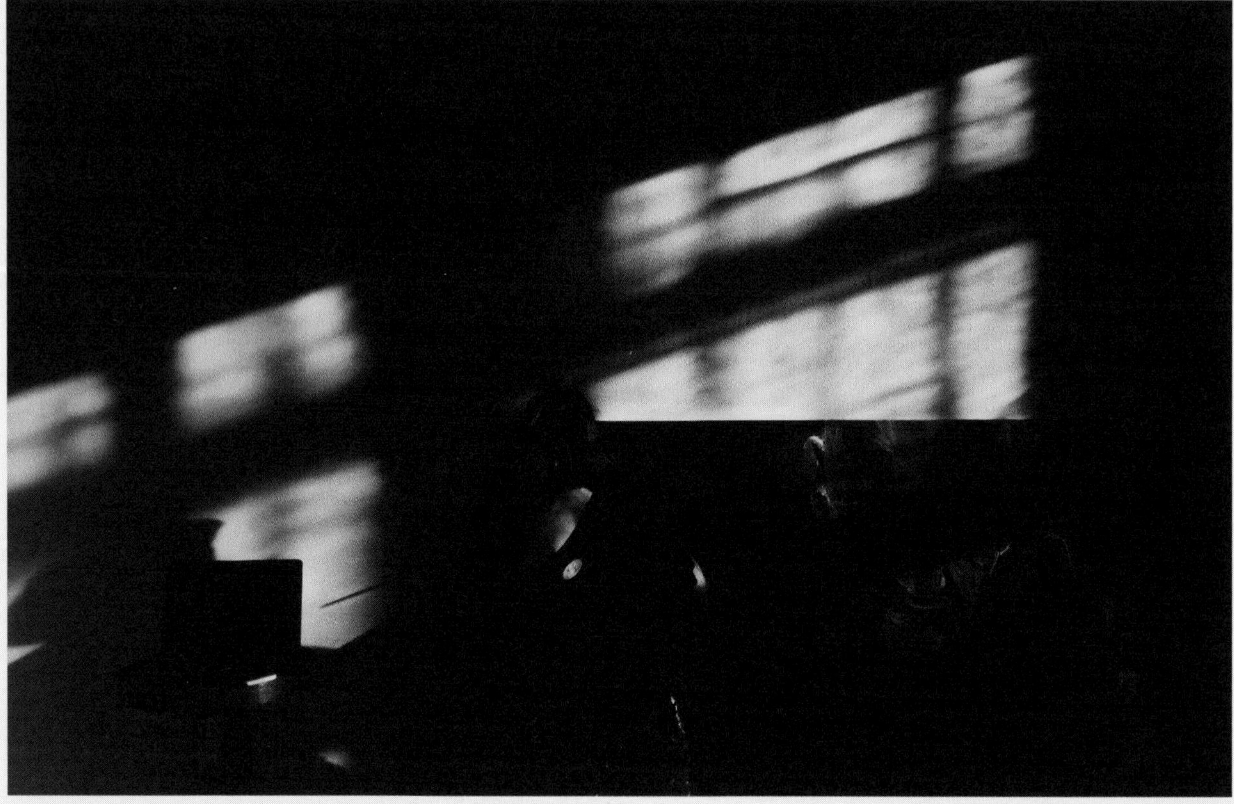

© Kris Lathouwers

INTRODUCTION

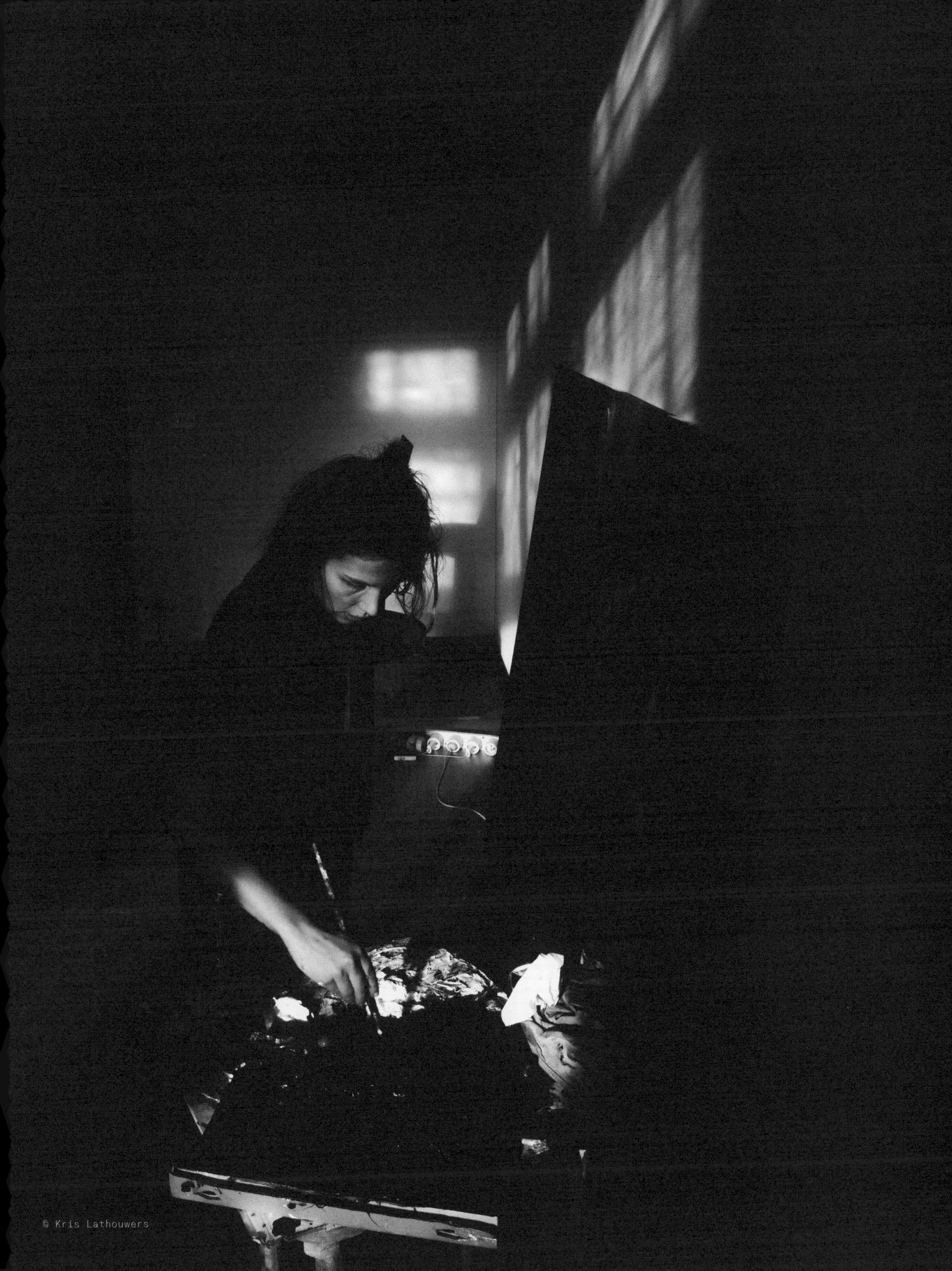
© Kris Lathouwers

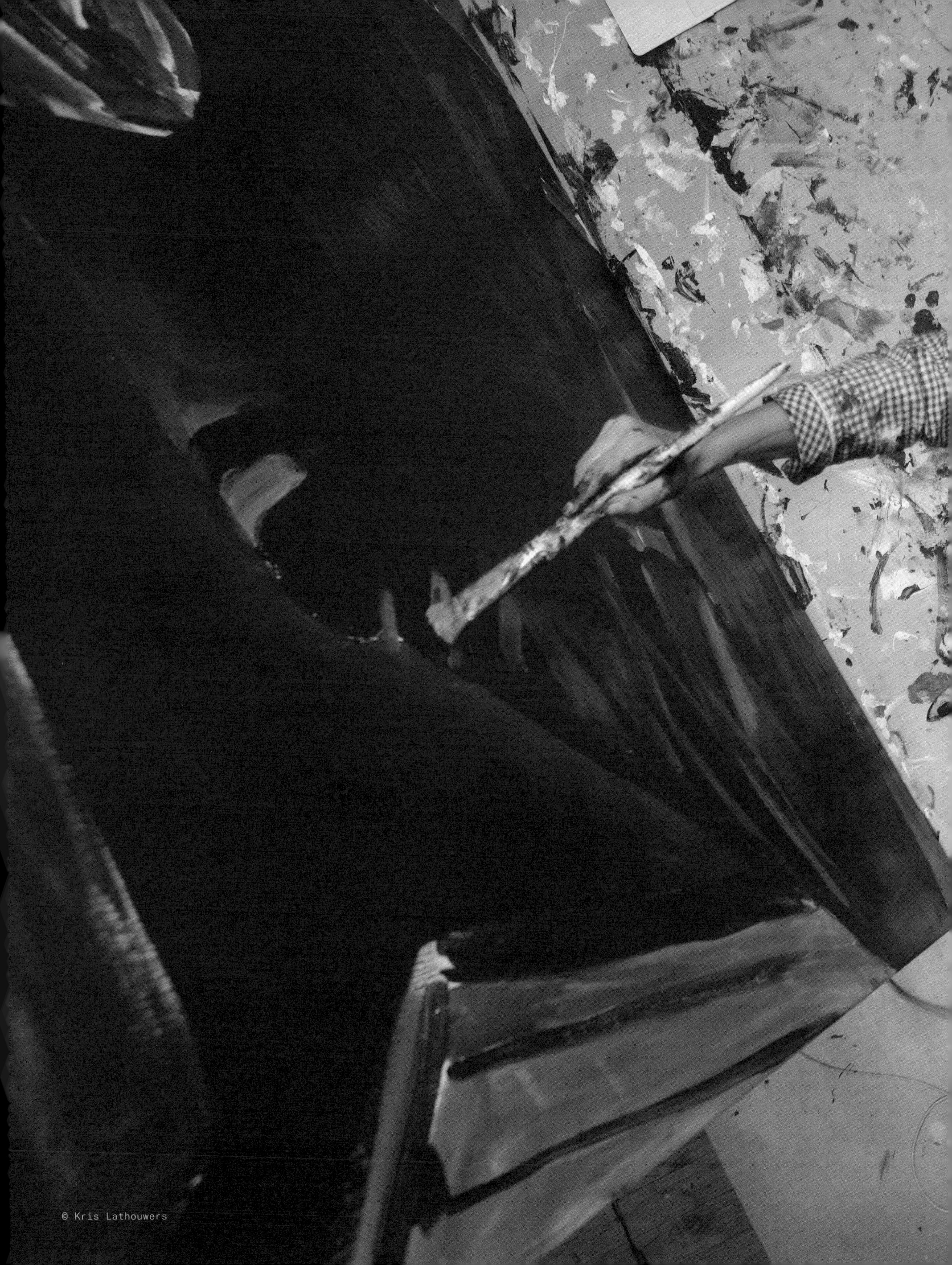
© Kris Lathouwers

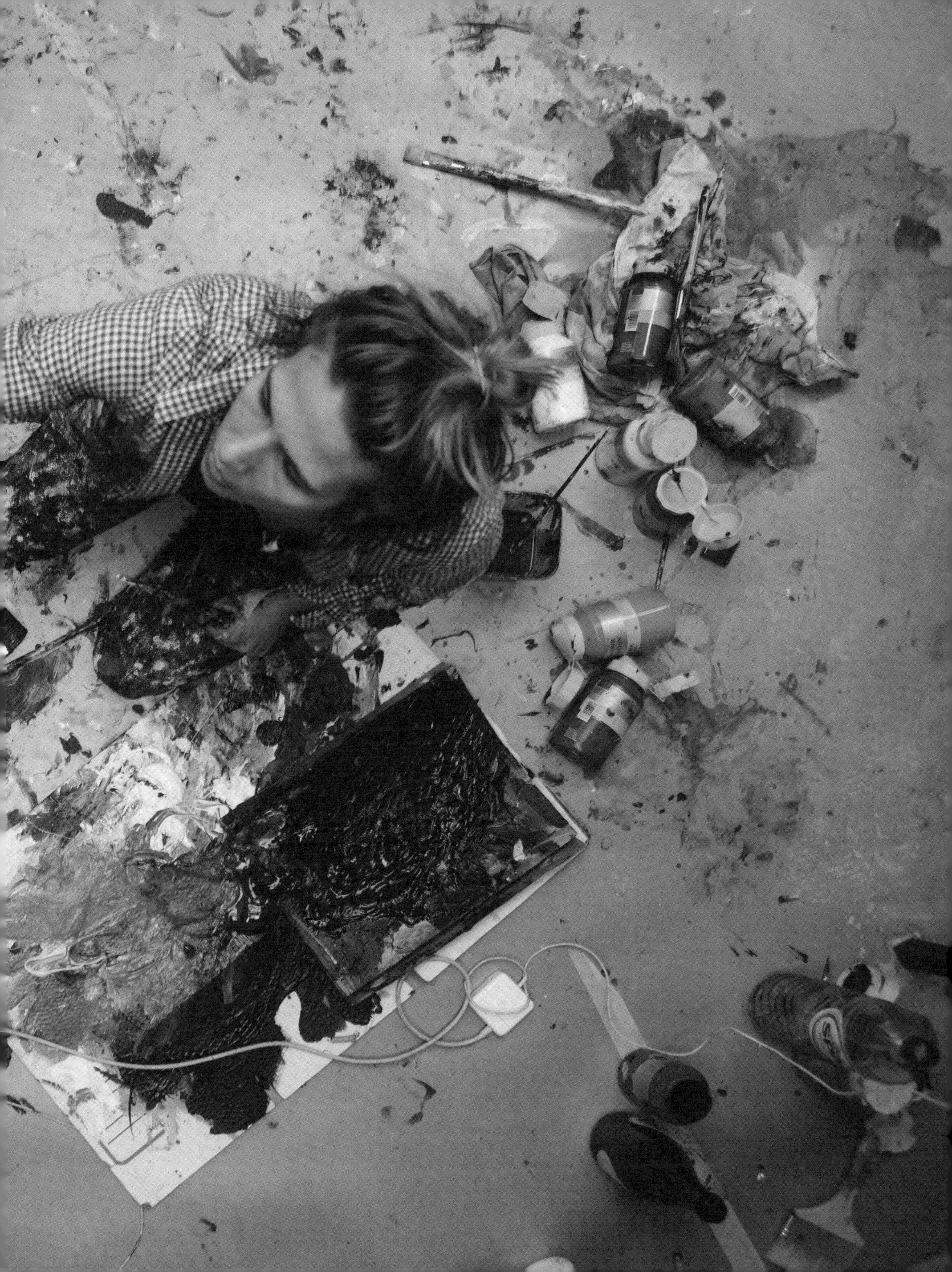

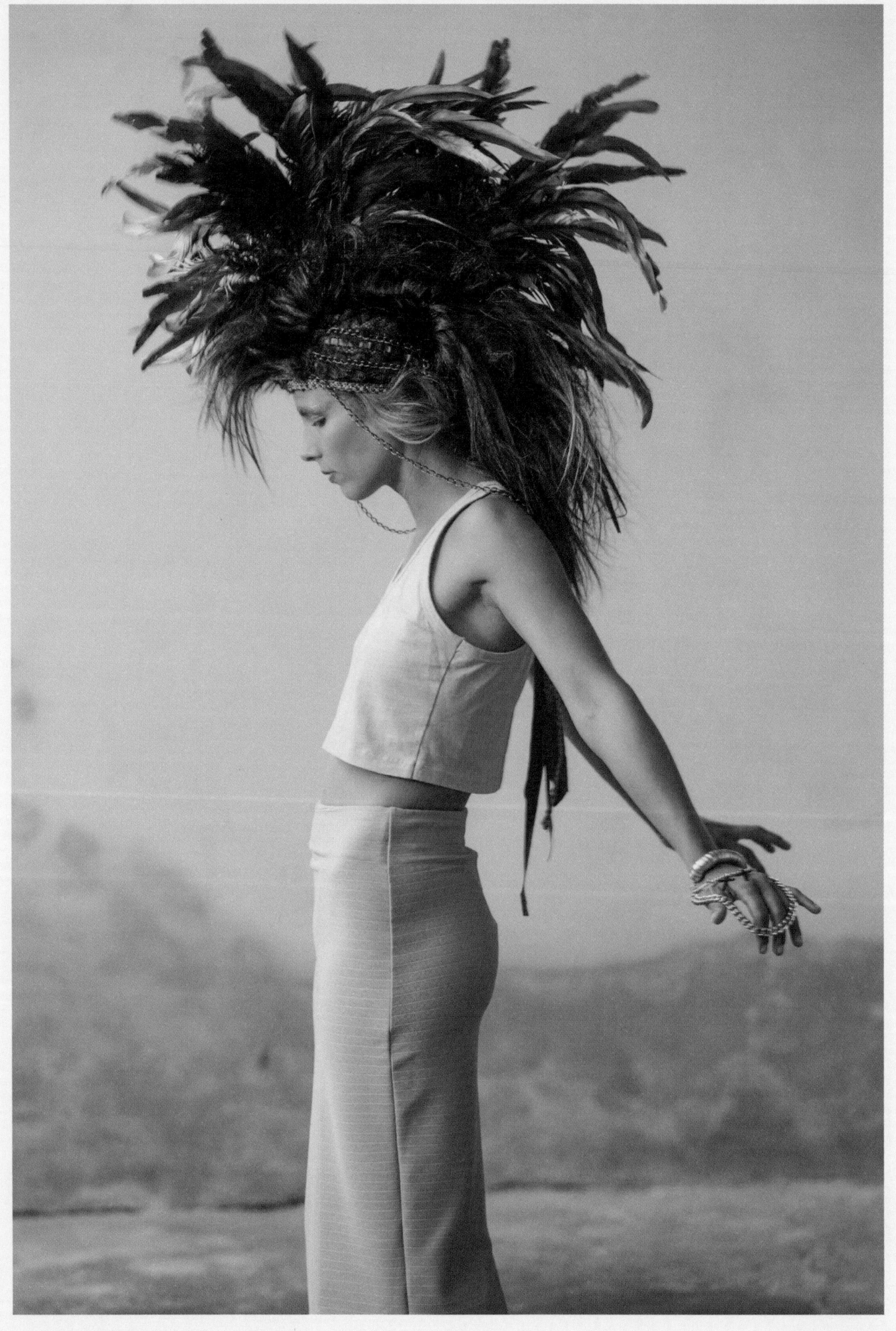

© Mike Steegmans

    INTRODUCTION

Rhapsody in White: Exploring the World of Charlotte De Cock

Léon Lemahieu

To capture the true essence of an artist, be
it a painter, a photographer, a dancer, a music-
maker, or any other, isn't a sinecure; however,
to capture the heart of the matter of a multidisciplinary, jack-of-all-(these) trades such as
Charlotte De Cock, seems to be a daunting task.
Still, by observing closely what she has observed
closely, accompanying her on her journeys, following her in her tracks over mountain, plain
and valley, listening to her music, attending
her performances, festivals and appearances,
and viewing her road-trip movies, the story of
Charlotte De Cock starts to tell itself.

Her first appearance upon the artistic scene was
in 2009 in the Frank Van Laere Gallery in Antwerp
with a series of Marie Antoinette paintings. The
showing was an instant breakthrough, with Martin
Schmidt from Gallery DiMeo in Paris calling her
style "Rock Baroque".

Her personal breakthrough came during a trip
to the Southwest of the USA. Overwhelmed by its
nature and captured by "the beauty and expres-
siveness of the Native American culture", she
started to paint several new series expressing
her devotion to this artistically adopted homeland
and its different cultures and countercultures.

At the same time, the urge for expressing herself in other artistic ways manifested itself,
resulting in photo shoots, musical festivals and
composing music herself, thematic events, performances, modeling, exploring voyages documented by
a traveling companion or on her own.

Witnessing all these facets of artistic talents,
witnessing her amazing outbursts of energy, one
realizes that she is a natural *multi-taskforce*
working directly from a necessity, an urgency
to express herself in so many different ways, a
versatility that challenges the public, knowing
that the career of many an artist flopped pre-
cisely because of switching styles, a move rather
not appreciated by the public, often limiting
an artist to one style or discipline.

However, that is her force, her signature.
Her capriciousness is the source of her creative
energy. It is not a question of *wanting* to do
this or that, but of *having* to do it; and, moreover, not of having to do this or that, but of
having to do them all. *It is a must, a necessity.*
The sum of all these activities forms her palette, a palette that changes constantly with
time—time being a constant element in her work
—a growing spectrum of artistic activities to
satisfy the needs of a quicksilver mind and body.

Yet the heart of her artistic personality lies
in her paintings.

 INTRODUCTION

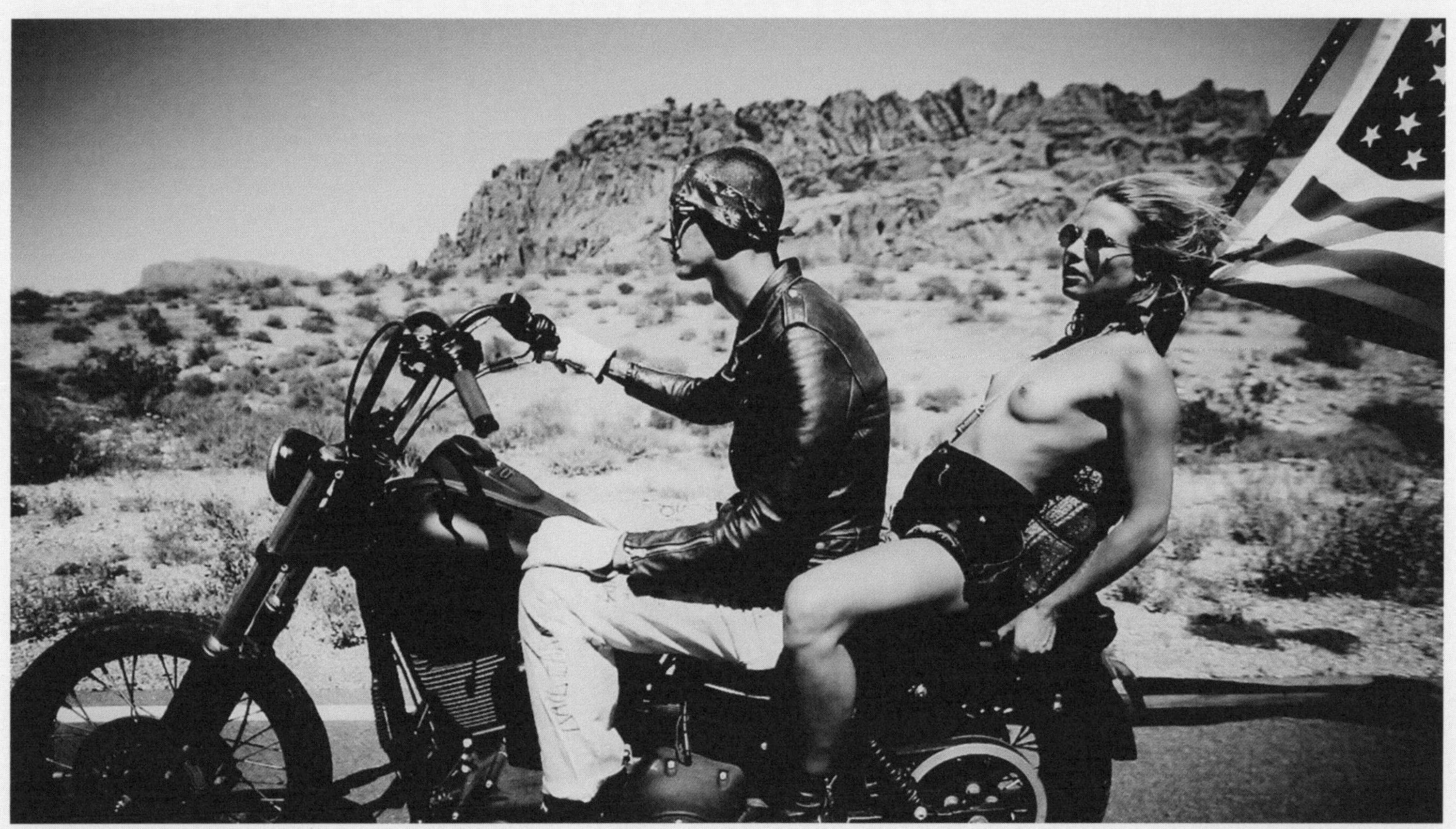

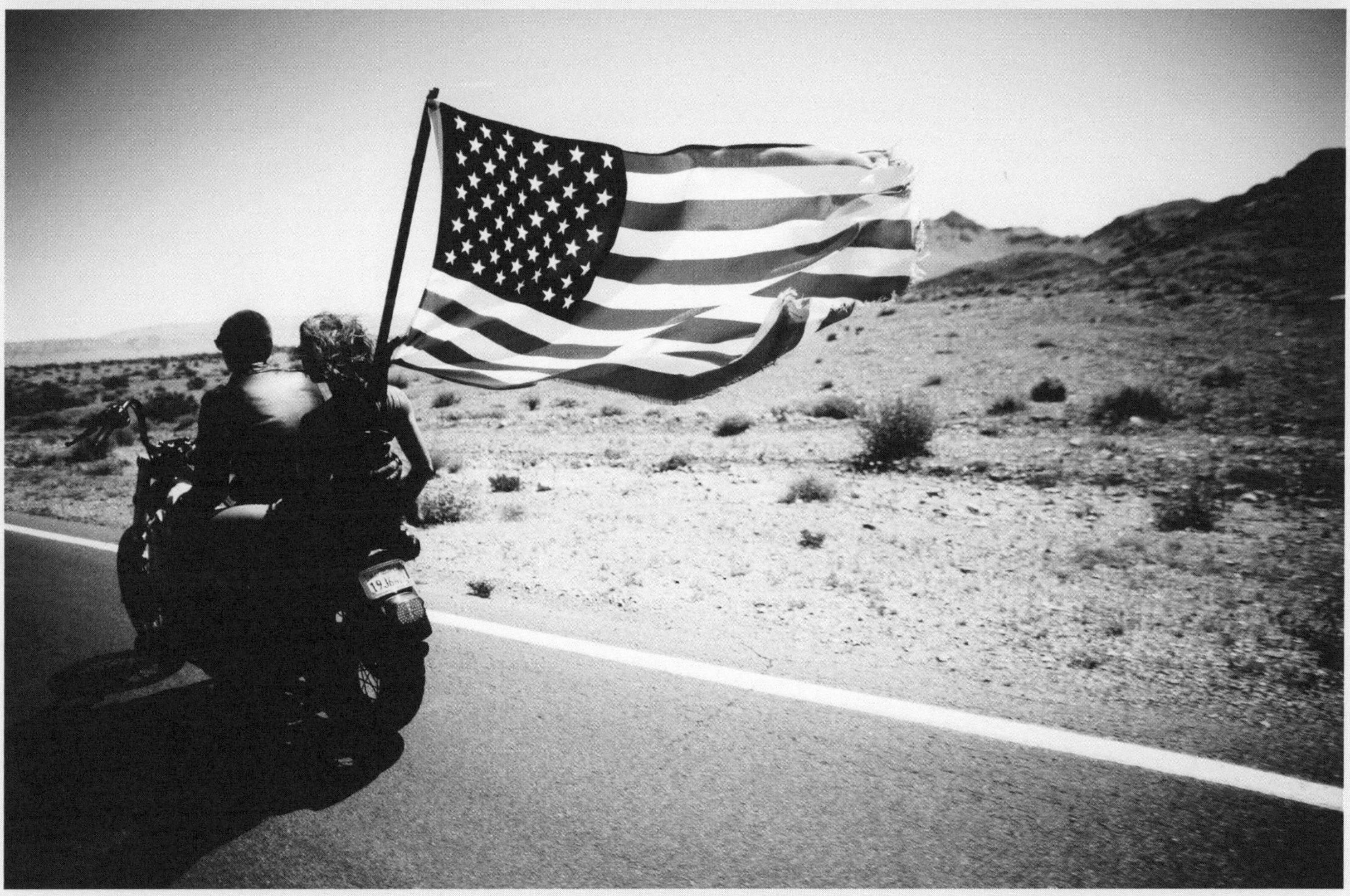

© Kris Lathouwers

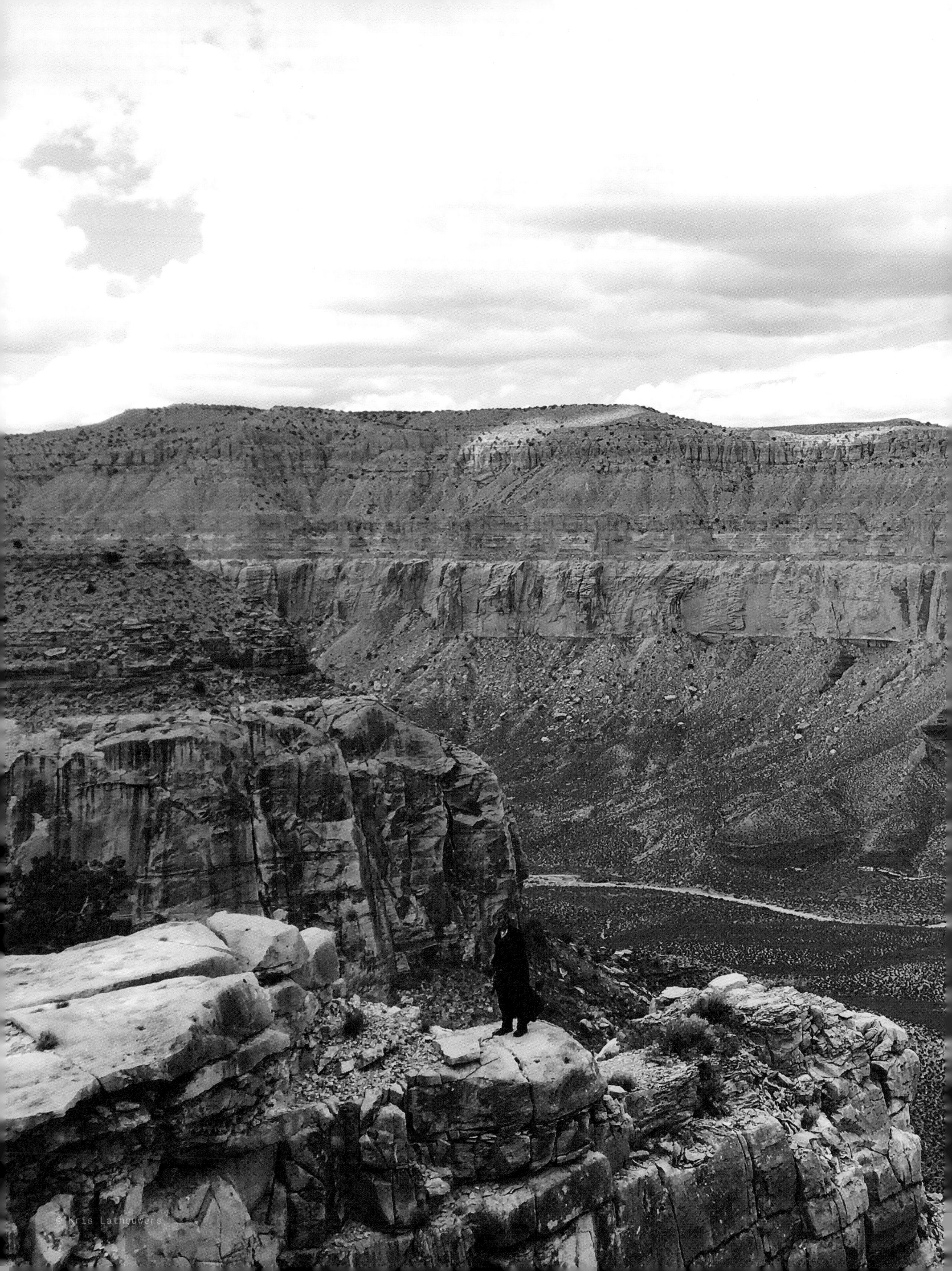

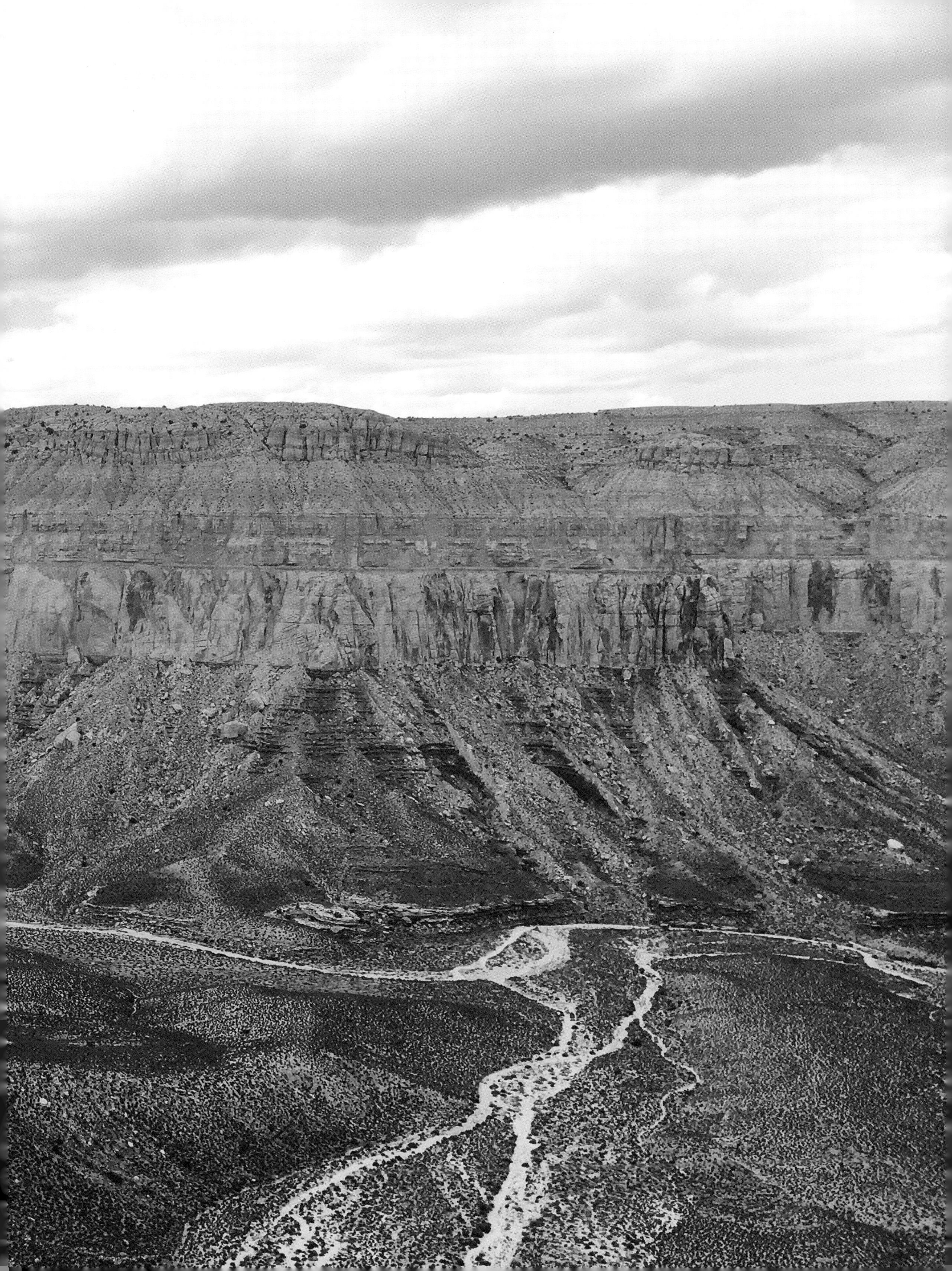

Early Work

Three series of paintings, called respectively *Marie Antoinette*, *La Chasse* and *Native Americans*, form what Charlotte De Cock calls her early work.

In these canvases, her *exercises de style*, often painted in a searching manner, but wherein the joy of painting is clearly visible; and, of which Charlotte claims to have nothing specific to say, several revealing aspects of her style and painterly technique, and the development of it, can be disclosed nevertheless.

In the first series, *Marie Antoinette*, all of these compositions are painted from existing images, stills from the eponymous movie made by Sofia Coppola.

Unlike in the cycle *Native Americans*, where she literally embodies her subject, posing as an American Indian herself, in the Marie Antoinette paintings she sticks to the image, however puts so much of herself in the painterly execution of it, that we can easily recognize them as camouflaged self-portraits, though the persons portrayed are actual actresses.

Marie Antoinette, an outsider at the last royal court of France, on the verge of revolution, a highly contested figure, a charming young lady, elegant, controversial in taste and manner, obsessed by fashion, trendsetting, fierce, humane, joyous, vain, lonesome, closed, enterprising yet naive; the towering, pre-surrealistic wigs; the fancy dresses and smart furniture; the sparkling jewelry and chandeliers; the gastronomic excesses; the atmosphere of permanent partying, ….

It isn't hard to see why these tableaux, filmed and interpreted by Coppola that is, in a rather romantic style, were so attractive to a young, burgeoning painter. Moreover, she paints them with great gusto, in a soft, cheerful palette, suiting the atmosphere of the court, in exuberant, ever so soft colors, the sweet, tasty, appetizing colors of the good life, of delicious food and wines, gastronomic voluptuous tableaux, where sex is a dessert; in courtly colors rich with smells, saturated with every shade of pleasure. They are funny and amusing, a pleasure for the eye.

However, it is the use of her whites that catches the eye. And with this white, the perception of change, a change of mood, a certain darkening of the mood, the more intriguing because she expresses that darkening with the use of white, of light—a first hint of her controversial nature….

I will focus upon one particular painting. In it we see Marie Antoinette, spread out in the grass, in a moment of absolute happiness, a real *Splendour in the Grass*, a lively illustration of William Wordsworth's poem ("…Thou Child of Joy") unaware of any treacherous intrigue or revolt, lying amidst a bed of white flowers, saturated with happiness, a happiness so exuberant, so filled with beatitude yet tied to eros, which is explicitly an erotic happiness, and which is undoubtedly the purest form of happiness there is, contrary to what the diabolic nonsense of the puritans want us, want her to believe, that it seems like if these little flowers are sparkling bubbles, bubbles of pure, uncontaminated joy.

A fountain of joy through the fountain of light through a fountain of white….No clue to her cruel end, everything in the scenery is lovely, no words of excuse, yet, for having stepped on the headsman's foot.

To have painted this in her newly required vigorous white makes the composition, and the joy expressed in it, all the more lusty and genuine. I suspect she painted it from and with the same energetic joy as is expressed in *Marie Antoinette*. Charlotte Antoinette.

From now on—and I don't allude to her episodes when literally living in castles, giving grand feasts—she is Marie Antoinette on her way to become Charlotte, the Queen.

With the *La Chasse* series, also painted from existing images, Charlotte continues to explore the possibilities of the use of white.

In *Come Back Darling* (100 x 70 cm, 2014), a smartly dressed hunter (Wellington boots, white jodhpurs, red jacket, cap) on a white horse enters the wood, surrounded by a pack of white-and-brown dogs, their tails in the air. The trees are dark, a dense, dark wood consisting of hardly elaborated, roughly painted bare trunks. There is a turning track surrounded by greenery and withered leaves; the scenery is quiet, though filled with life. The life is in the dogs, sniffing for game, but still packed together, in the muscled bum of the horse, and in the back of the disciplined, erect rider. Man, horse and dogs form a triangle of flesh, of lively, human and beastly muscles, bursting with energy, with dynamism, but perfectly in control, perfectly calm. Everything in this painting is vertical, erect: the trees, the man, the horse, the dogs and their tails. It is the beginning of the hunt.

In a similar painting, *240Yearsbeforeyourtime* (100x100 cm, 2014), set in a magnificent snowy landscape, a nobleman on his horse returns from a hunt, dressed in a sharp, red jacket, quietly seated on a quietly stepping brown horse, his dogs freely running around, no less relaxed than man and horse. There is no tension or nervousness whatsoever related to a hunt.

A majority of the painting is white, but it is of such a rich variety of white, what I call her "shades of white" that it gives this utterly quiet, utterly white landscape a tension and nervousness nevertheless. The trick, perhaps, lies in the variety of forms, the perspective, in the depths. You have the road that turns into the forest, with a clear cart track; the snow-clad leaves left of the road, like a shrubbery of white gloves with the fingers down; the snow-clad pine trees on the right have a totally different, flatter pattern than the leaves on the left, finer and denser, a more solid foliage; then there are the branches, filling the upper part of the painting, and although a lot of them must be dead branches, their freakish shapes and sharp ends, pointed to each other like swords, give the

composition tension; then there is the white,
the light at the end of the road, like a mist,
a misty future. This is the end of the hunt.

Game: the very word, already, indicating that
for these upper-class folks not only to hunt is
a game, but the prey itself, the poor persecuted
animal, is (a) game; and killing became a
ritualized sport, where one is neatly and
properly dressed up, like soldiers, especially
the soldiers in Maria Antoinette's time, in
finely tailored costumes, well-groomed men fit
for the kill—a game indeed.

In another, utterly charming composition,
we see a fox—the game—looking in surprise,
perhaps challenging the approaching horseman,
who is aiming to shoot it. Again, the setting
is an overwhelmingly serene winter landscape,
consisting of bare, snow-clad trees, giving no
shelter to the poor, hunted fox. Yet, there seems
to be no threat, mainly because of the white
branches, radiating peace.

In these early compositions, already, nature
is overwhelming, breathing freedom or the cry
for it, something she will further refine in
her *Journeys* and American landscapes, and
anticipating her events and festivals, such
as the Barefoot festival.

In her *Native Americans*, or *Feathers*-series,
Charlotte, painting herself as a Native American,
becoming that chief, even when depicted in
provocative, erotic poses, as in that diptych
where she re-doubles herself in one, elegant
movement from one canvas to the other, she
handles her whites in an almost sculptural way.

Where, in the beginning, these whites contain
little softening specks of color, as in the
Marie Antoinette paintings (still full of courtly
smells from lying in between silken bed sheets),
with the nature of the subject changing, slowly
these colored specks disappear, and the white
becomes a pure, hard, unsophisticated, militant
white, requiring a harsher style of painting,
a tougher kind of brush technique, this palette
and technique better fitting her new subjects.

The use of white, of light, of blinding white
light. Perhaps it happened by accident, whilst
depicting these stills from the movie: the white
dresses and white, powdered wigs and faces;
or whilst painting the white dogs following a

white horse, or the white *fleur-de-lis* in the
field, the little white sheep, the snow on tree-
branches, or the Indian feathers.

There is, of course, a long tradition, in the
Low Countries (The Netherlands and Flanders),
to which she belongs, of painters of light, of
painters of white. Contrarily to what one may
think, the intensity of the light, in The Low
Countries, on a normal clear day, is harder,
fiercer, than in for instance California or
Nevada, on a very sunny day, under a burning hot
sun. The reason for that is quite simple: because
there is so much water in The Low Countries,
nearly every place borders on water, the air is
permanently saturated with very fine particles
of water, like water-dust, reflecting the light,
spreading the light, even with a weak sun, in a
kind of turbo-charged way, spreading it all over
the picture. That kind of light, very specific
for The Low Countries, is unique. Films have been
made about this phenomenon.

All the seventeenth-century painters knew about
this phenomenon. There is another De Cock from
Antwerp, a sixteenth-century painter, who knew
already how to apply this light, this white.
Charlotte discovered it whilst painting her
early work. Her artistic roots are there.
Le tout Charlotte est là, déjà!
(LÉON LEMAHIEU)

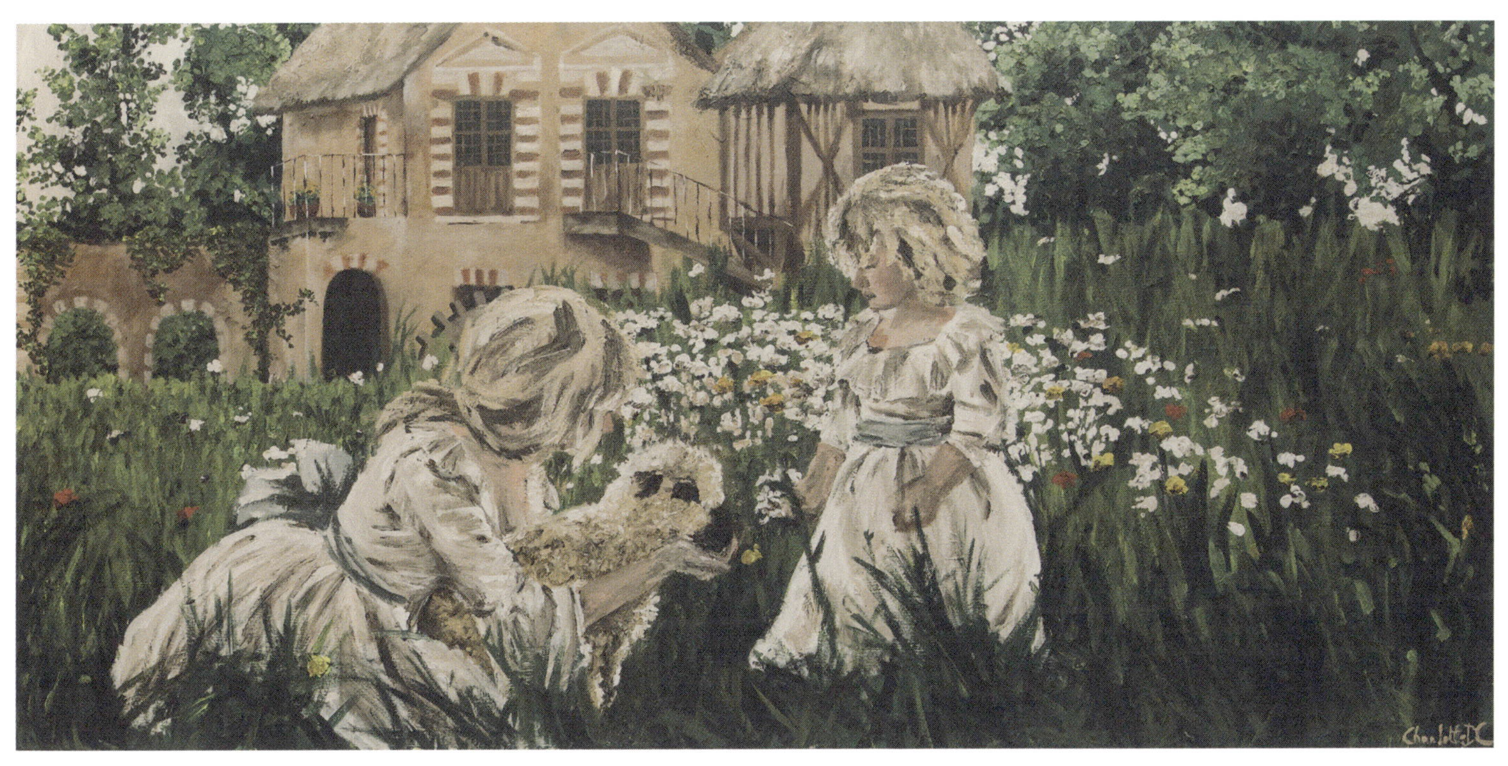

My Black Sheep, Marie Antoinette series,
100 x 200 cm, 2009

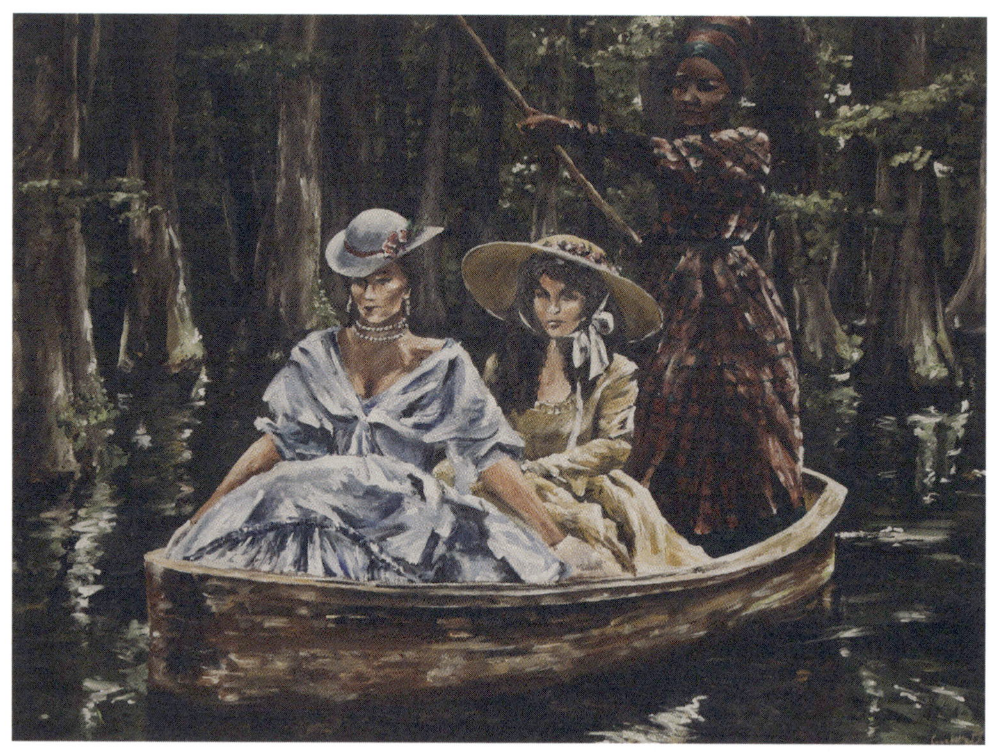

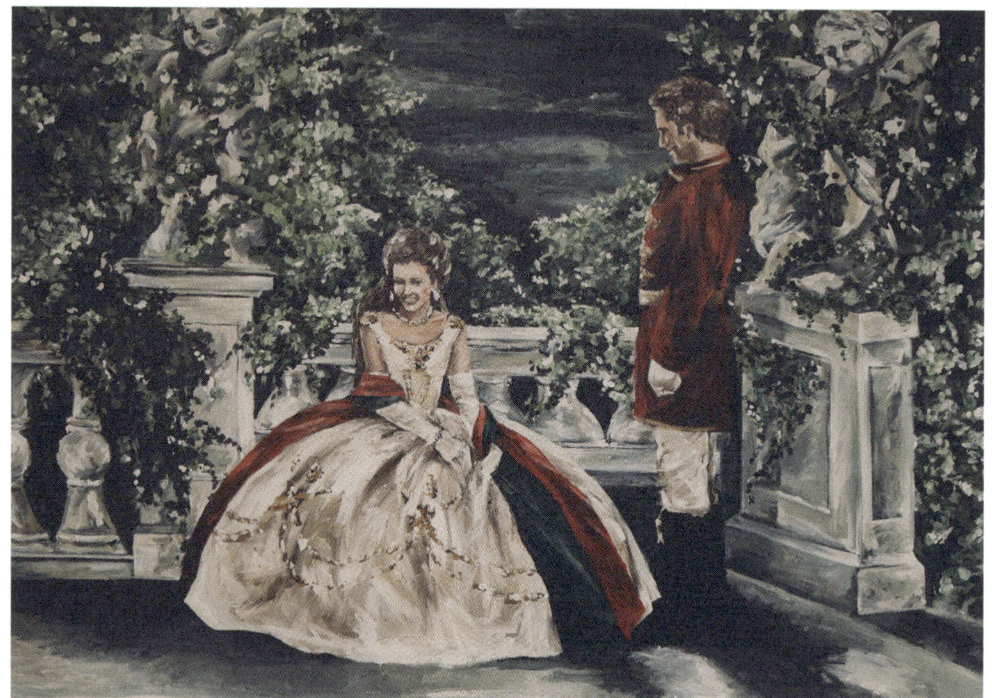

Going Home, Marie Antoinette series,
200 x 150 cm, 2009

There Is No One like You, Marie Antoinette
series, 200 x 150 cm, 2009

1. EARLY WORK

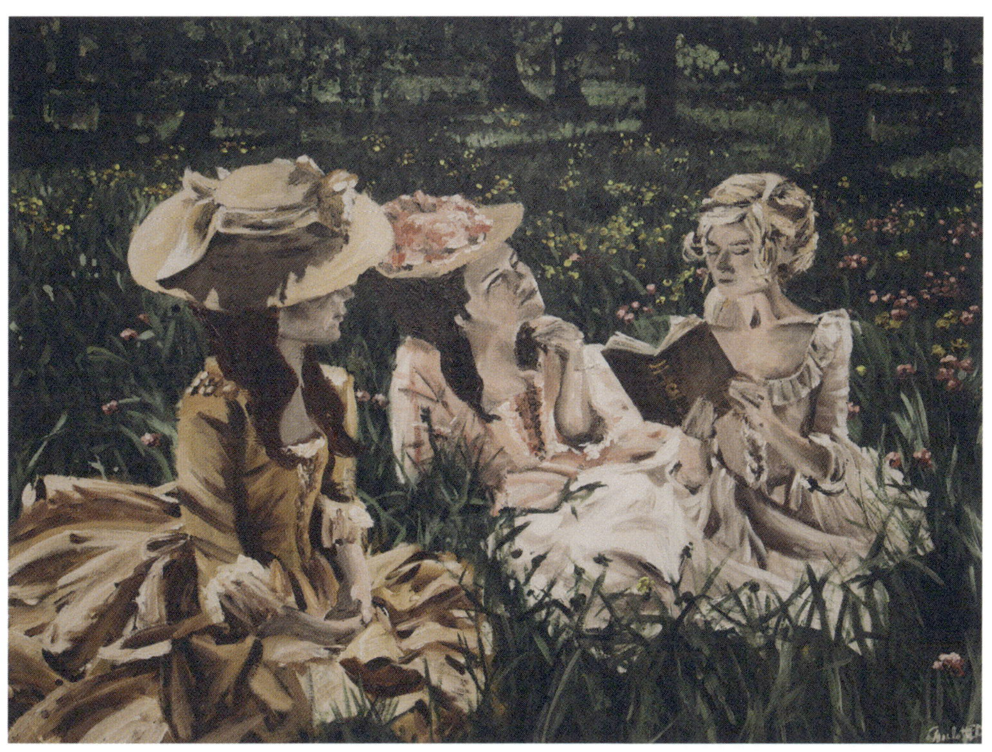

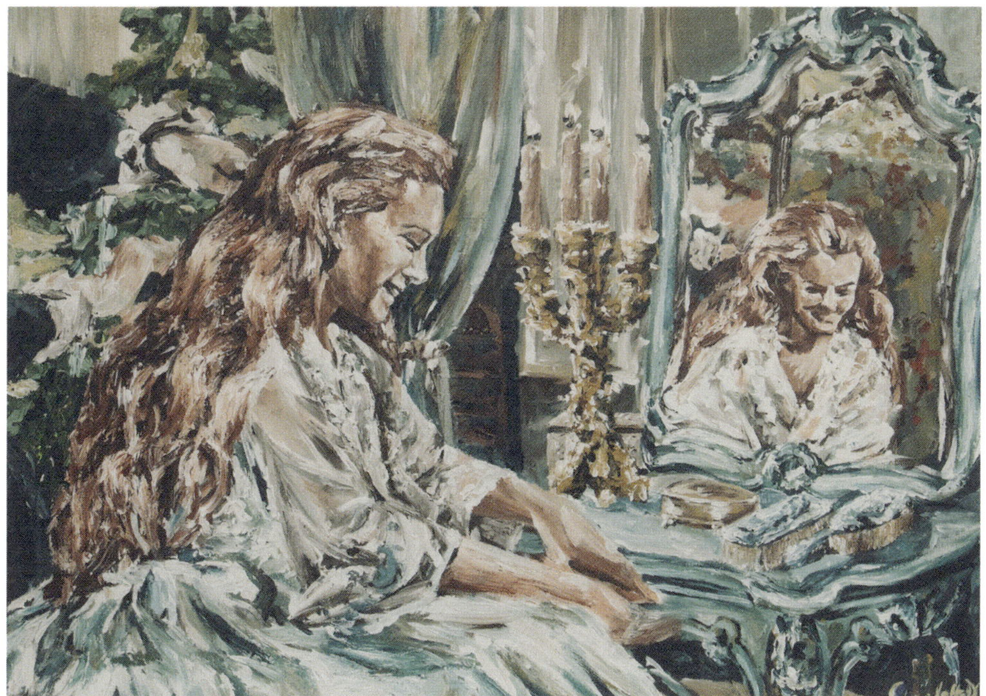

This Could Be so Beautiful, Marie
Antoinette series, 200 x 150 cm, 2009

Angel Baby, Marie Antoinette series,
100 x 80 cm, 2009

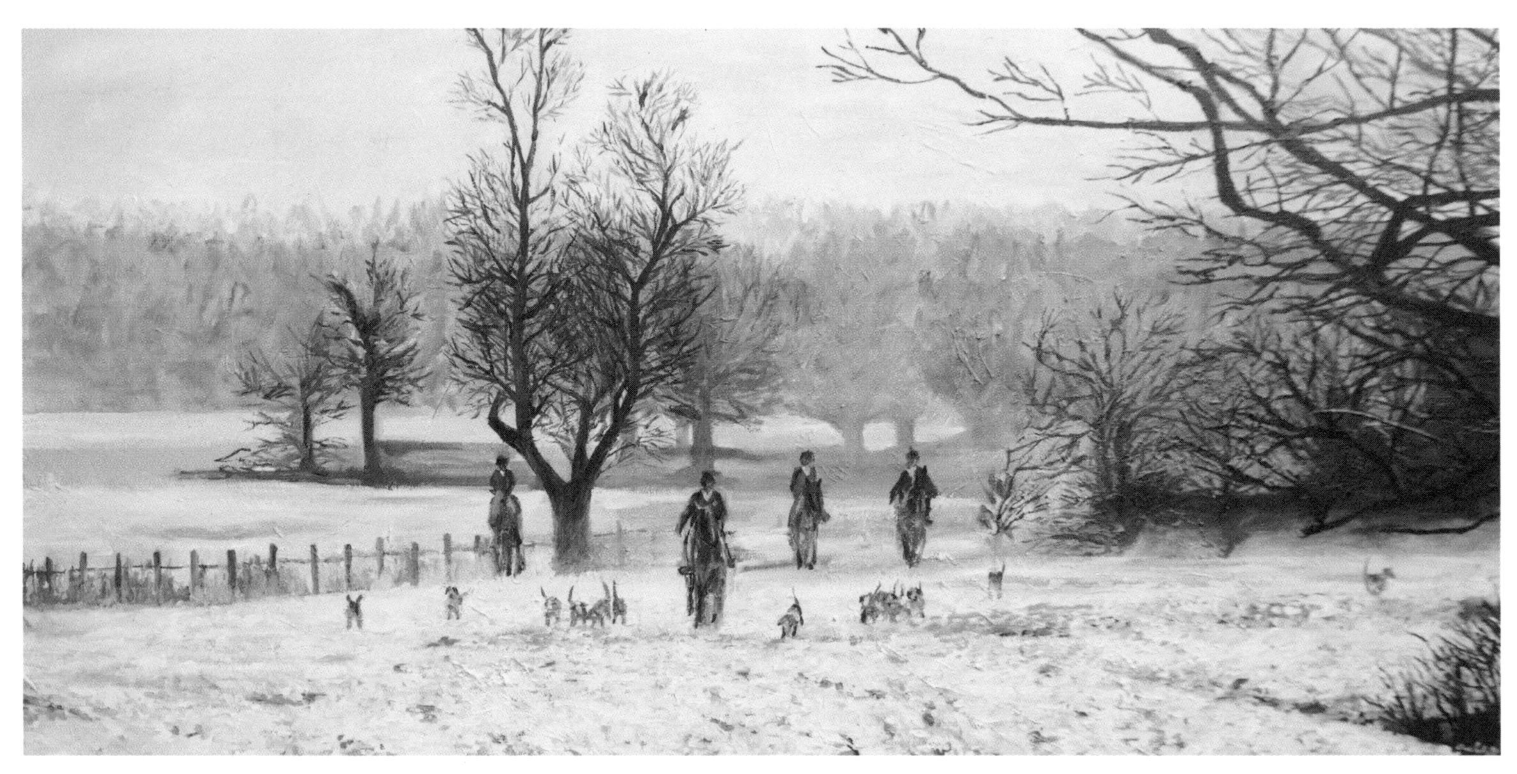

Sultans of Swing, La Chasse series, acrylic
on canvas, 200 x 100 cm, 2010

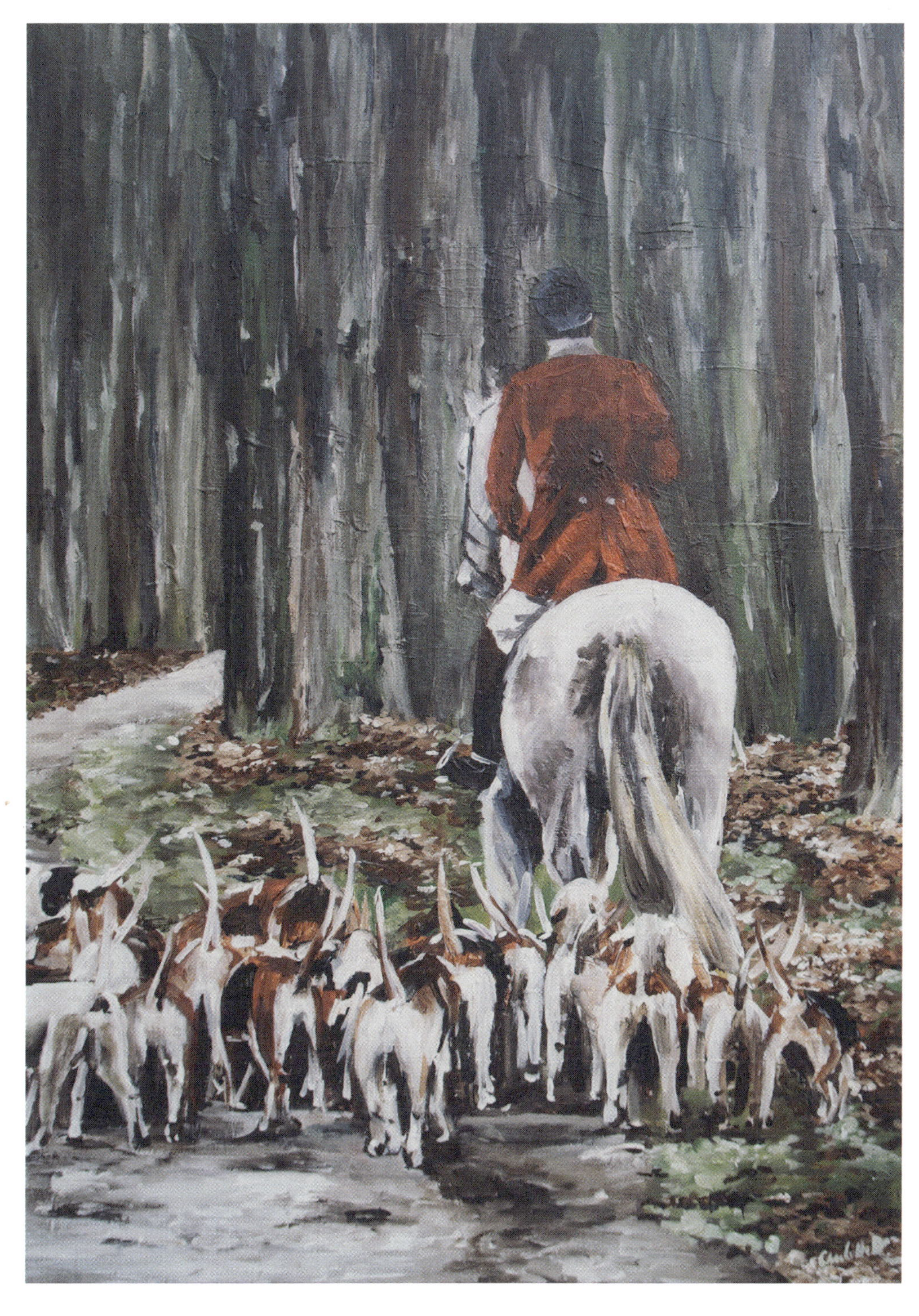

240 Years before your Time,
La Chasse series, acrylic on canvas,
100 x 80 cm, 2011

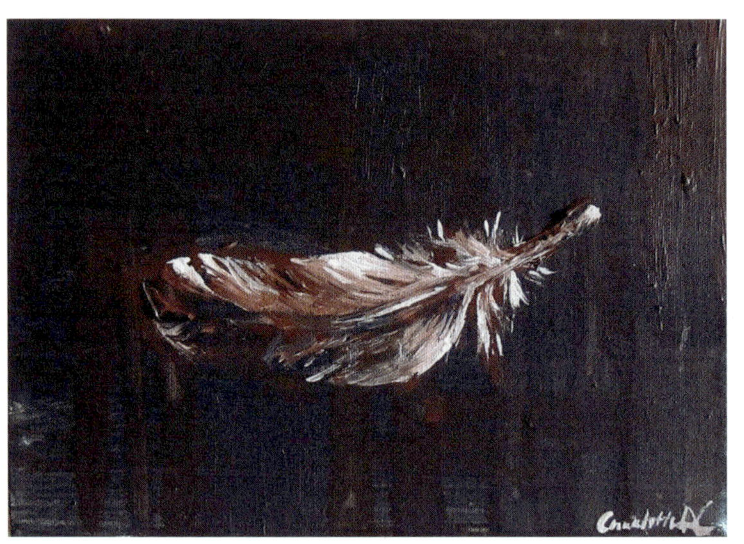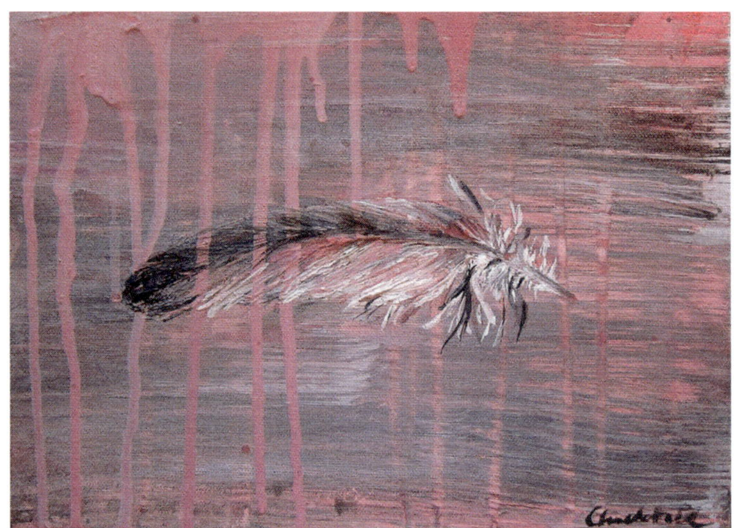

1. EARLY WORK

LEFT *Baby*, Feathers series,
acrylic on canvas, 30 x 20 cm, 2013

RIGHT *Love*, Feathers series,
acrylic on canvas, 30 x 20 cm, 2013

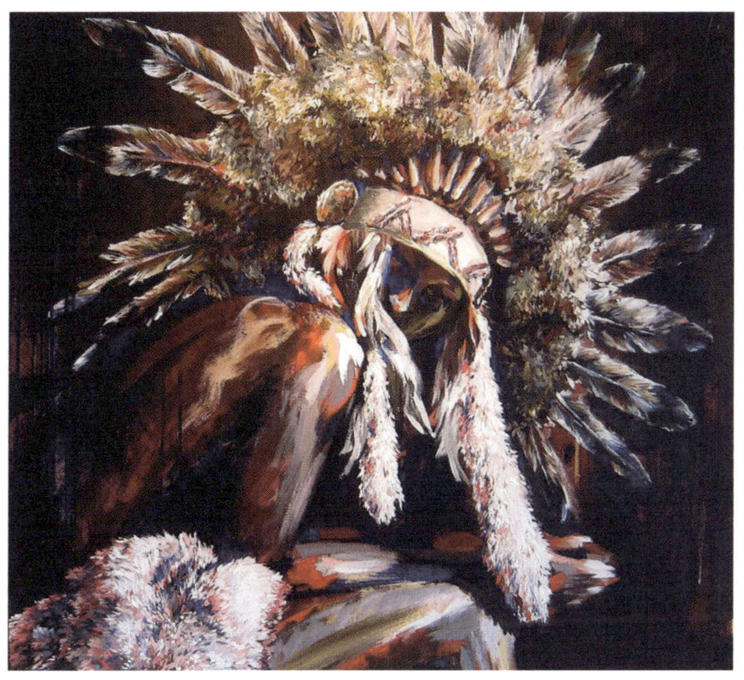 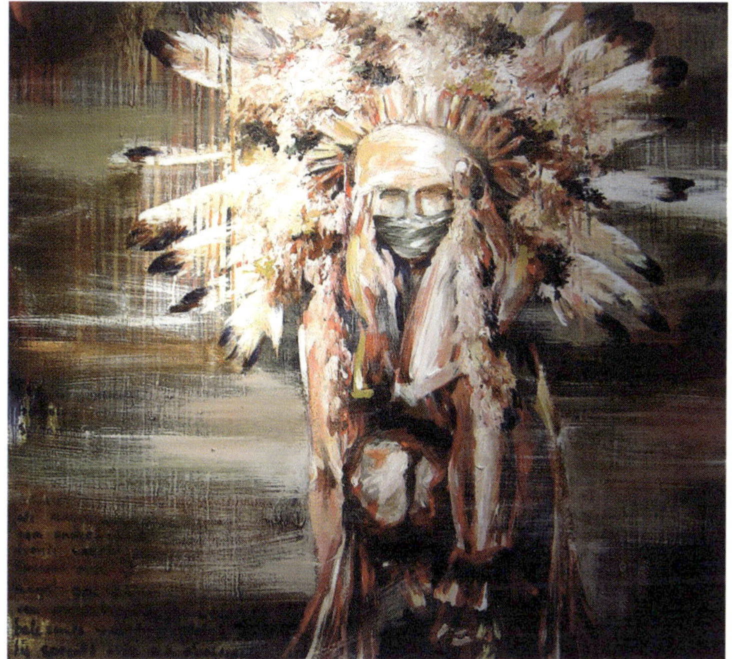

LEFT *I Want You*, Feathers series, acrylic on
canvas, 100 x 100 cm, 2013

RIGHT *I Want You (II)*, Feathers series,
acrylic on canvas, 100 x 100 cm, 2013

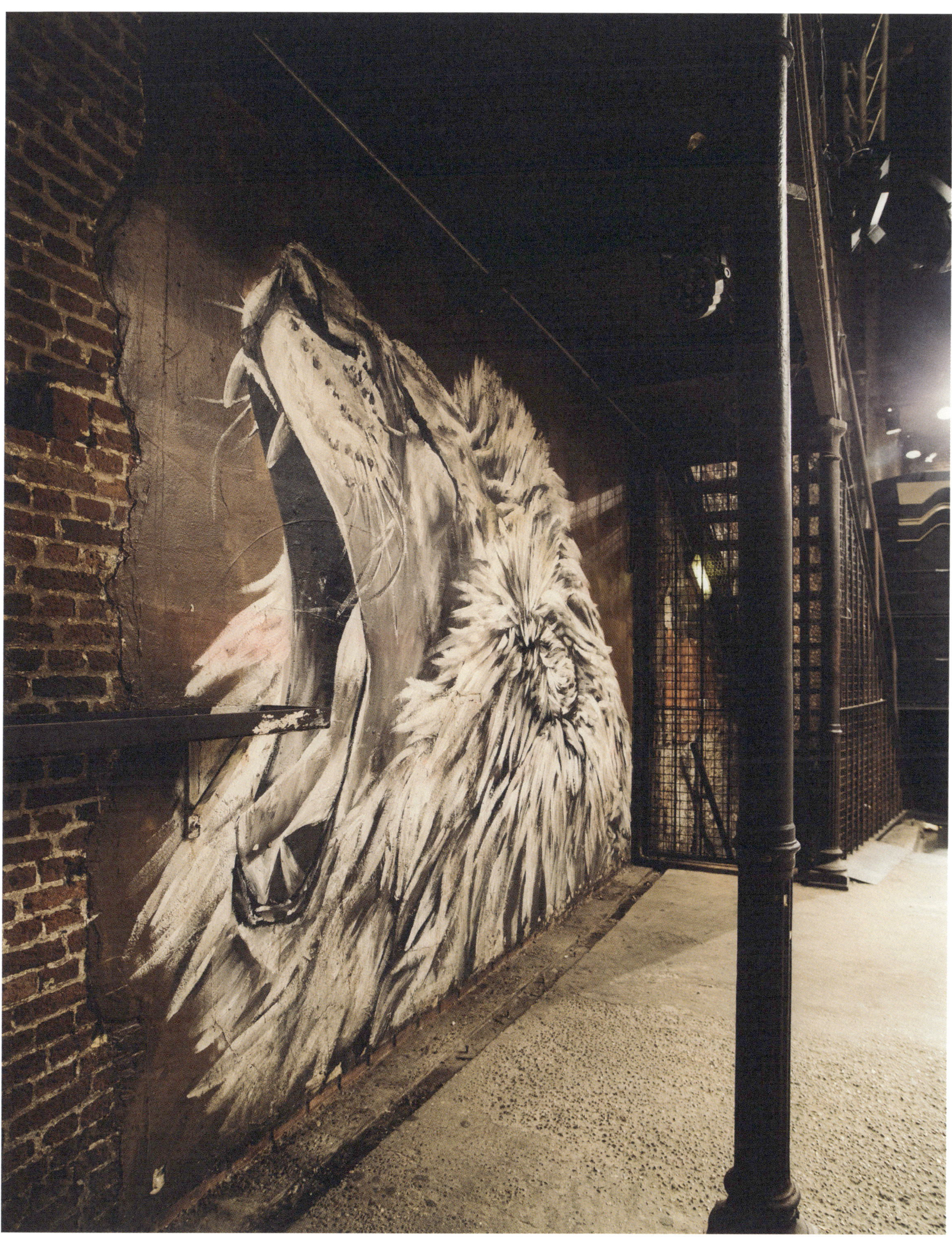

Hugo, mural at Café d'Anvers, Antwerp,
300 x 400 cm, 2016, © Kris Lathouwers

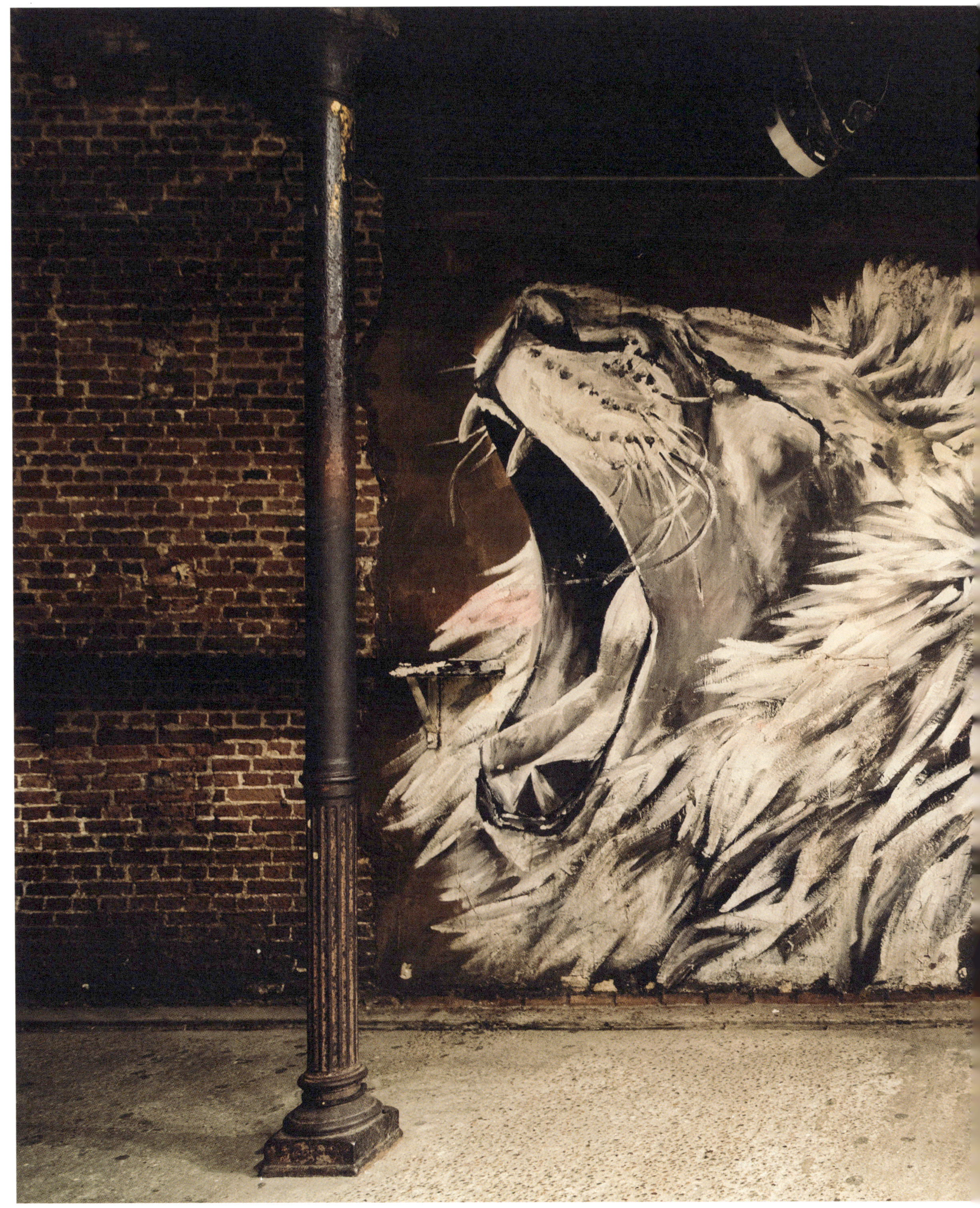

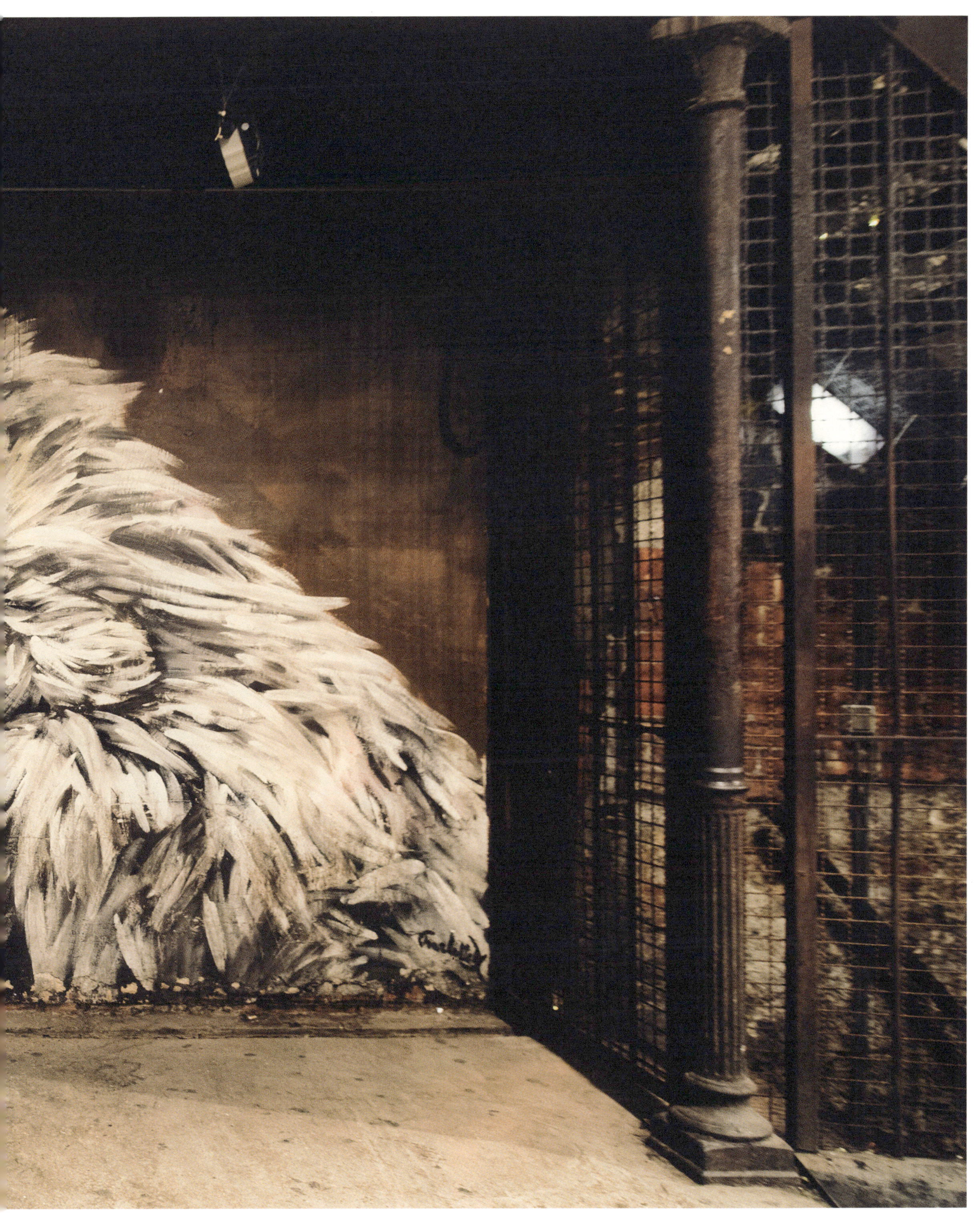

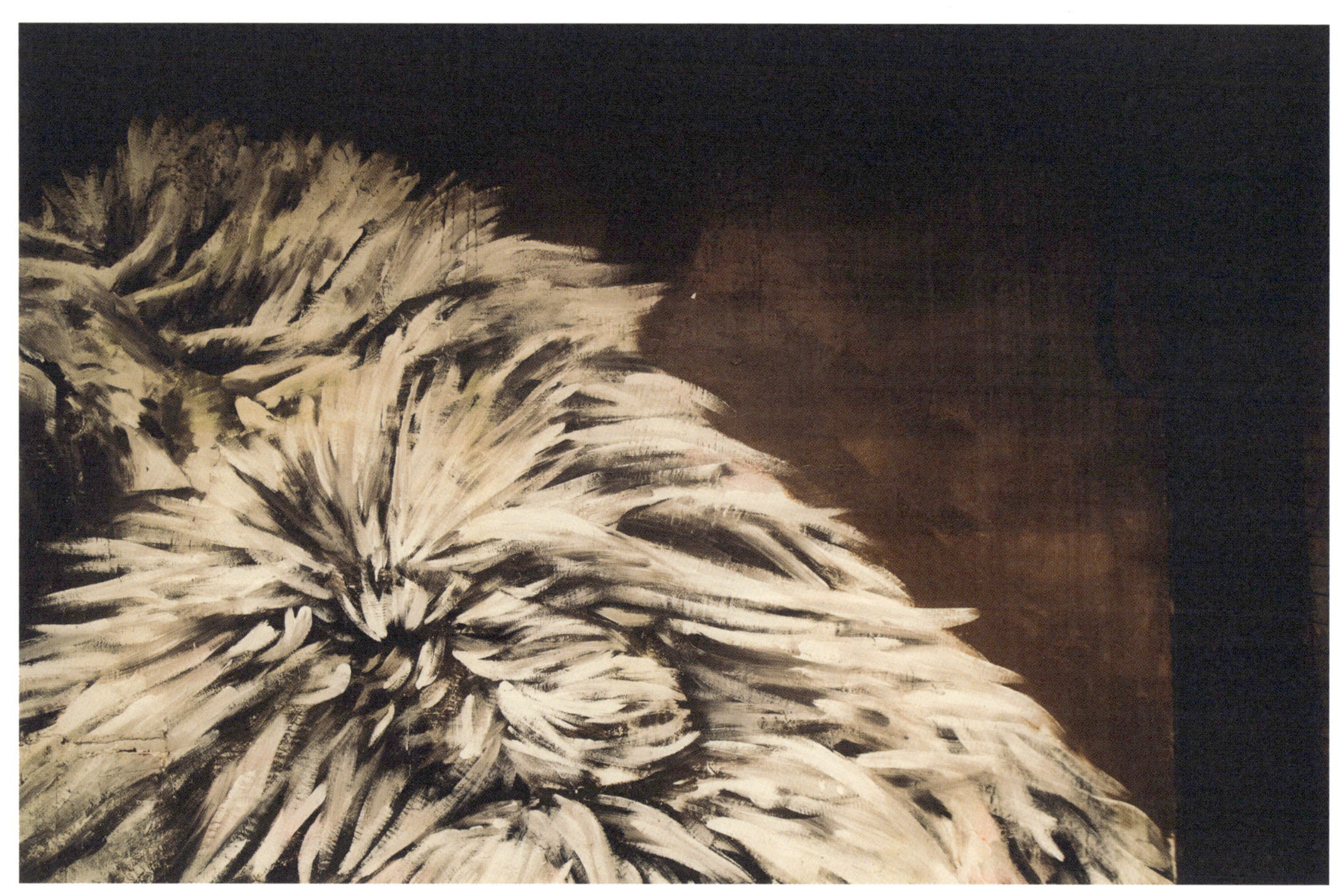

MURALS

Hugo (detail), mural, 300 x 400 cm,
2016, © Kris Lathouwers

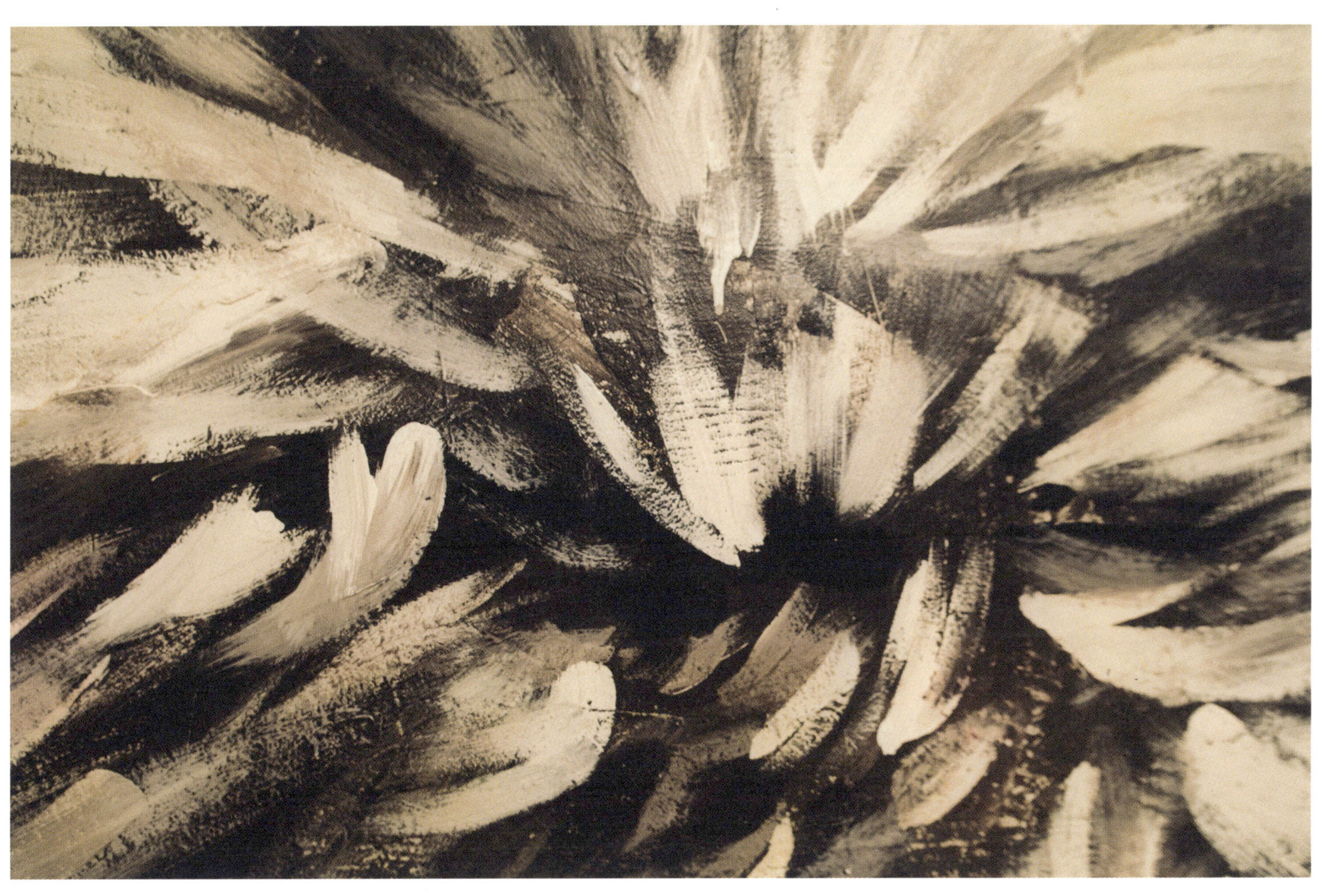

Hugo (detail), mural, 300 x 400 cm,
2016, © Kris Lathouwers

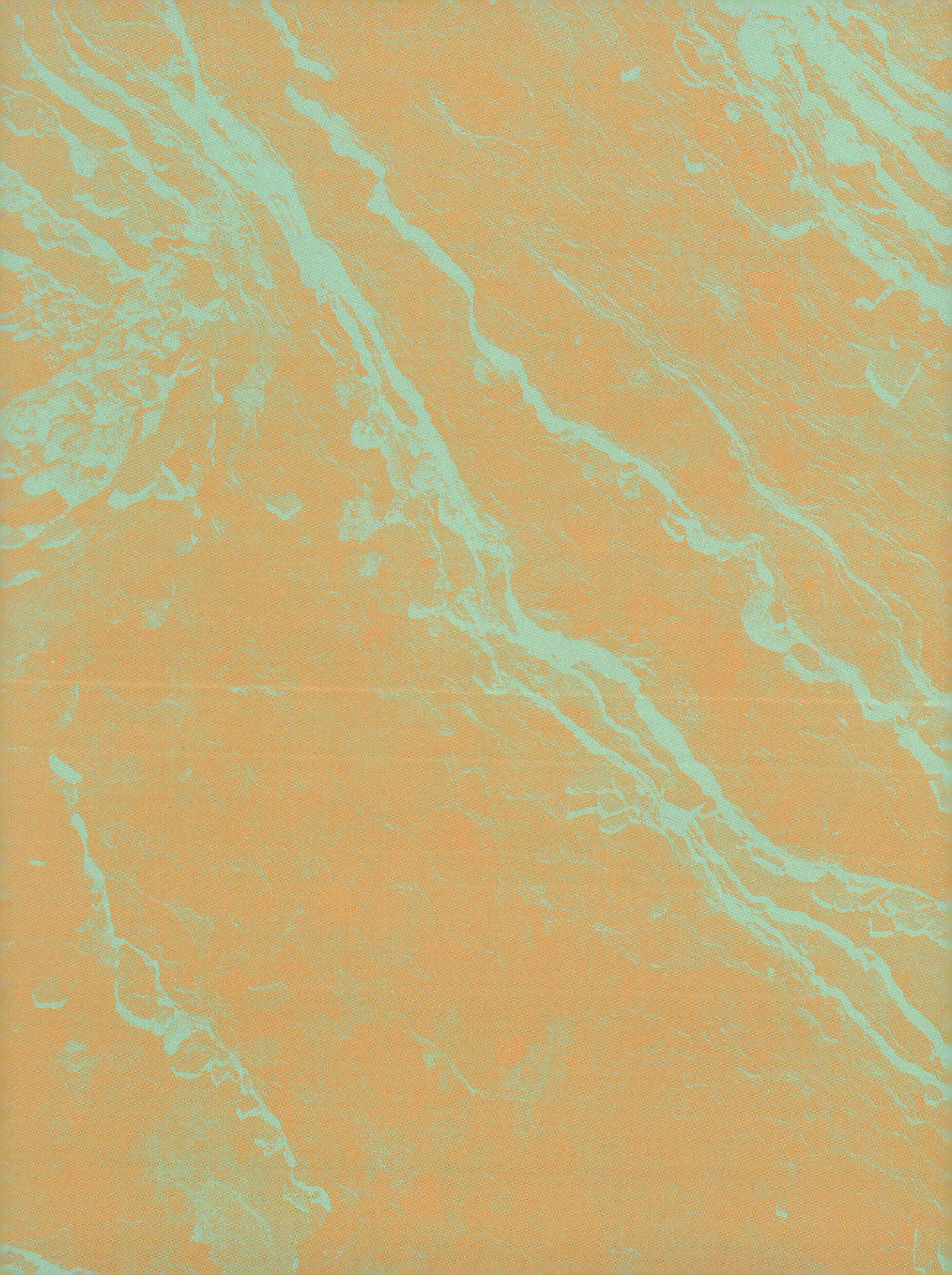

Thirteen Masters

In her *13 Masters* series, Charlotte painted
13 male artists representing the voice of a
generation through arts, music, acting, writing
and photography. Several of these artists are
internationally successful, but like De Cock
choose to stick to their home base of Antwerp.

The original idea was to make a series about
the local café-culture threatened with
extinction. This international port once was
the proud owner of a café on every corner; pub
crawling being the local sport for centuries.
So, she started with making pictures of her
favorite painters in their favorite café, for
all of these artists, being good denizens of
Antwerp, are fervent barflies. However, soon
their personalities overtook the cafés to become
purported subjects onto themselves.

It became a fascinating challenge for this young
painter to portray these masters of their trade,
the creators behind their creations, freed from
the demands of their audiences or the claims
of their collectors, and to paint them with her
sober black-and-white palette. As a result, of
course, it gave her career a nice boost.

Not unlike one of her so-called "masters",
Fred Bervoets, the focus in her paintings is
on herself. Eventually one could perceive these
portraits of artists as self-portraits: Charlotte
(painted) as Luc Tuymans, as Fred Bervoets, as
Koen van den Broek, as Guy Van Bossche. As these
are all men, and most of them of a fatherly age,
one could consider them also as self-portraits
being her father, the father she never really
knew, painting herself in the skin of possible,
or desirable, father figures; reason, perhaps,
why the eyes are never really alive….
(LÉON LEMAHIEU)

Fred & Damiaan

"Artists aim high. Painter Fred Bervoets and actor Damiaan De Schrijver
are critically acclaimed to the moon and back, but actually they're
folksy people with both feet on the ground. I wanted to capture them
not in their working space, but in their comfort space. Damiaan holding
Fred is a sugar-sweet message of true friendship. This visual is what
I brought back from a green field to my atelier."

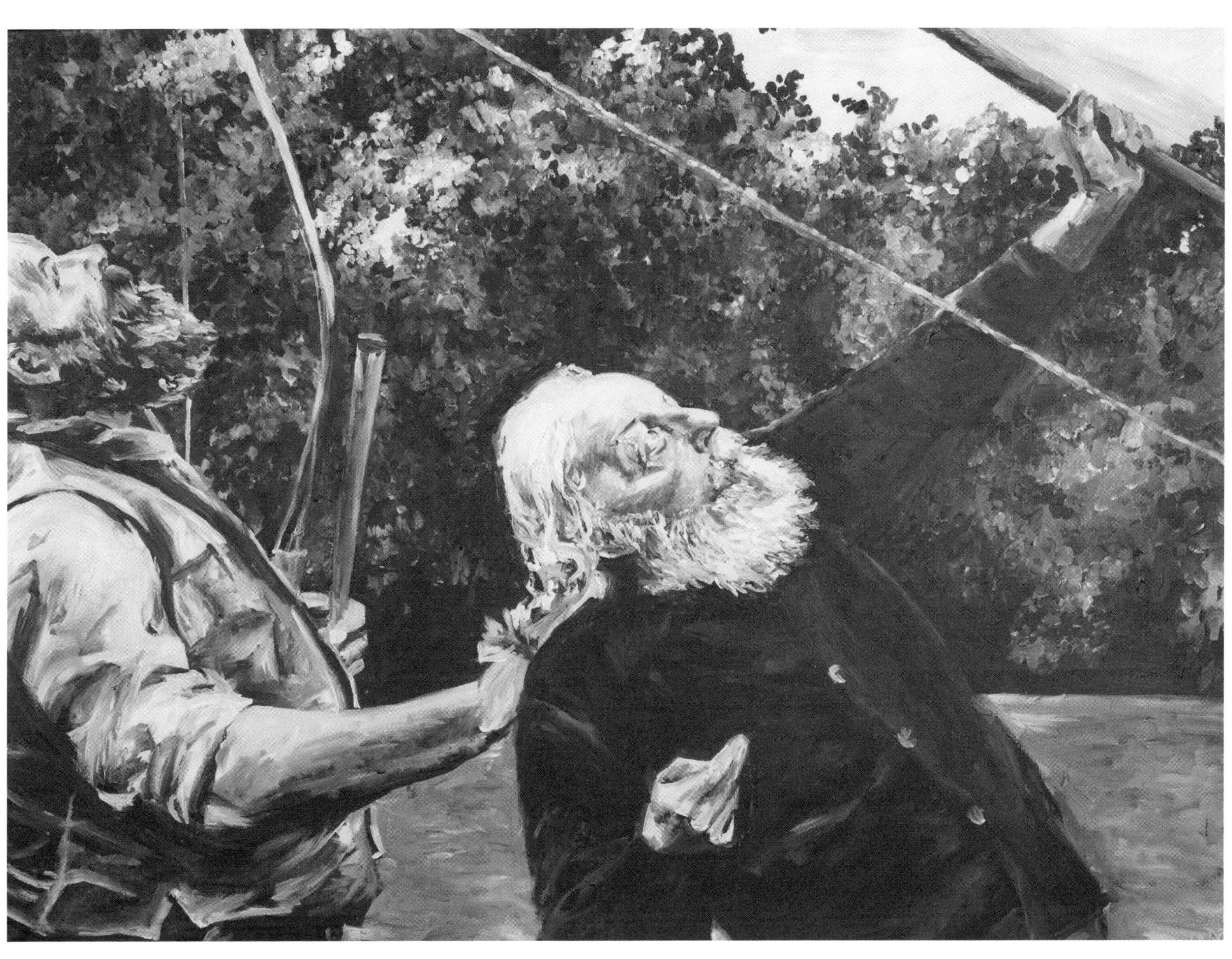

Fred & Damiaan, 13 Masters series, acrylic
on canvas, 200 x 150 cm, 2015

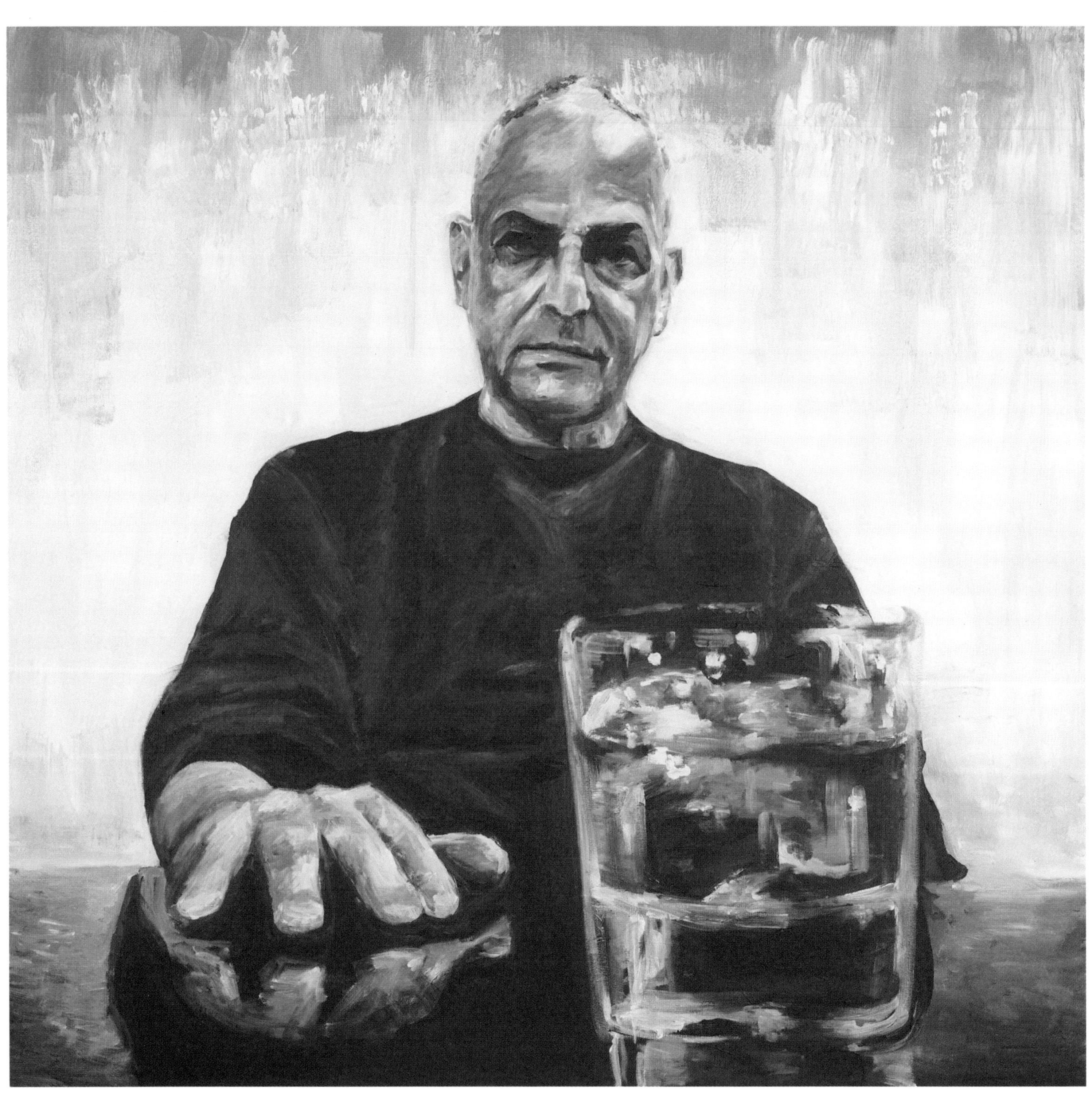

2. THIRTEEN MASTERS

Luc, 13 Masters series, 150 x 150 cm, 2015

Luc

"Imagine: one of your all-time heroes agrees to have his portrait
painted? After the initial personal high, where do I begin?
Luc Tuymans is one of the world's most respected painters,
renowned from Chicago to Hong Kong, but I decided to meet him
in his watering hole—back home in Antwerp. Little humor in
his seriousness—yet if you know Luc, you would understand why.
Big heart, strong man, no mercy. So grateful."

Robbe

"Life is unpredictable. Film director Robbe De Hert has seen his
heights. Once he cheered up Belgium with his movies. Now life eats
him up. However, this guy is still a fighter. He may be an old man
(ten points on my coolissimo-meter), but what I like the most about
him? He still actually *makes* things (eleven points). He doesn't
just *have* the vibe—he *owns* the vibe. There's no disease more lethal
than a disease called passion."

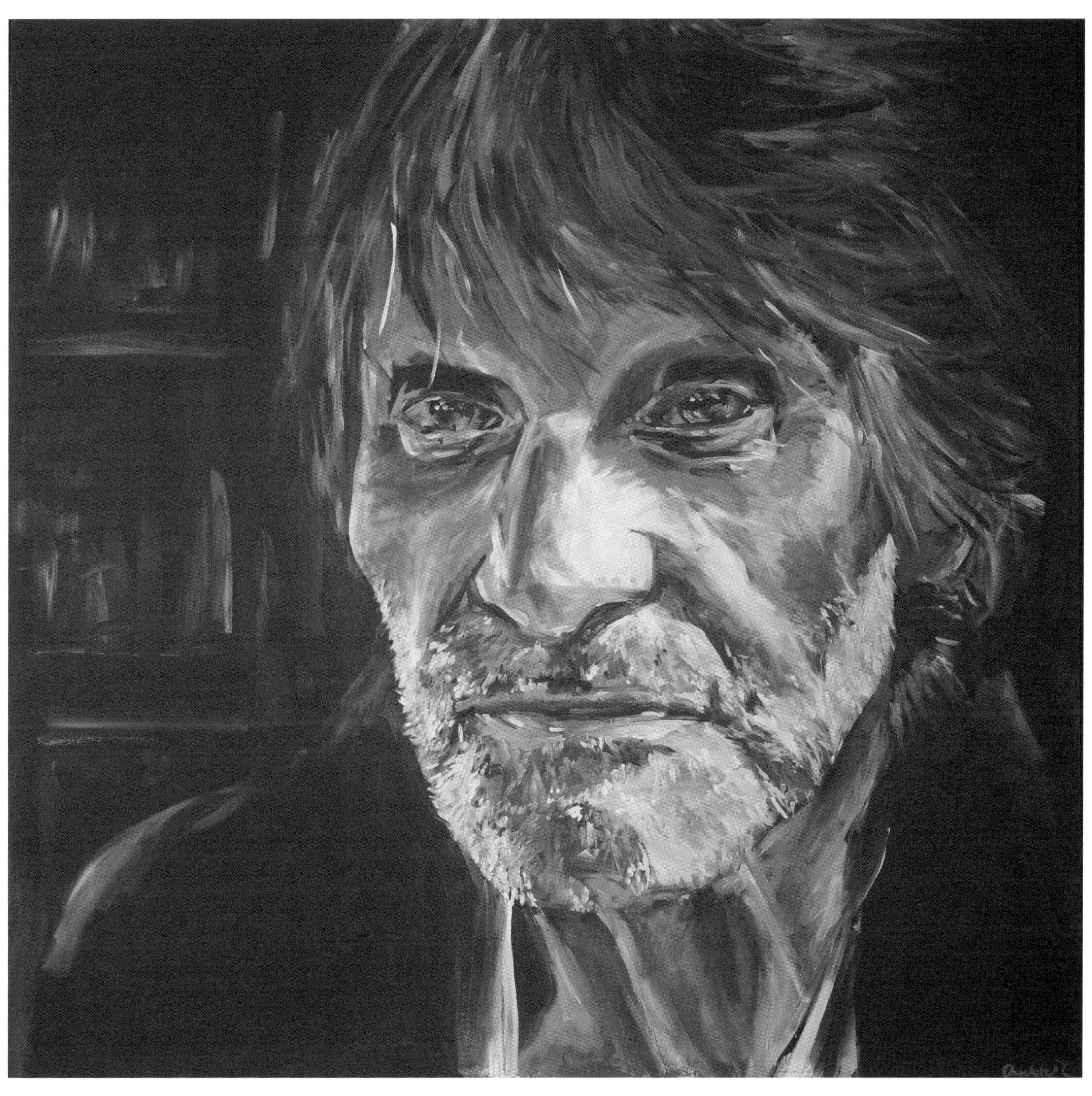

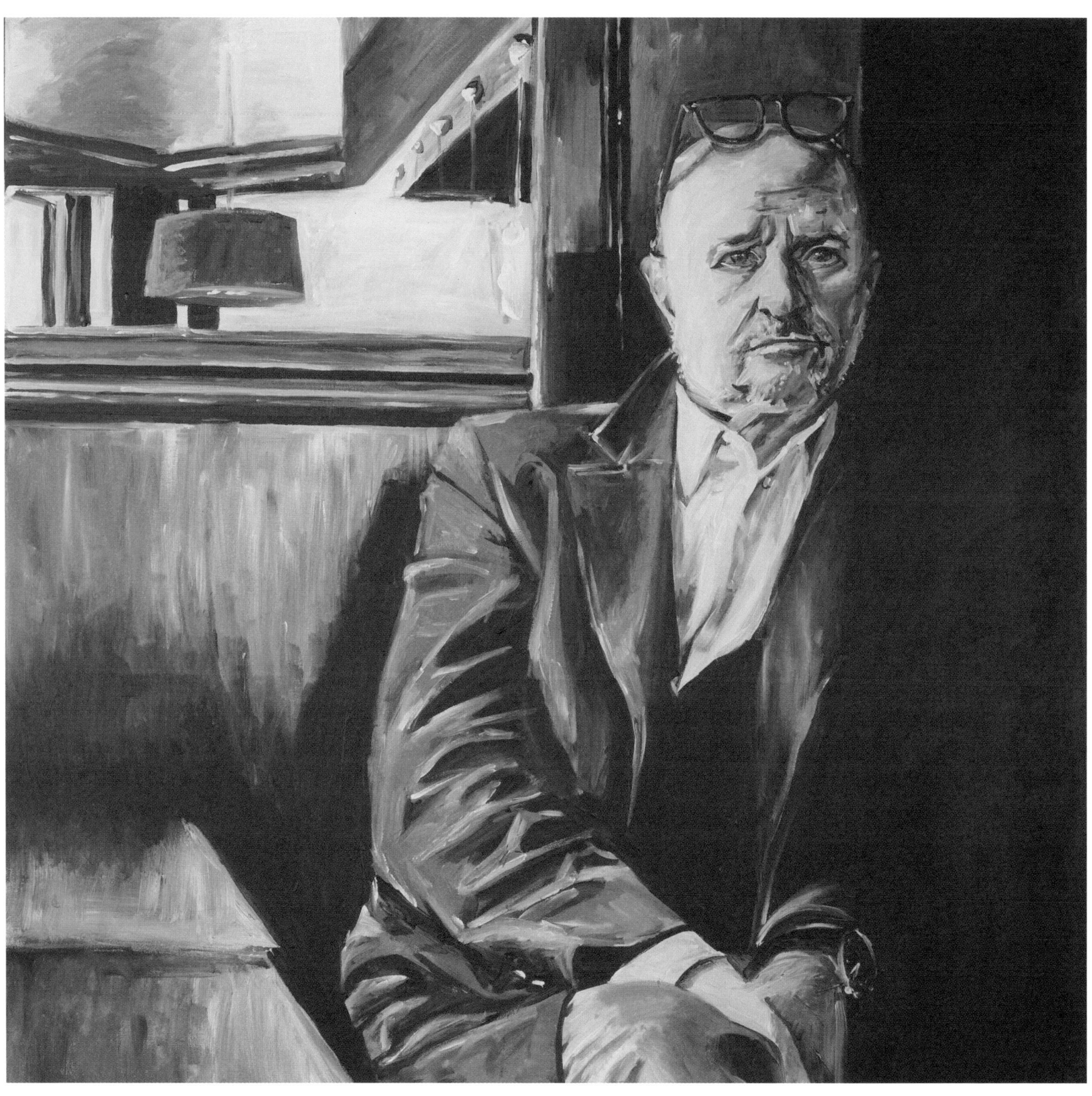

2. THIRTEEN MASTERS

Guy, 13 Masters series, 150 x 150 cm, 2015

Guy

"Intriguing, inspiring, relentless, stubborn. Guy Van Bossche
captures reality in a way that makes me happy. That's exactly
why I wanted him in my Masters collection. His work will invite
you to see more than a painting; a story and an imagination that
transcends the paint upon the canvas."

Ludo

"How happy can one get over a painting? Artist Ludo Mich is exactly
this—a big man with a big, big smile. I'm so proud to have captured
him this way. Large plus for this guy: he was a friend of my
beloved dad's, back in the historical, iconic yet foggy nights in
Antwerp, and I just love listening to his stories and I will never
get enough from this inspiring guy."

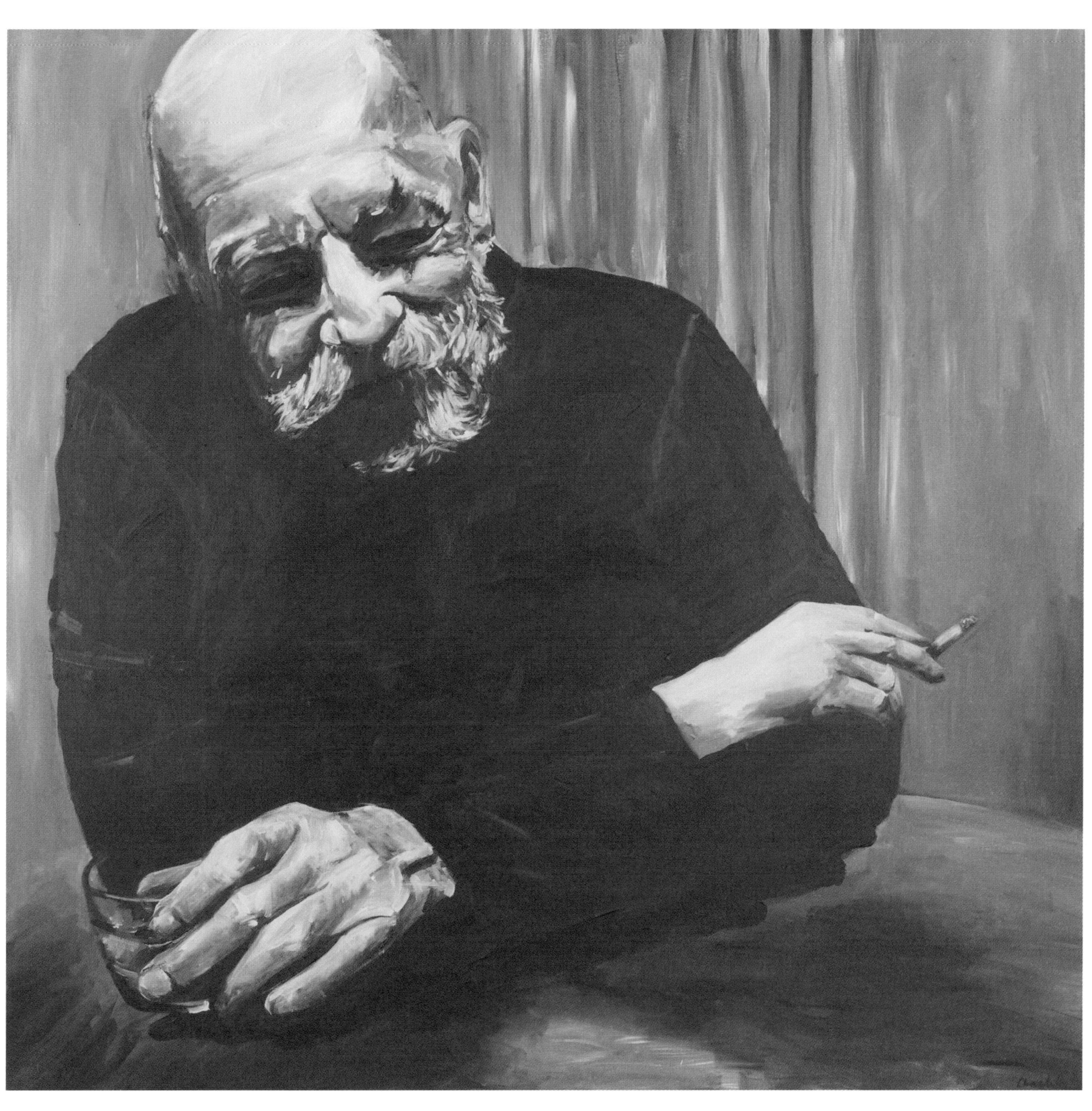

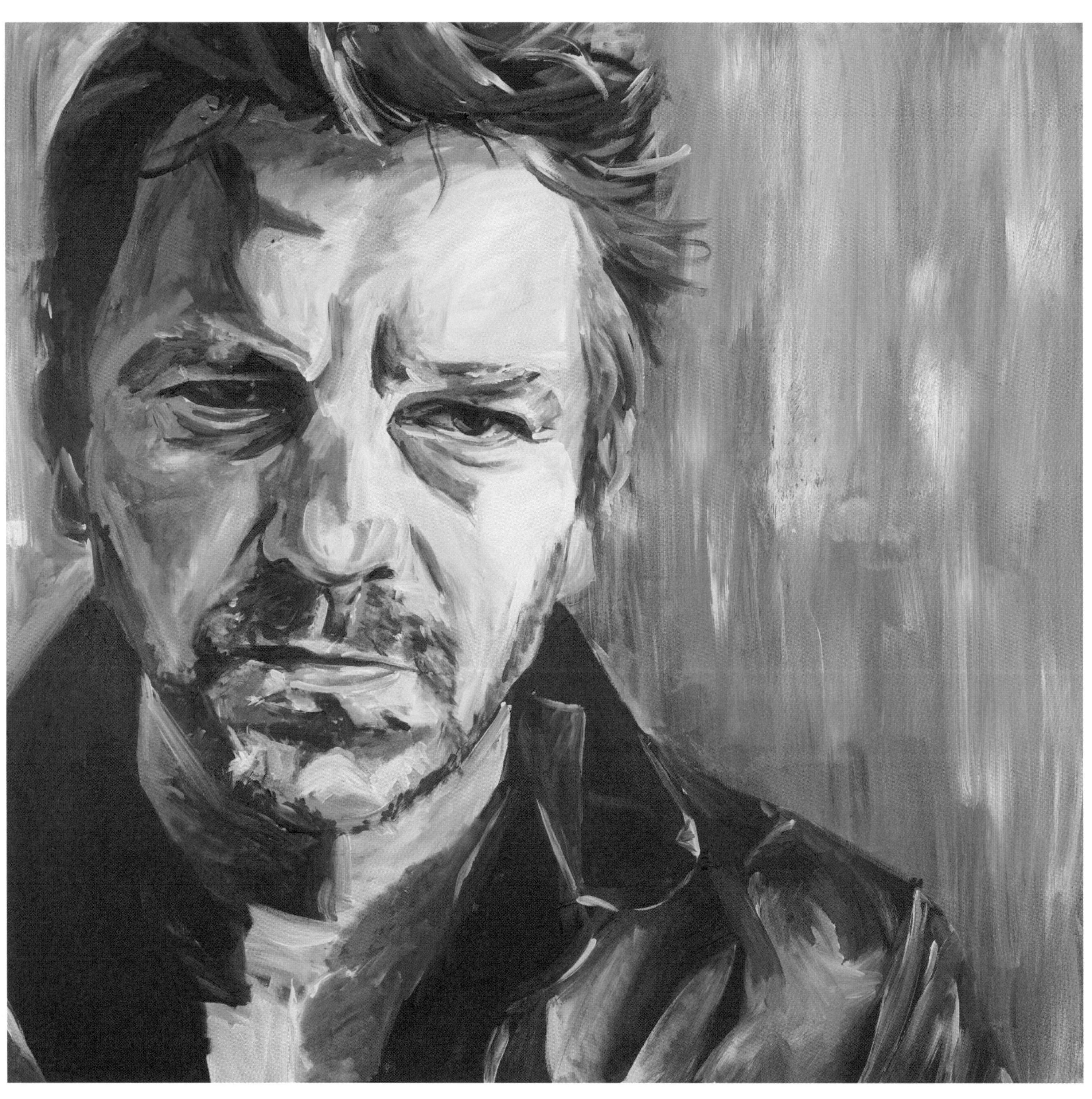

Tom

"Tom Barman is where screaming rock music meets a Fellini
experimental film, where art meets a black leather jacket, where
a Lazy Red Cheeks cocktail leads to steamy sex at 5 A.M. I'm a
big fan of dEUS. This was the first Antwerp band to rock the world
and I admire him so much. Small detail: Tom orders 20 DVD's a week
and he's nothing less than a movie professor *cum laude*. One of my
ambitions is to make my own feature film and I hope one day he will
help me with the process."

Wim

"There are mainstream movies (which I enjoy on lazy Sundays under
a blanket on my couch) and there are movies that challenge you to
think differently. Wim Catrysse's work is the latter. The awesome
way he uses light, camera, character and point-of-view are truly
artistic. Understanding him isn't always easy, but isn't that the
purpose of art?"

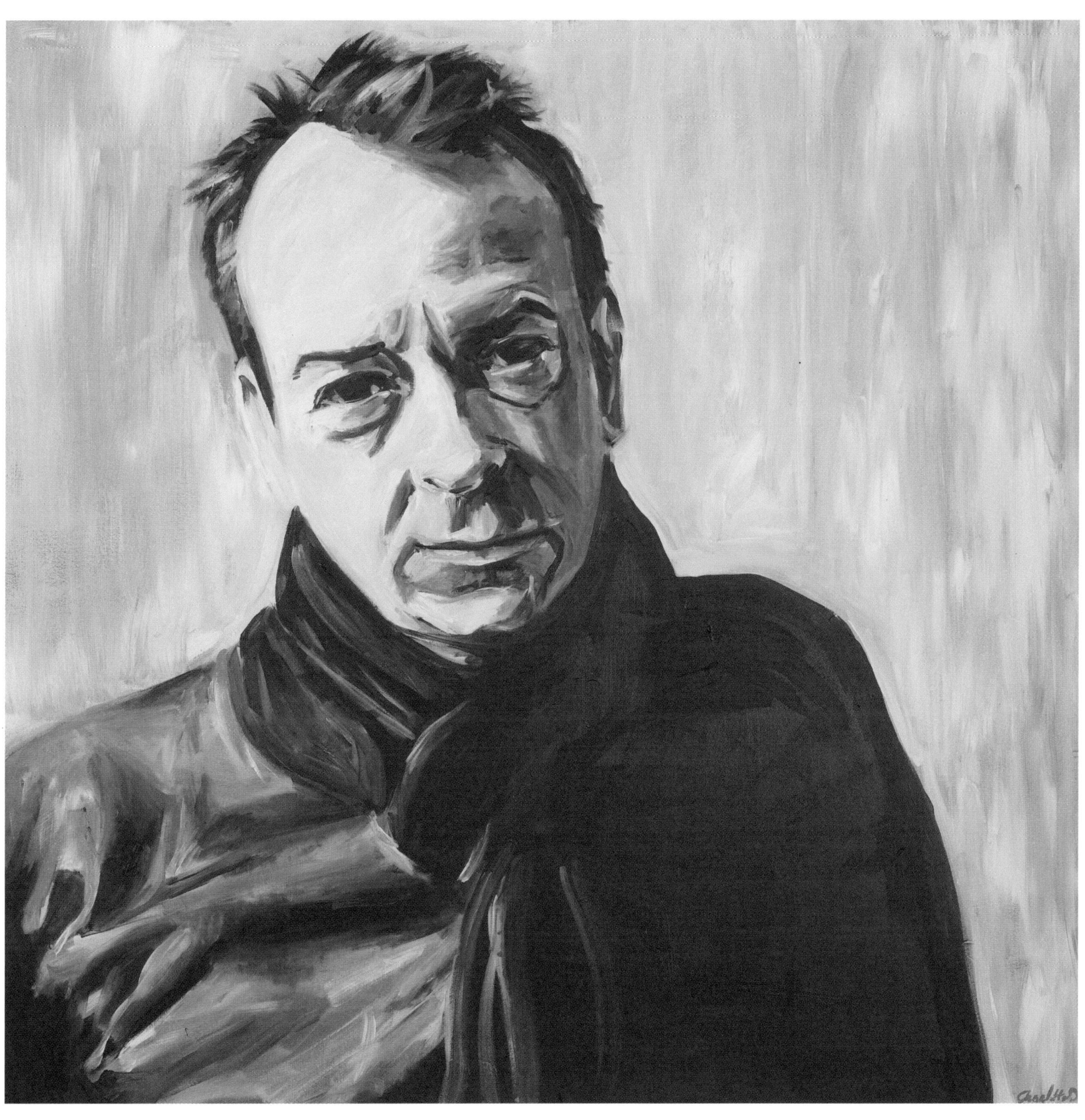

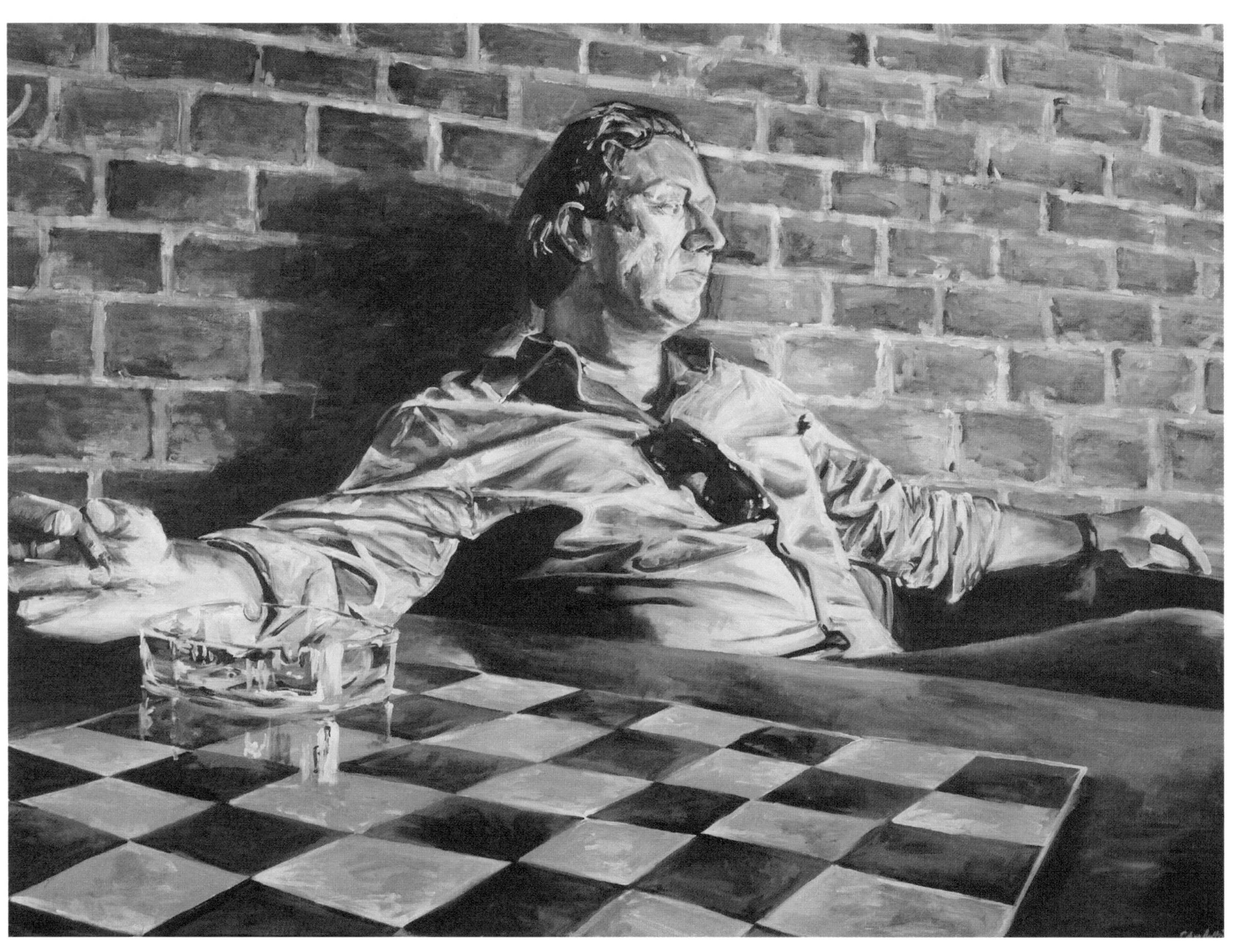

     2. THIRTEEN MASTERS   *Koen*, 13 Masters series, 200 x 150 cm, 2015

Koen

"Every artist needs a wake-up call once and a while. My ass got
kicked by painter Koen van den Broek. He dropped by in my atelier
to tell me I needed to get out of my comfort zone. Coming from
one of Belgium's greatest, these words pushed me into the right
direction. And, while he may seem laid back in the painting,
Koen is a hard worker who has dedicated his life to making
beautiful things."

Jan

"From acting in an award-winning movie to a graduating student's
short film: Jan Decleir will use his talent with equal dedication.
I felt blessed having the opportunity to paint Antwerp's most
iconic actor. Jan is portrayed in the bar he visits for 50 years
and this is exactly who he is: friendly, professional, a *bon
vivant*. Far from the spotlights, but such awesome talent doesn't
need cocktail parties and magazine covers."

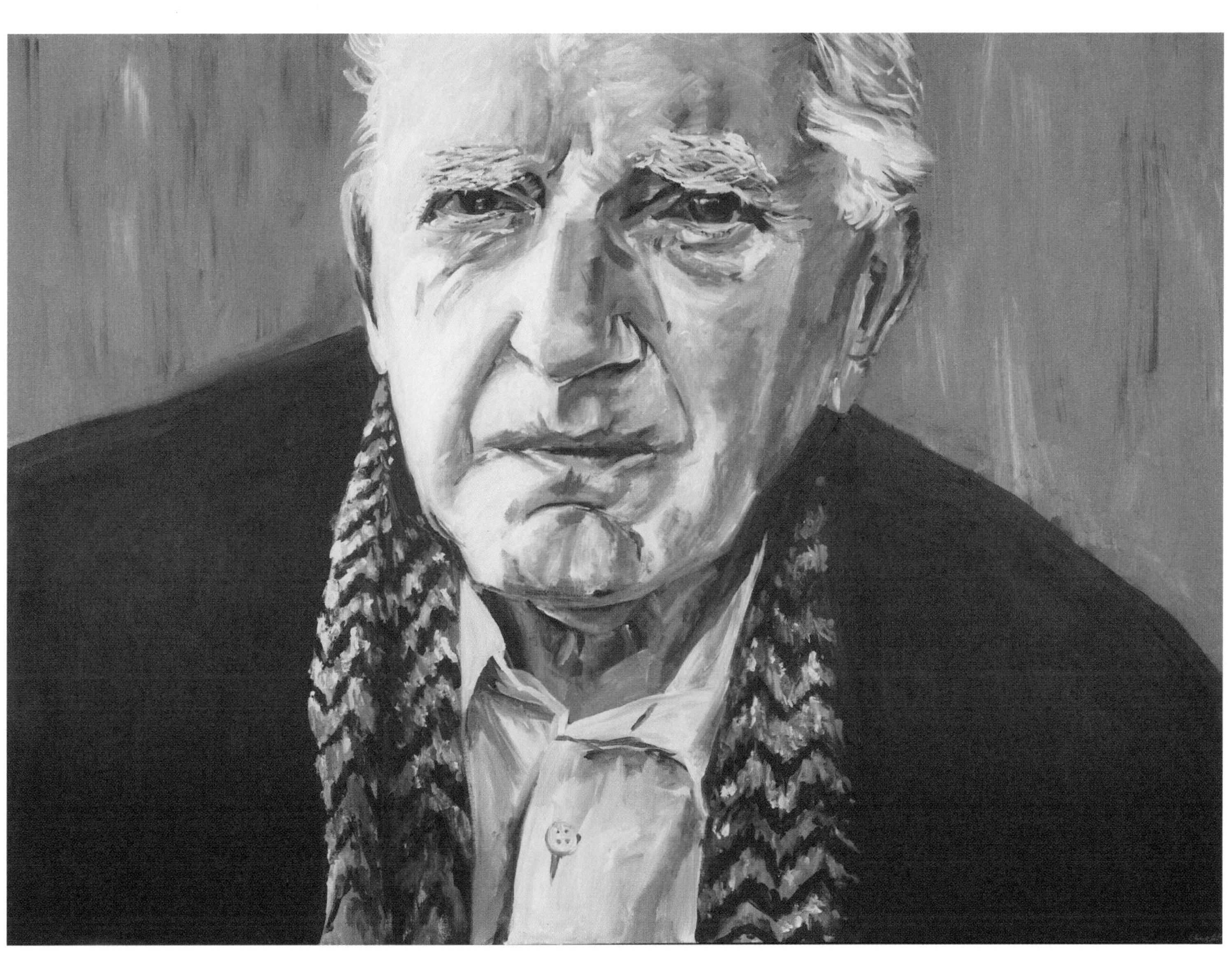

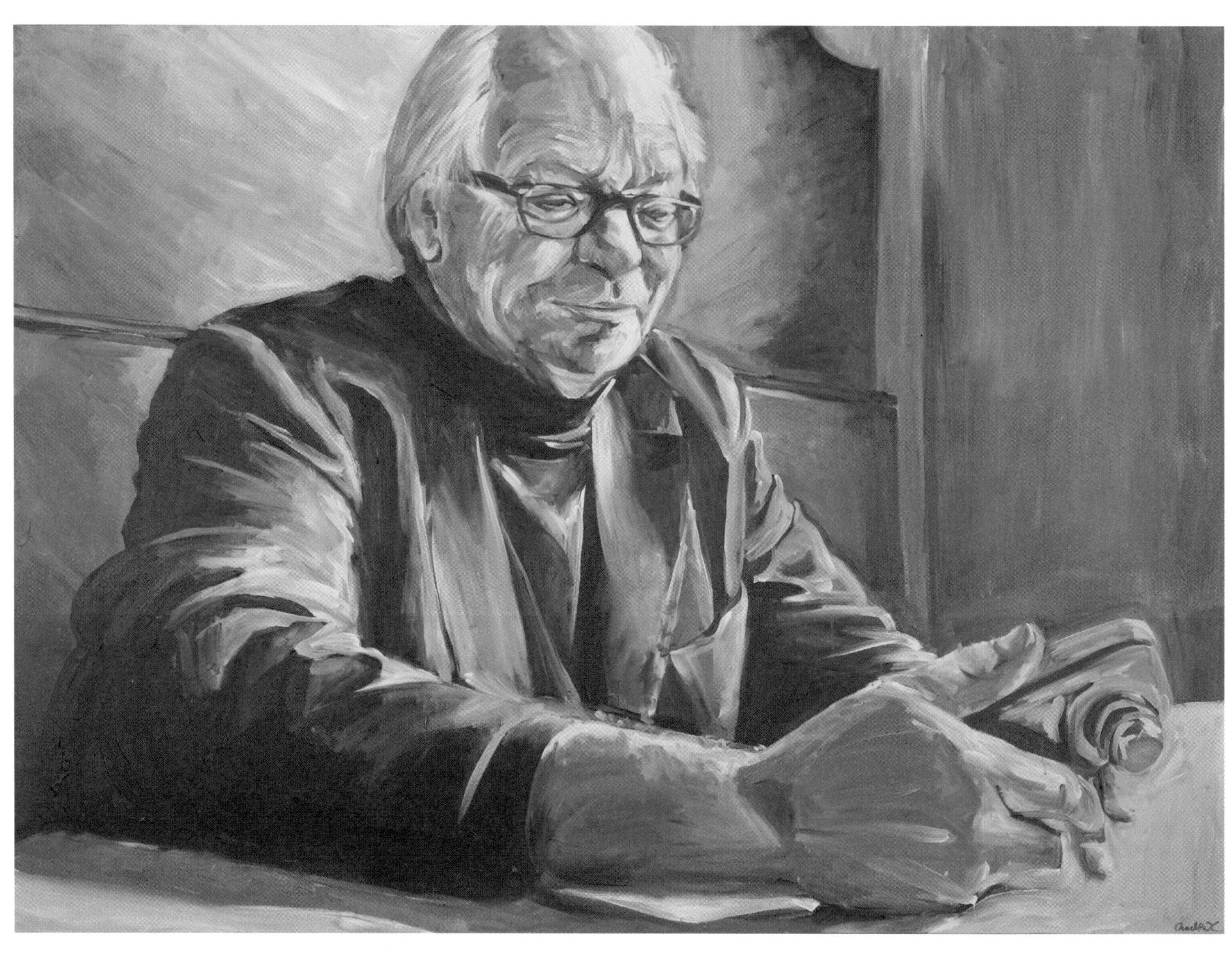

　　2. THIRTEEN MASTERS

Herman, 13 Masters series,
200 x 150 cm, 2015

Herman

"Funny. While I was photographing him, photographer Herman
Selleslags was taking pictures of me. He may not be a man of many
words, but his eyes and his lens have captured a thousand stories
that speak for themselves. It's so nice to exchange ideas with
someone who works with light, contrast, decor, props and faces—just
like myself. Both of us are free thinkers, but we are limited to
just capturing one moment. We're on the same level as to how we get
the maximum out of that split second."

Jeroen

"Our own Man In Black doesn't require much light or set dressing.
His face is as expressive as his words on paper. I captured
author Jeroen Olyslaegers at Troubleyn, Jan Fabre's theatre
company. Jeroen is the only artist in this selection who works
with words. Actually, his job is not that different from painting
—both of us tell stories, plain and simple. This painting is as
dark as it gets."

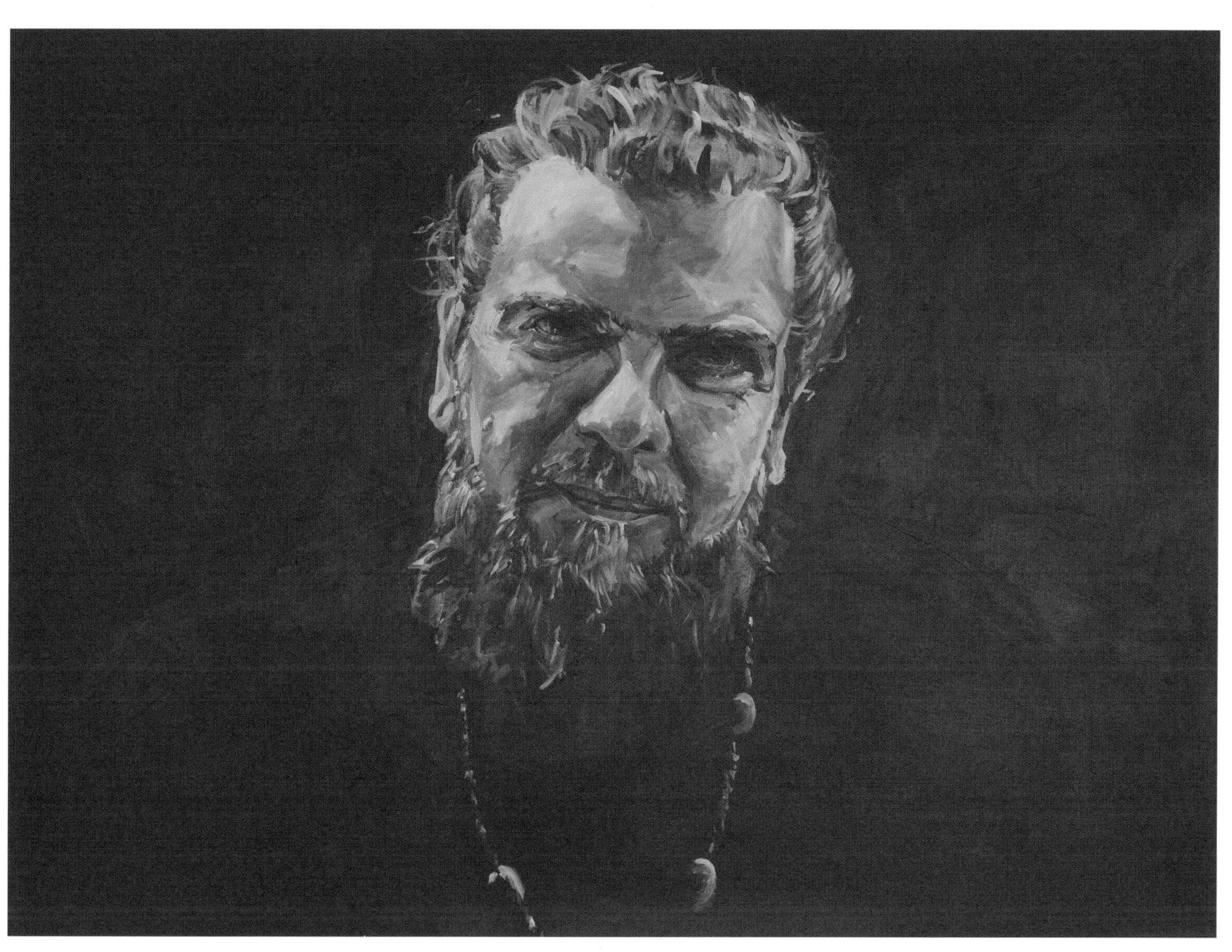

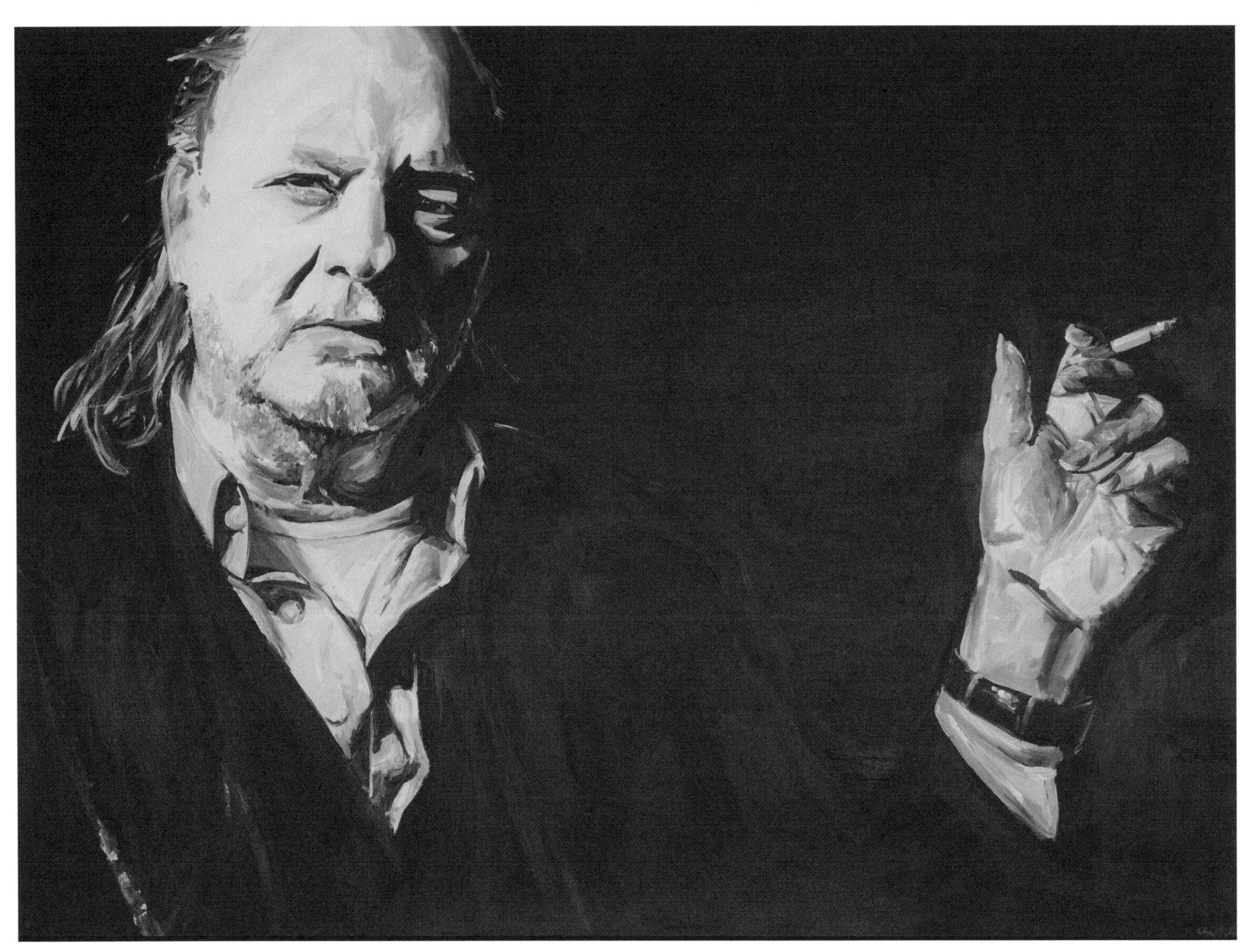

2. THIRTEEN MASTERS

Guillaume, 13 Masters series,
200 x 150 cm, 2015

Guillaume

"I just love autodidacts. Just like painter Guillaume Bijl,
I taught myself how to paint. I believe there's no better way
to develop your own style; you're not influenced by anybody.
Morevoer, I am not a big fan of the consumption society.
Guillaume is not afraid to make beautiful artwork out of waste
material. He's independent and a great source of ideas."

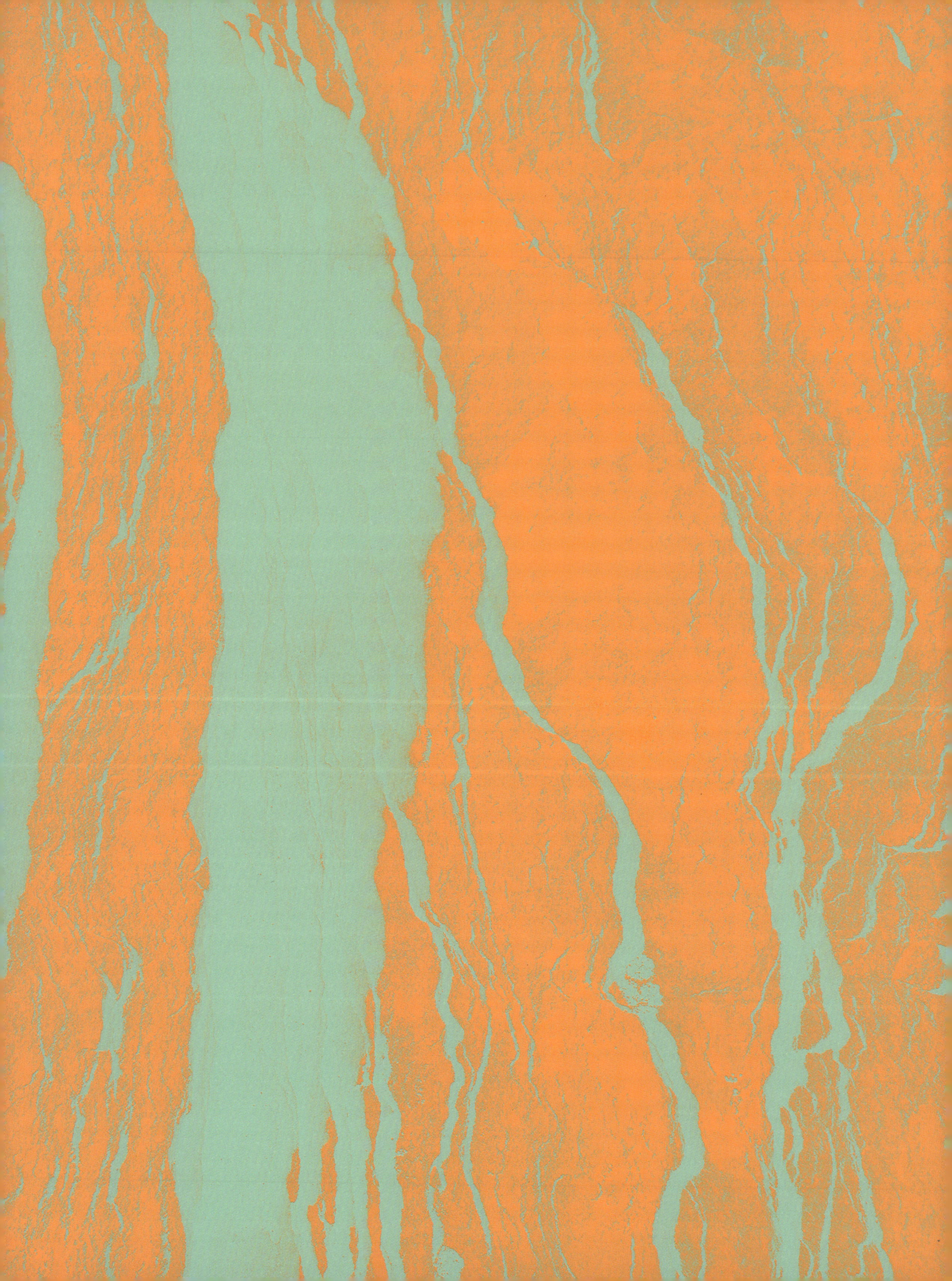

My California

My California

Paintings pt. 1

In *My California*, De Cock, in order to find new sources of inspiration, traveled through the deserts, on the lookout for members of the Native American Culture, and stumbled upon those representing White American Counterculture instead, ending up in deserted holiday spots, a clandestine military field illegally claimed by guys building their own planes, in little towns made of trash, in scrapheaps turned into art or into a concert hall. Places that certain people would call rat holes, or worse: shitholes.

We're talking about places such as Slab City, near Salvation Mountain, CA, where the residents make a creative re-use of the junk the military hastily dumped in the ground when they left, or Bombay Beach, in the Sonoran Desert, east of Salton Sea, a place destined to become a beach resort for the stars of high society such as Marilyn Monroe, but due to climatological changes became deserted, desolate, with dead fish all over the beach, as we can witness in the video teaser for *Daoud*.

The names alone of these places, or what resounds of them, are sheer poetry. Ballarat, around Panamint Springs, a supply point for miners, once harbored 500 inhabitants, now only one: Rock. This solitary man is the guardian of this little ghost town.

In *El Rodeo* (200x120 cm), we find Rock posing
before an old, rusty truck, mountains in the
background. Despite the fact that the other
paintings in this Californian series are pretty
colorful, this one is, once more, mainly executed
in whites and grays, perhaps in order to stress
the situation: the loneliness of place and man.
The truck was Charles Manson's escape-vehicle;
the white splotches, the bullet holes…

These old guys are rebels, or rather: renegades.
But whilst the official definition of renegade
(Webster's) is: traitor, deserter, the etymology
of the word indicates something totally
different: re-*negare*: say no, again. Say NO!,
again. Don't accept (the rules, the chains, the
bullshit). Say "No" to it, over and over again.

De Cock (re)places these outcasts, these marginal
peoples in their proper context: people who
gave up urban comforts to (re)gain something
more valuable: their freedom; which includes
the freedom to be free of artificial needs, of
all the artificial needs of an artificial world
filled with artificial people; a *modus vivendi*
she underlines in her notebooks,"…*the less
you need, the happier you will be*, or quoting
Bukowski: … *'The less I needed, the better I
felt'* and *'adventure begins when comfort has
left you.'"*

Now, I don't think comfort has really left
Charlotte, for as we can see in these pictures,
even the sands of the Mesquite dunes, or the
hard, cracked, sun-dried soil of the Californian
desert receives her elegant naked body as a
cashmere covered mattress.

Her trips through the Californian desert, up to
Big Sur, where Henry Miller lived, (writer of
controversial, forbidden books, being the first
writer to contest the American Dream, especially
with his "The air-conditioned Nightmare"), were
no nightmare at all. But Miller is, or should
be, one of her Masters nevertheless. His *Paradise
Lost*, the third part of the Big Sur trilogy,
would have suited Charlotte, and the old satyr
would have welcomed her in his Californian
residence with a large, *satyr*-ical smile…

There is one "selfie" painting of Charlotte
giving the finger, a finger to norm and
convention, political correctness and common
decency, whilst unscrupulously using all the
structures and facilities that conventional
society has laid out (for her), like the
smartphone, with its multifunctional facilities,
one on them being making selfies: that is to whom
the finger is meant for. This, too, would have
pleased the old master.

(LÉON LEMAHIEU)

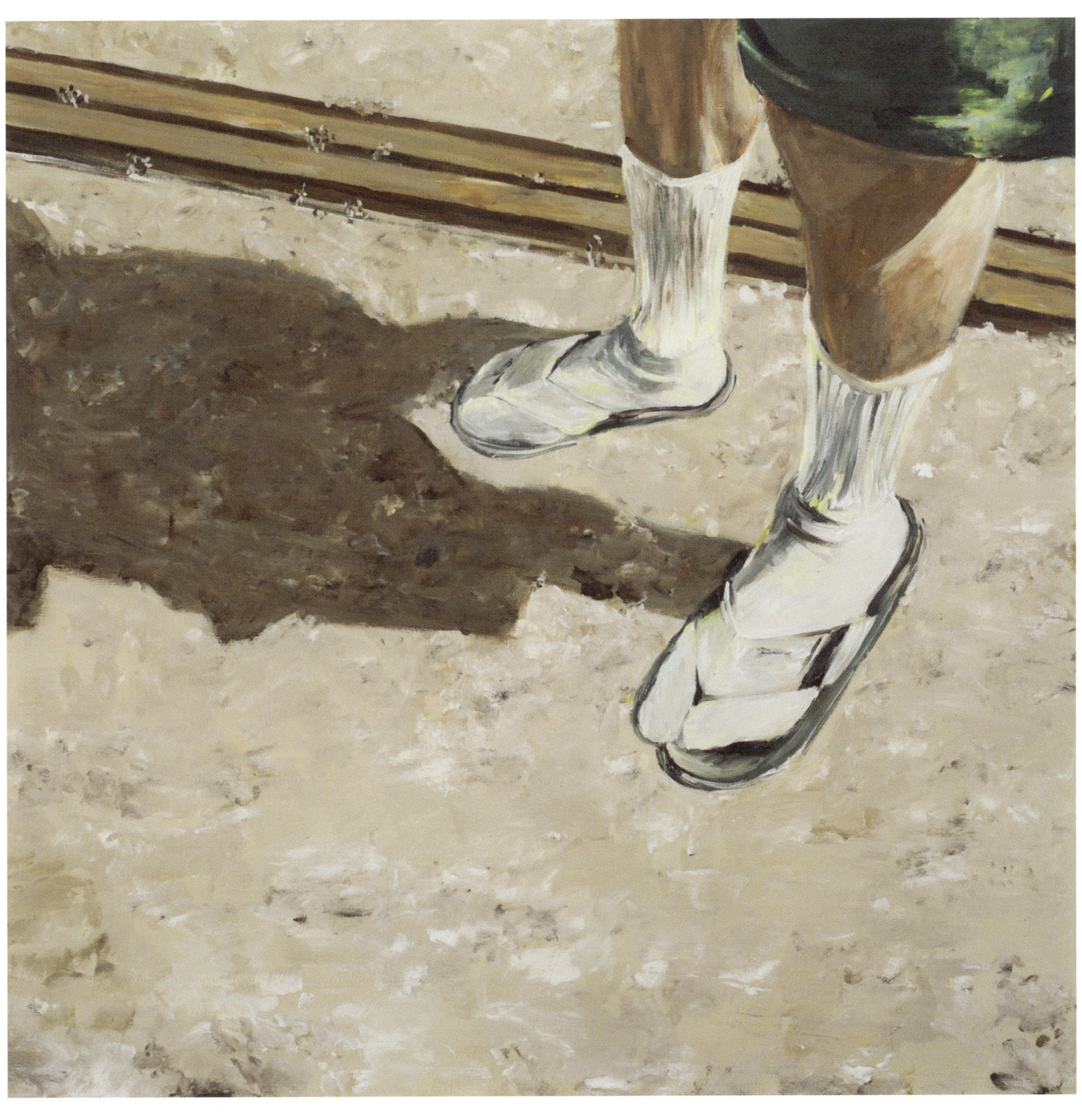

Regular John, My California series,
acrylic on canvas, 160 x 160 cm, 2016

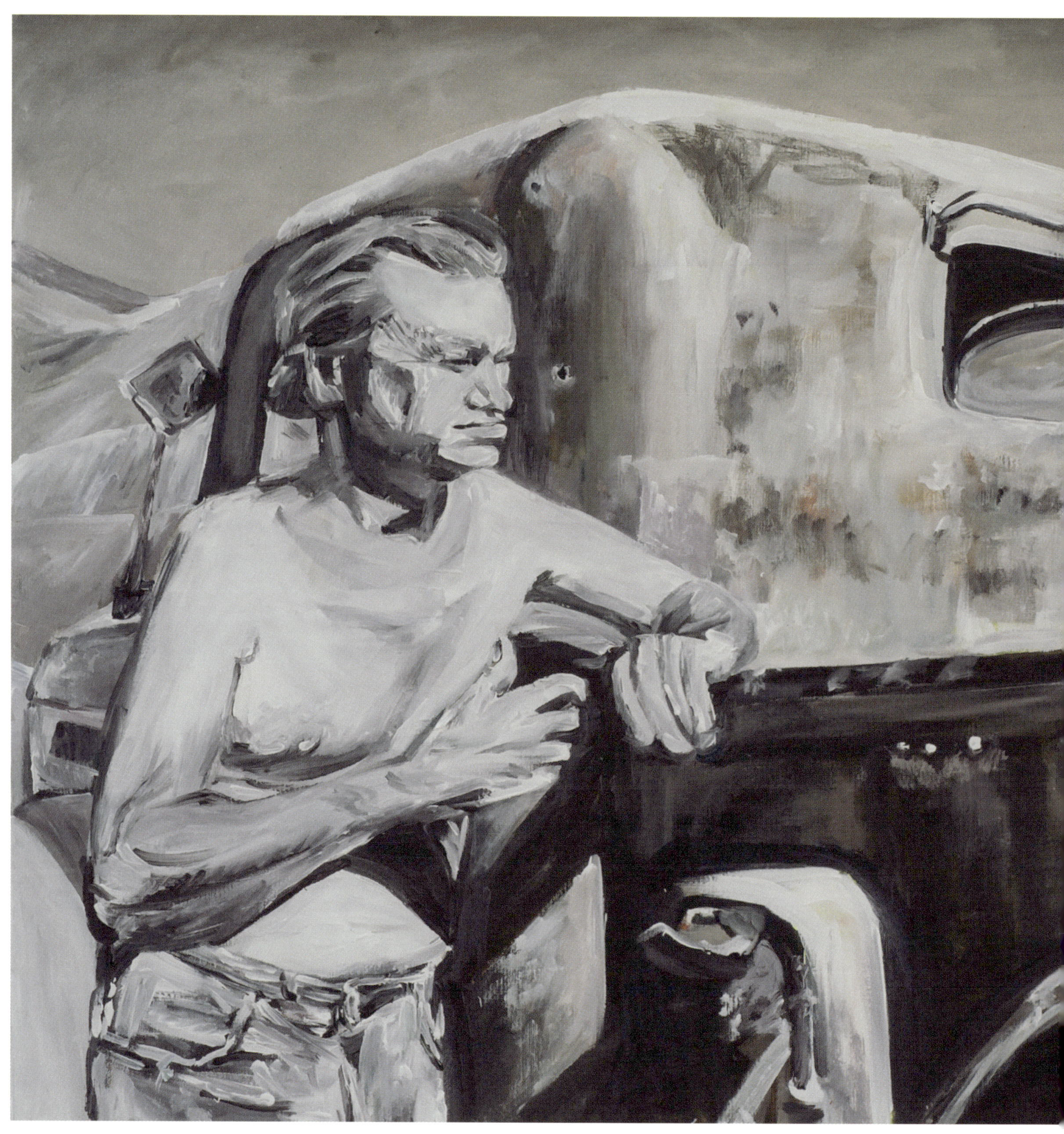

3. MY CALIFORNIA: PAINTINGS PT. 1

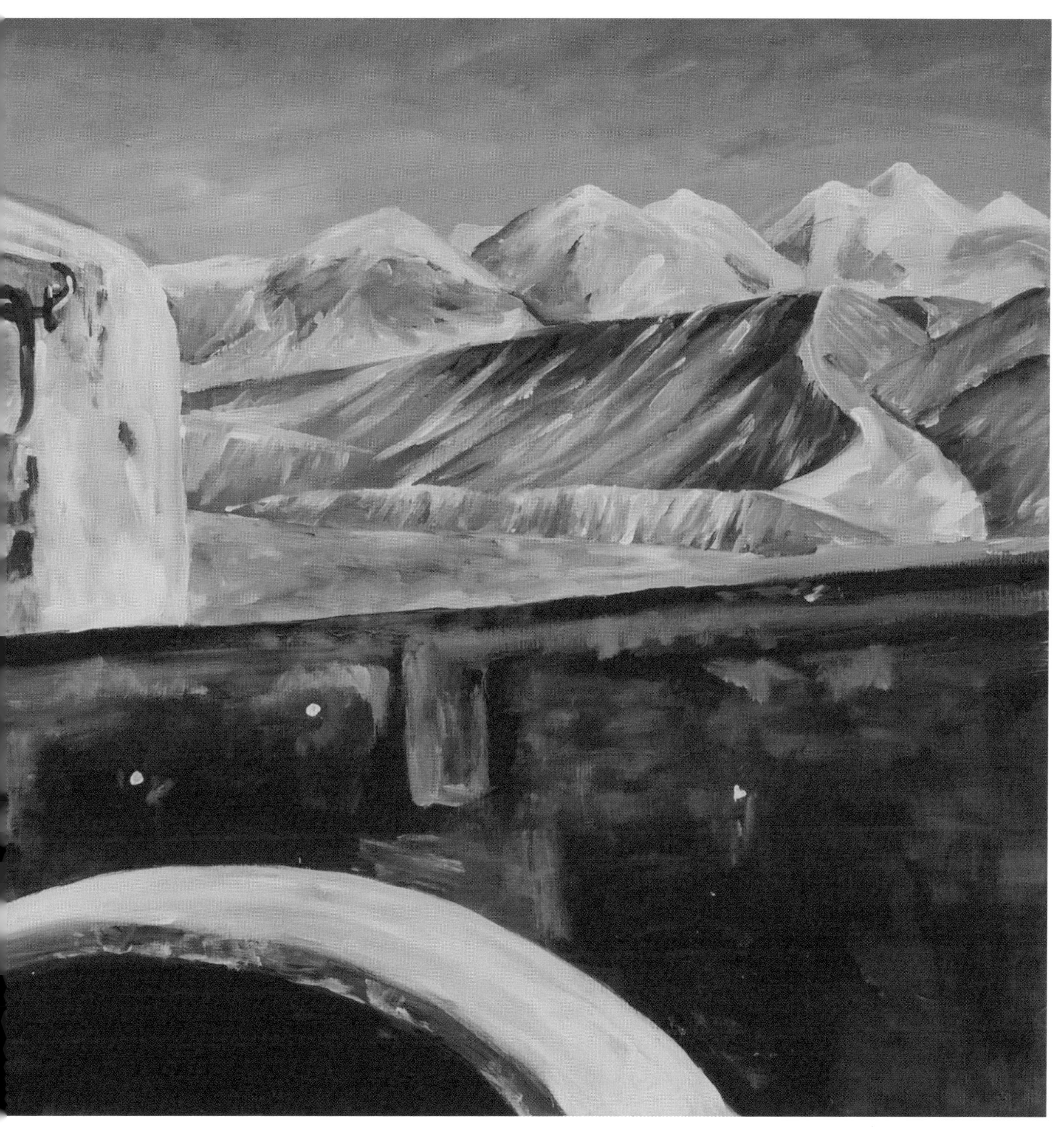

El Rodeo, My California series,
acrylic on canvas, 200 x 120 cm, 2016

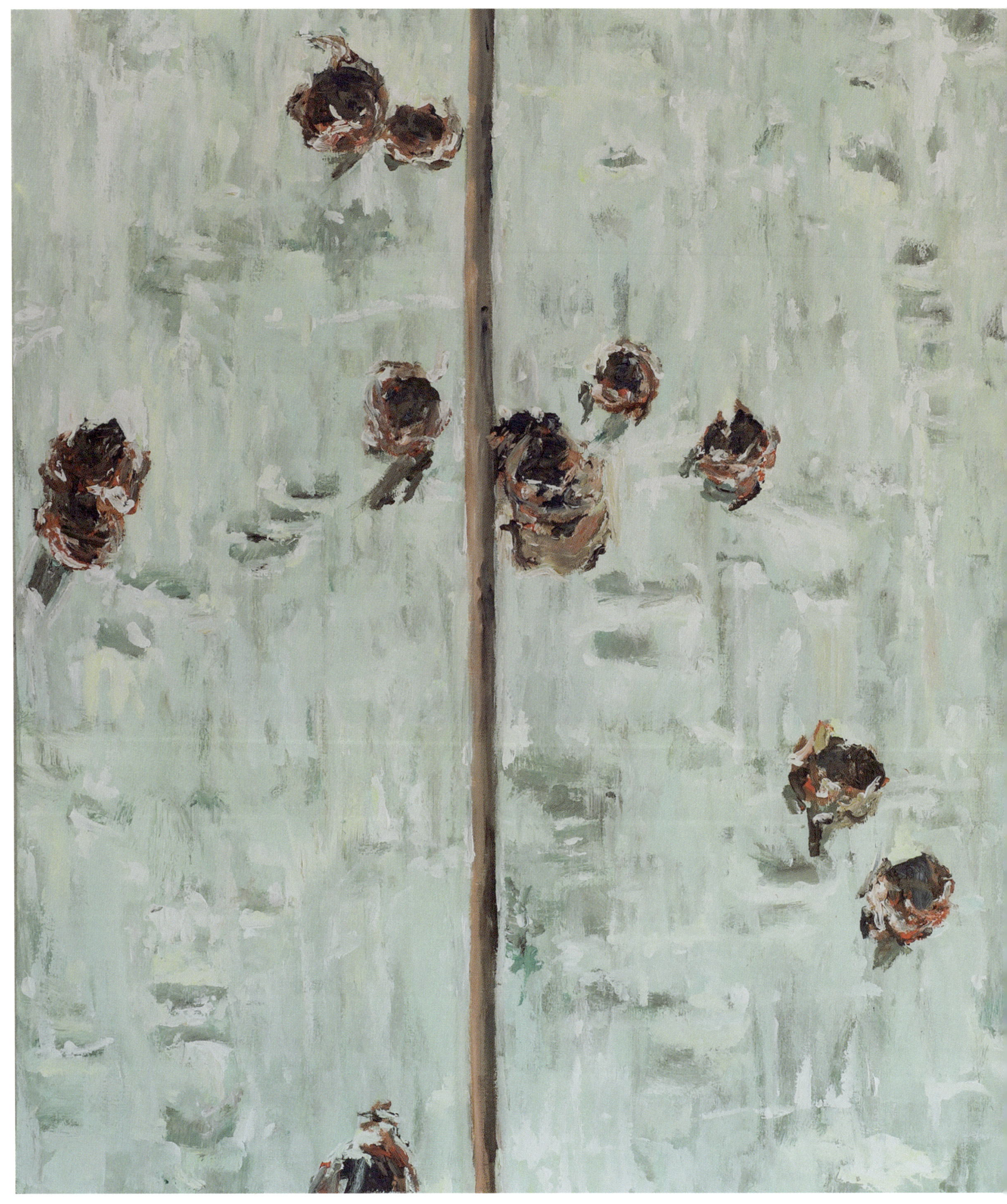

 3. MY CALIFORNIA: PAINTINGS PT. 1

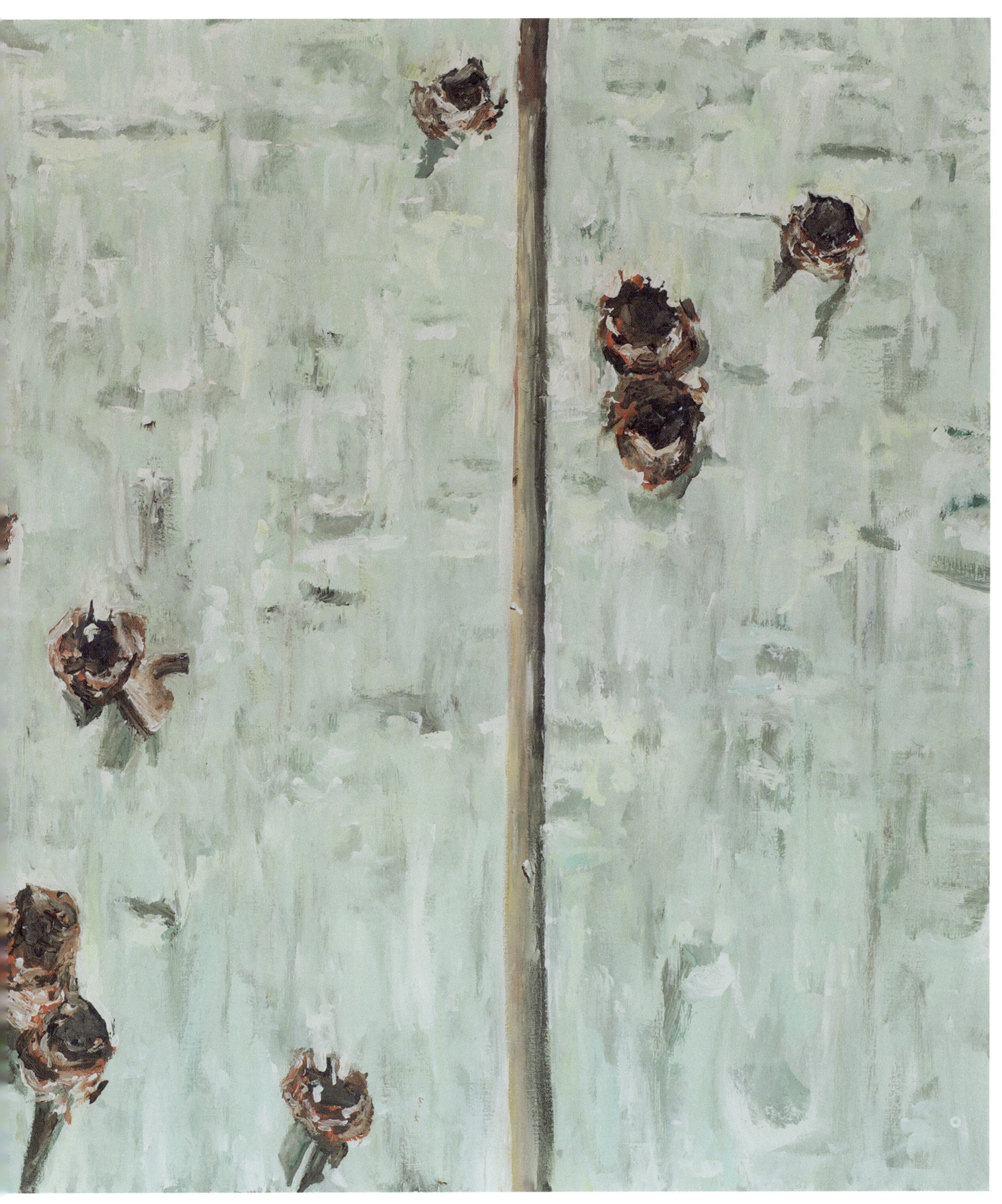

Gunman, My California series,
acrylic on canvas, 250 x 140 cm, 2016

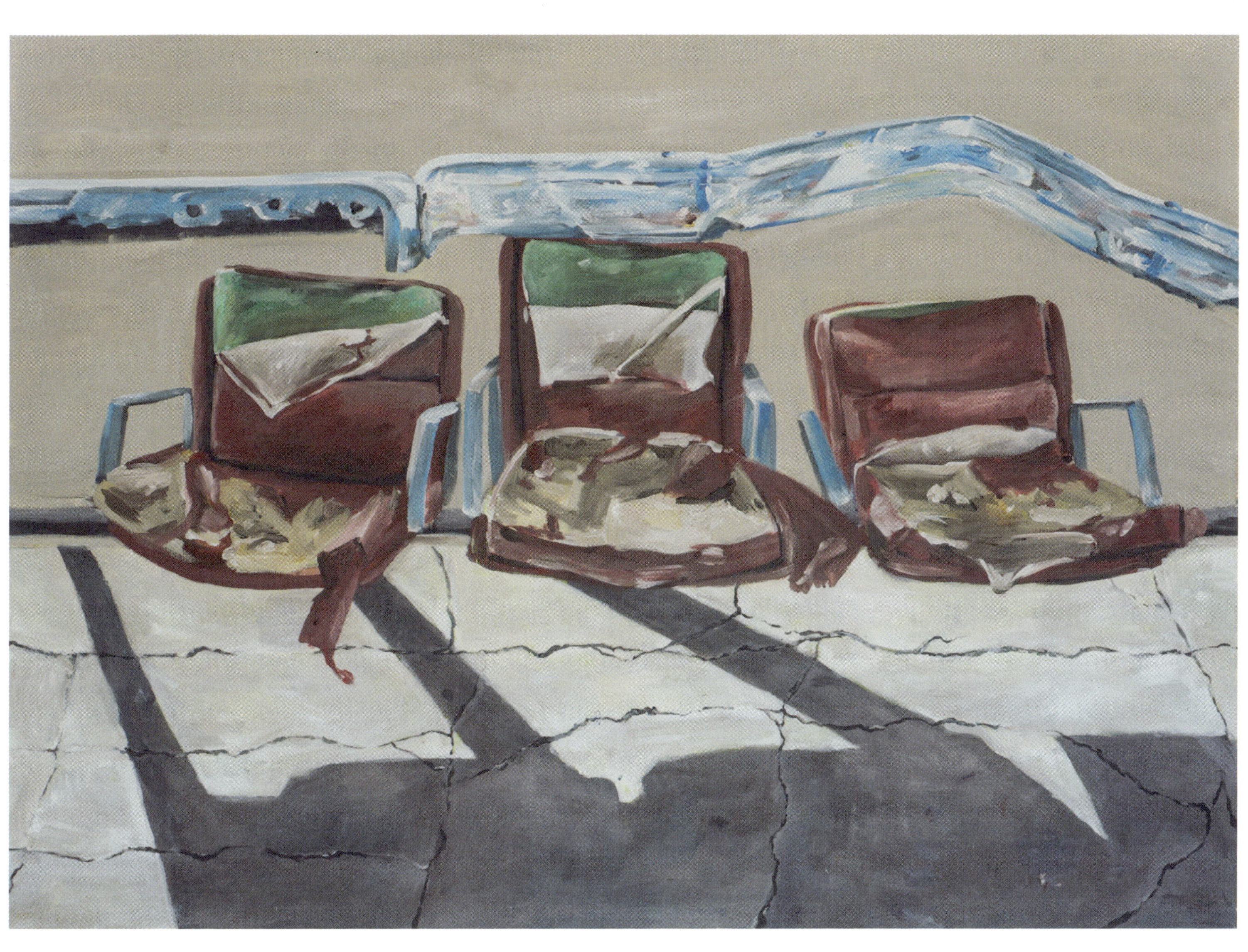

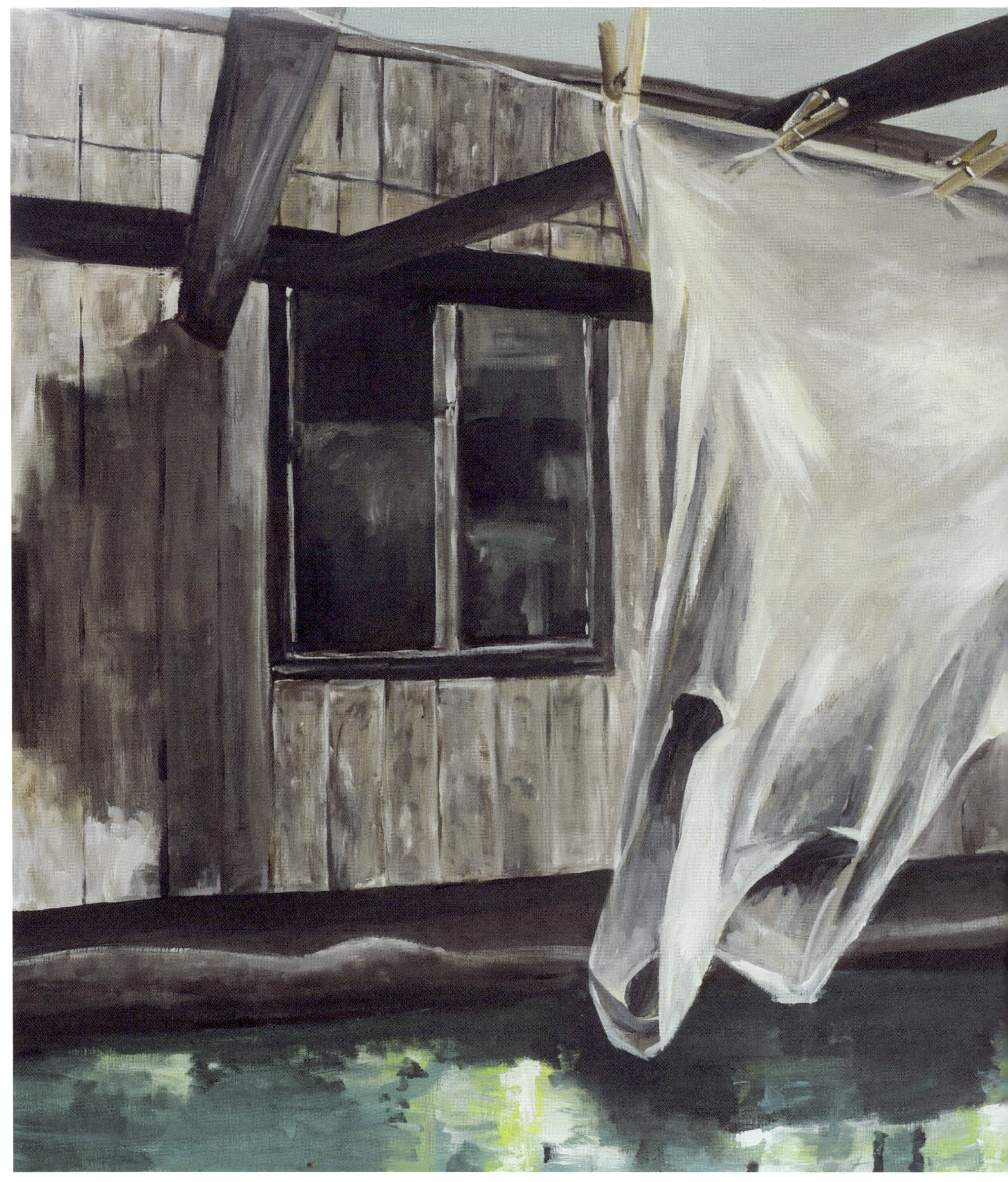

3. MY CALIFORNIA: PAINTINGS PT. 1

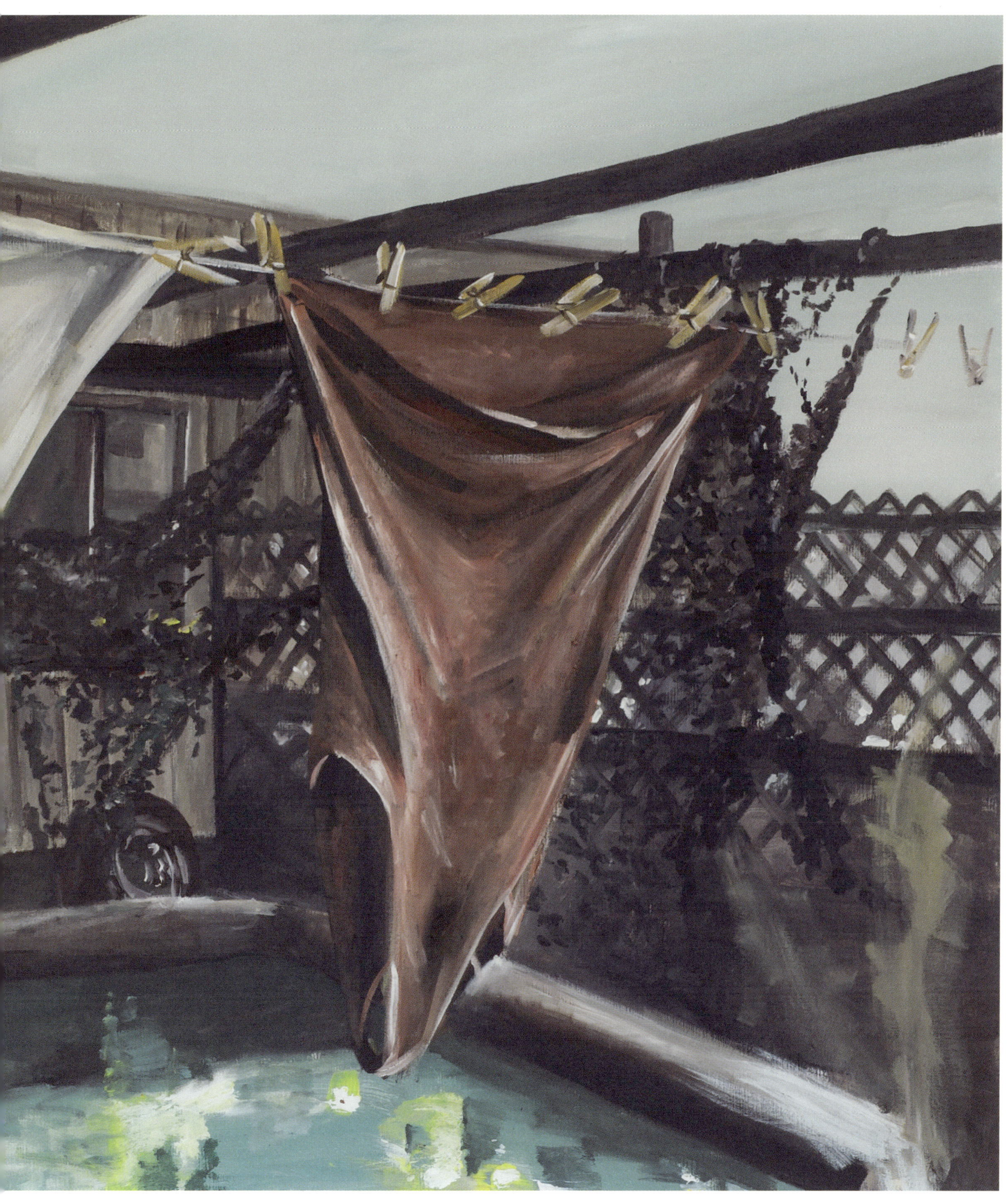

Scumbag Blues, My California series,
acrylic on canvas, 250 x 140 cm, 2016

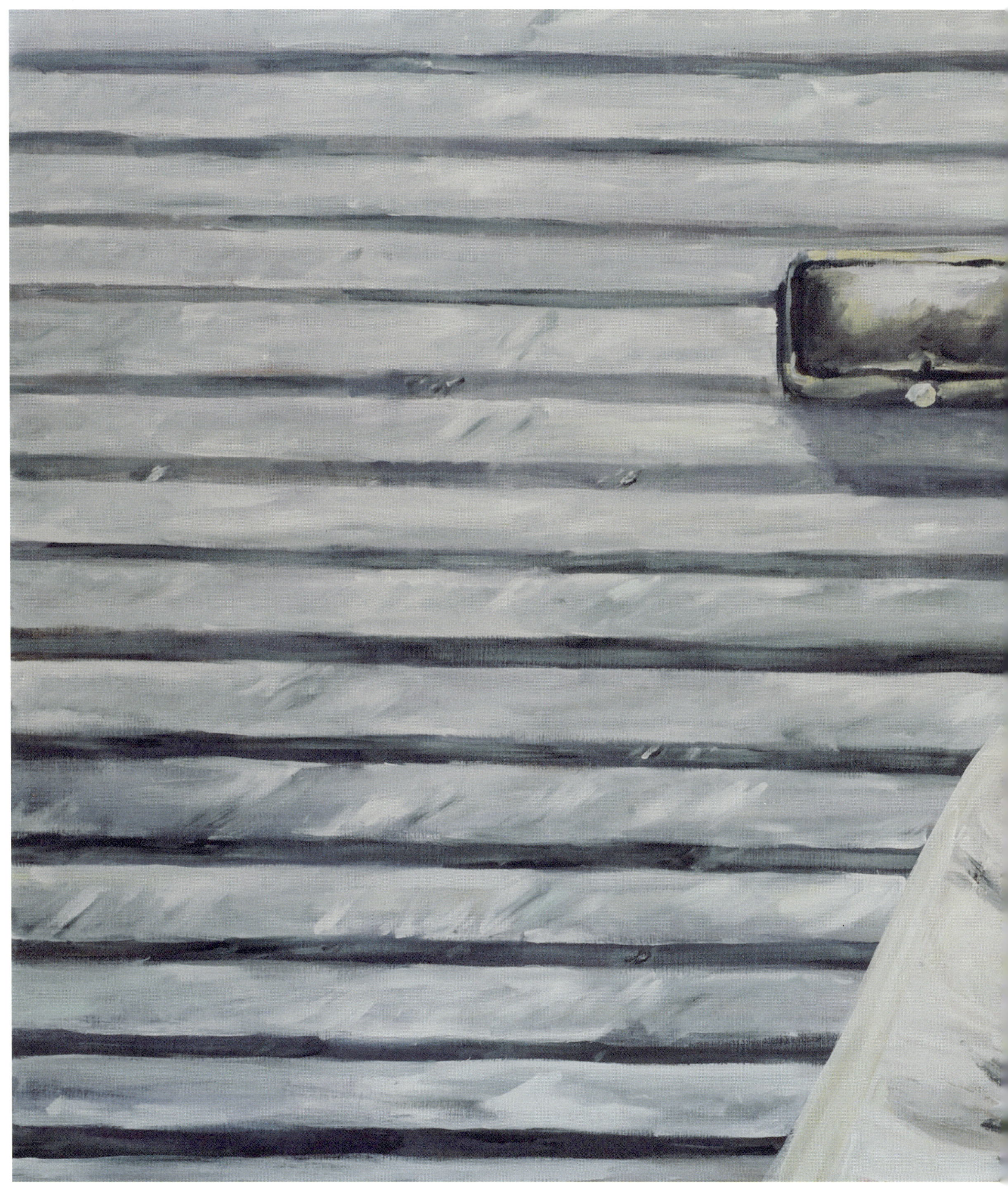

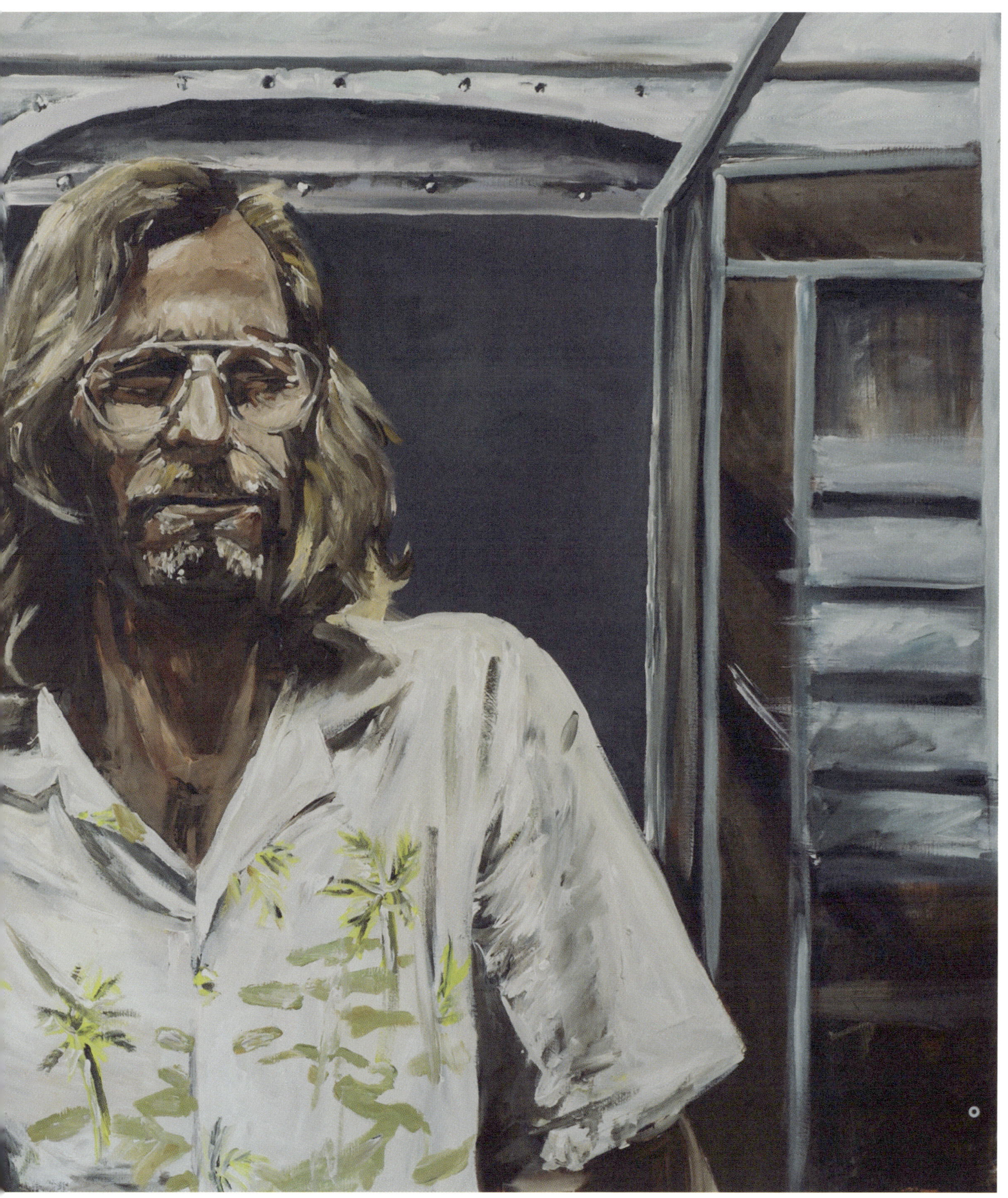

San Berdoo Sunburn, My California series,
acrylic on canvas, 250 x 140 cm, 2016

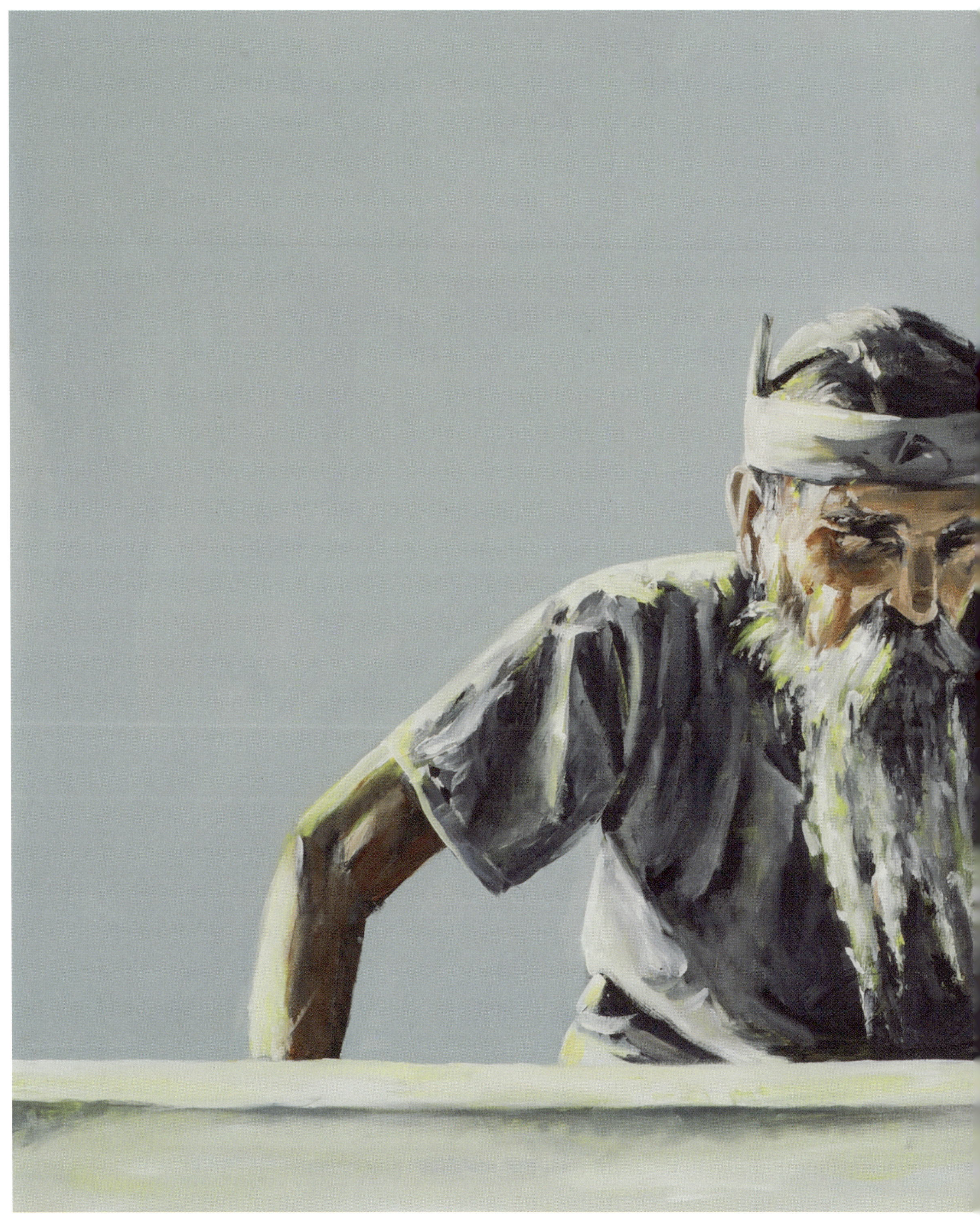

3. MY CALIFORNIA: PAINTINGS PT. 1

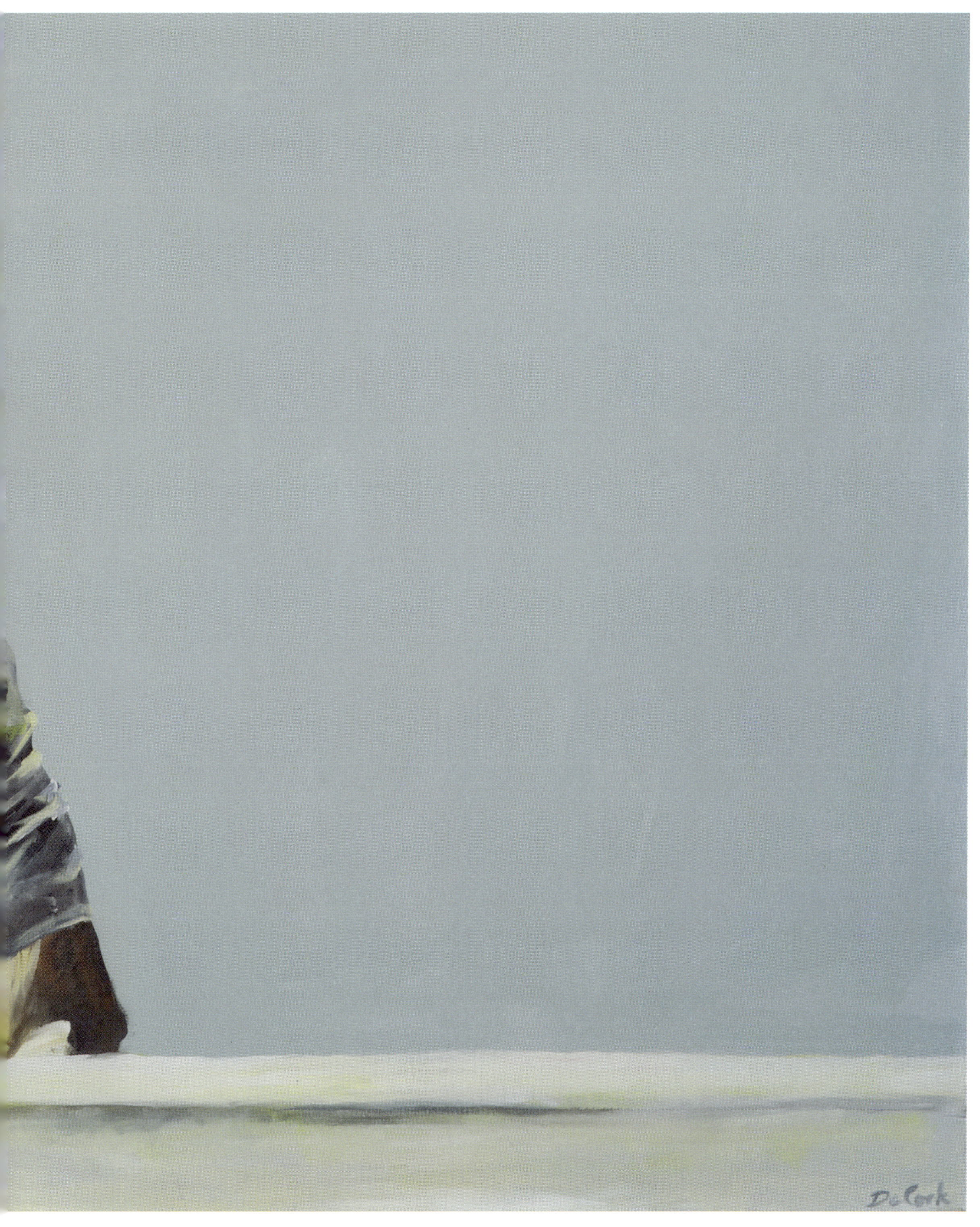

The Lost Art of Keeping a Secret,
My California series, acrylic on canvas,
200 x 120 cm, 2016

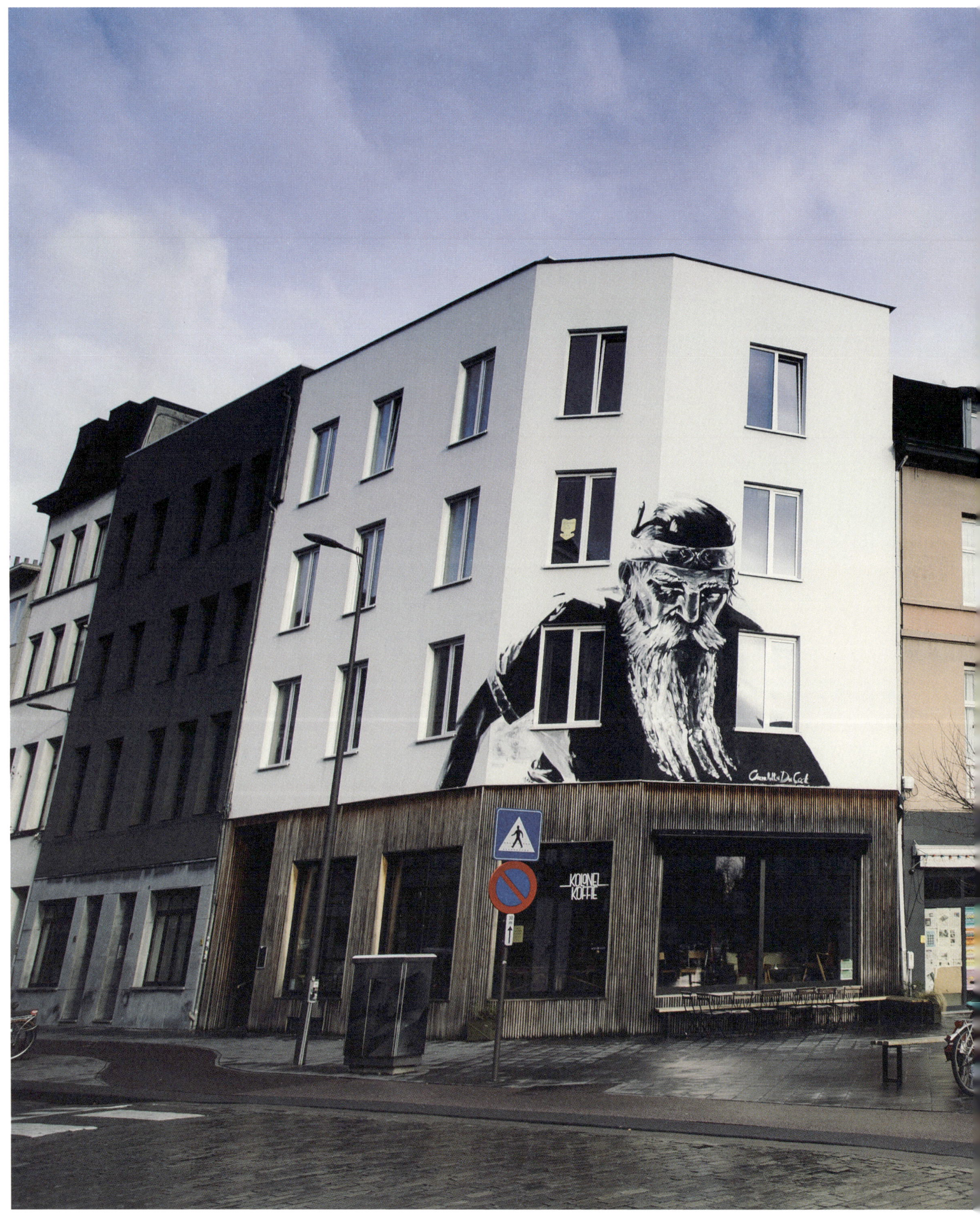

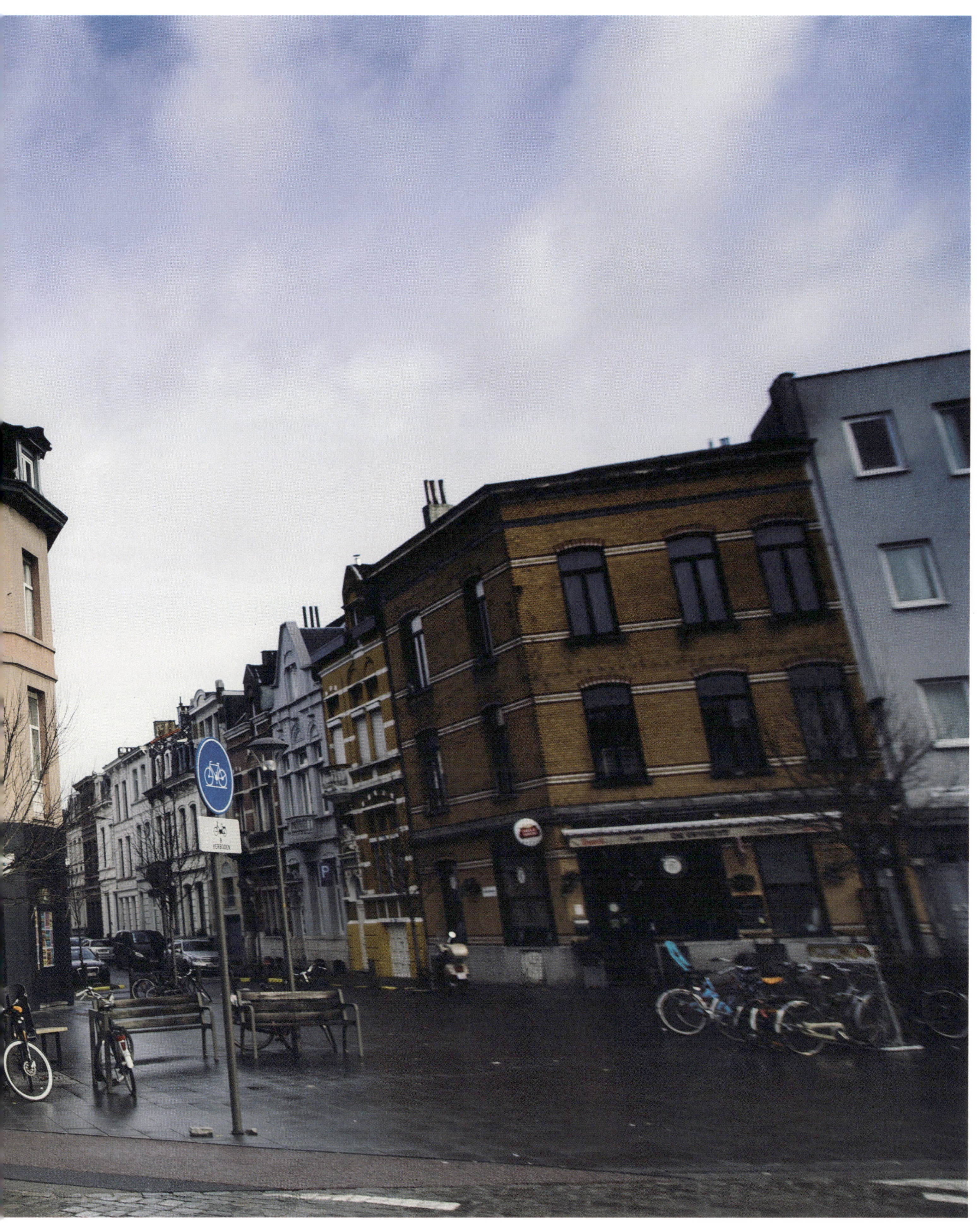

Kolonel, mural at Troonplaats, Antwerp,
800 x 800 cm, 2016, © Kris Lathouwers

My California

Documentary

"Our society is turning more and more
individualistic and materialistic. Due to
social media we are becoming rather antisocial
than social. We are losing actual face-to-
face communication. Materialization is getting
worse these days. We are applying for more and
more loans to get things we don't really need.
We think we need two cars, a big home with a
dishwasher and juicer to make us happy. But in
the end we're constantly working to make our
dreams come true and don't really have the time
to enjoy them."

"I also struggle with these things. I also buy
things I don't need and find myself scrolling
Facebook like a zombie, wasting time. Some time
ago I discovered a few places in the middle of
the desert where people were living without
the standards we call 'normal.' They live of
the grid, in places they call: 'The last free
place on earth'. There is no wifi or dishwasher
and they built their homes themselves with
recuperated material. I had the honor to meet
these amazing souls and spent time listening to
their stories. After a few days wandering around
these 'villages' I realized these people actually
communicated. True happiness reigned these places."

"I took photos on this trip, converted them into
paintings and put up an exhibition. After that,
I went back with a camera and gave everyone
prints of 'their' painting."

"With this documentary I want to spread the
message of these inspirational souls …"
(CHARLOTTE DE COCK)

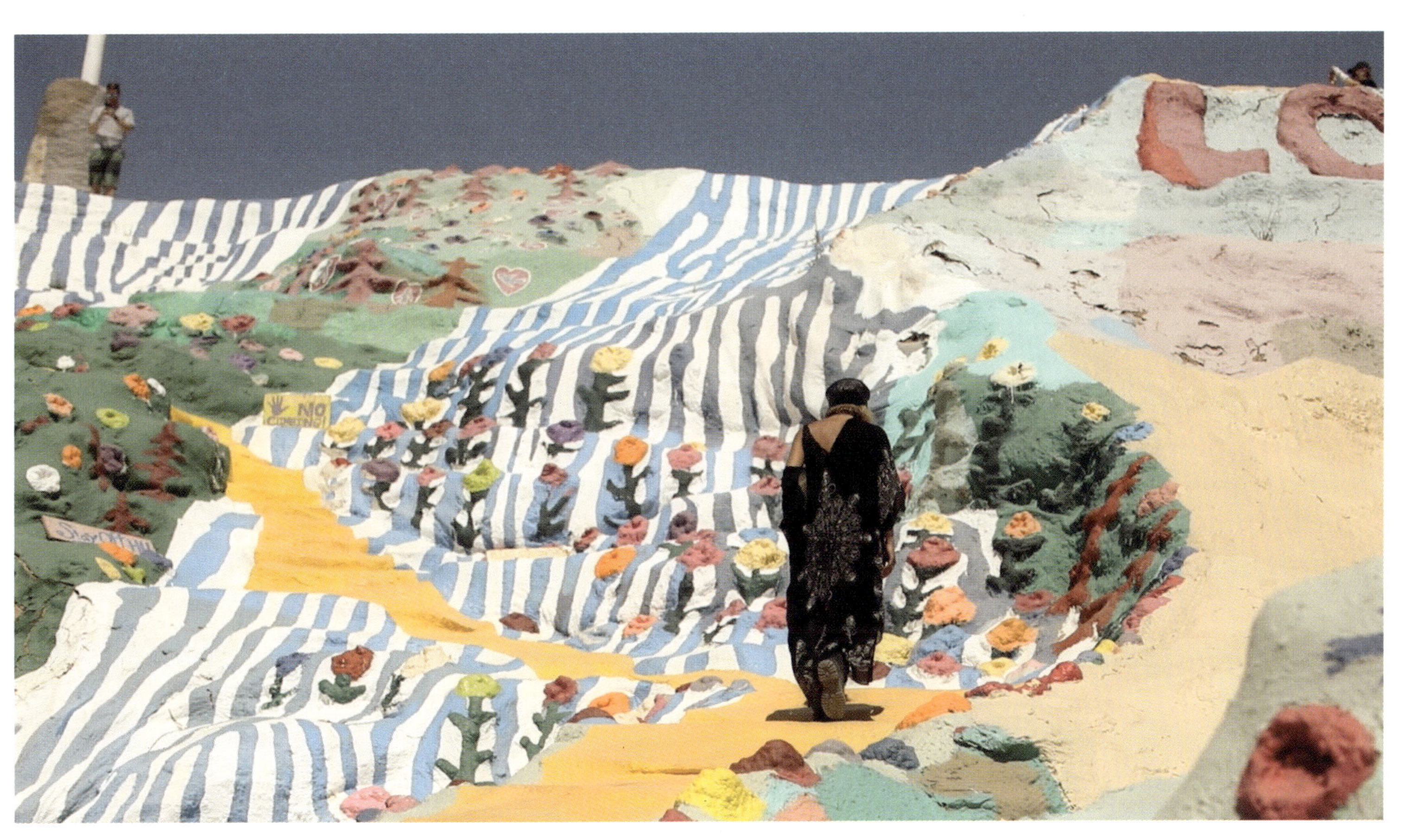

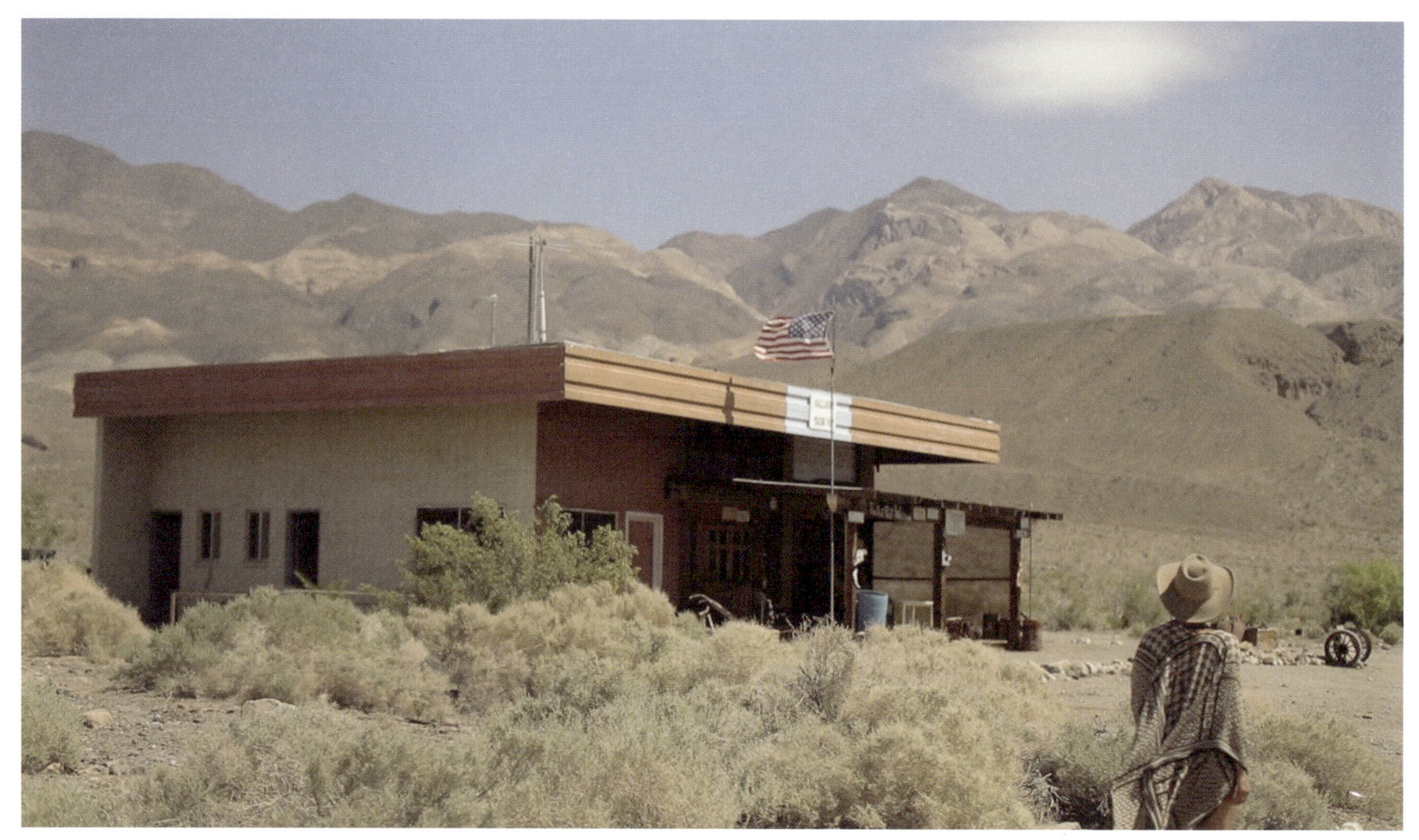

Ballarat

Still of video by Kris Lathouwers, 2017

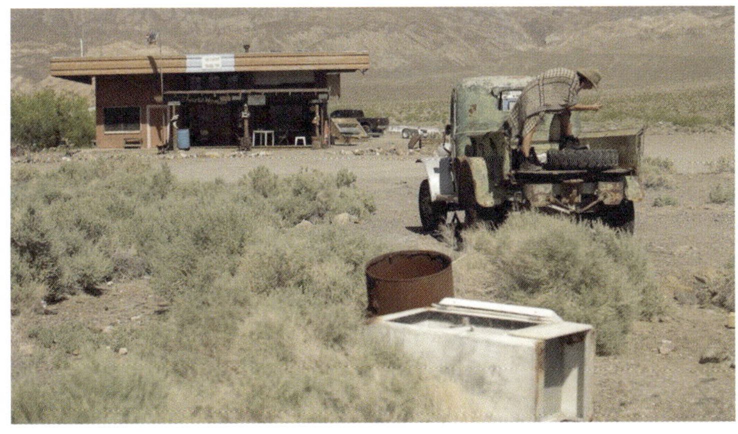
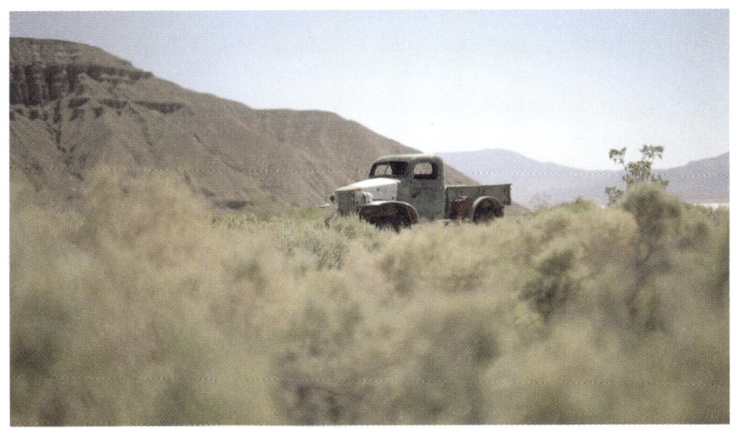
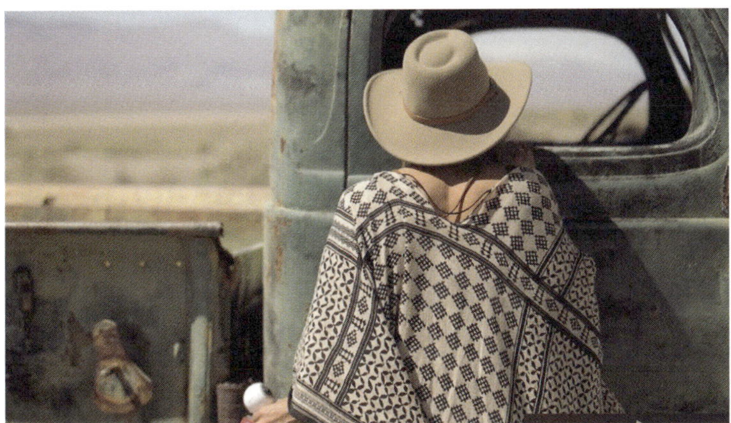
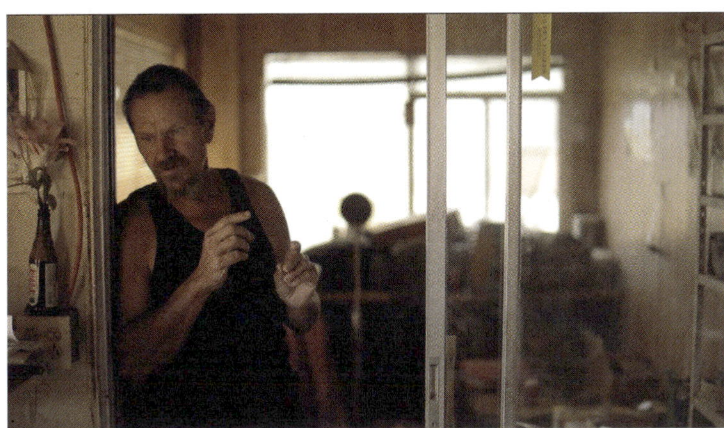
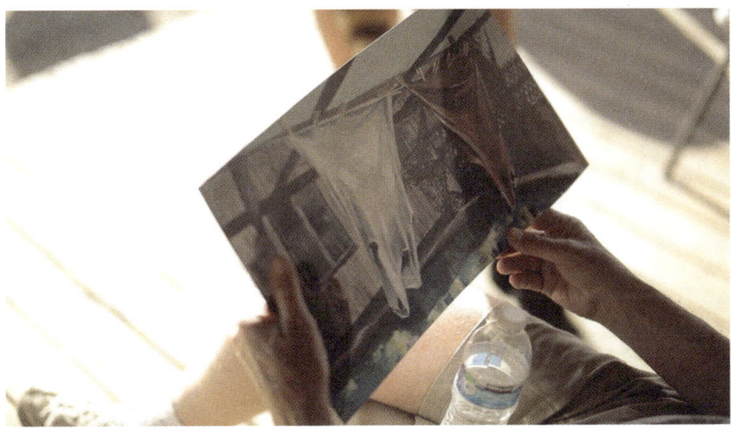
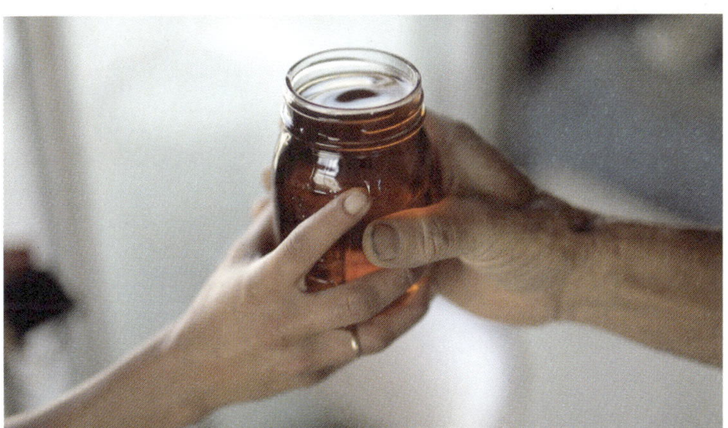
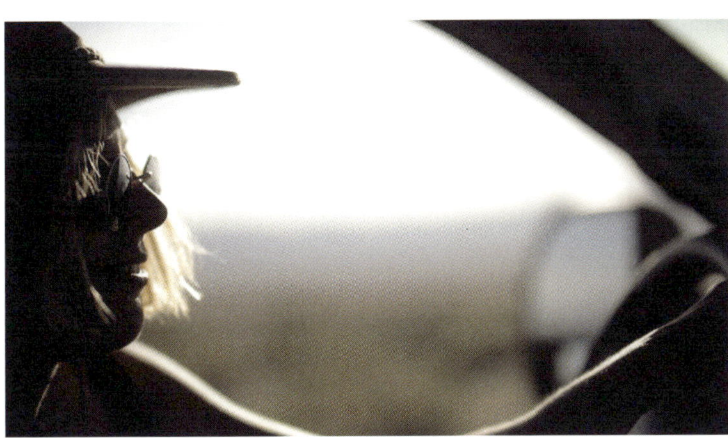
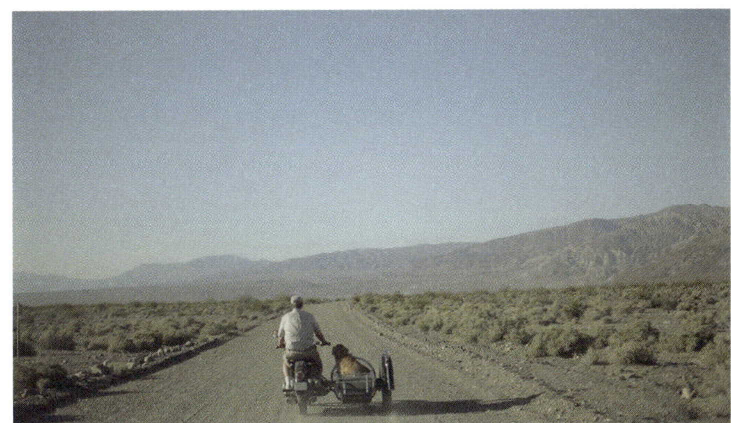

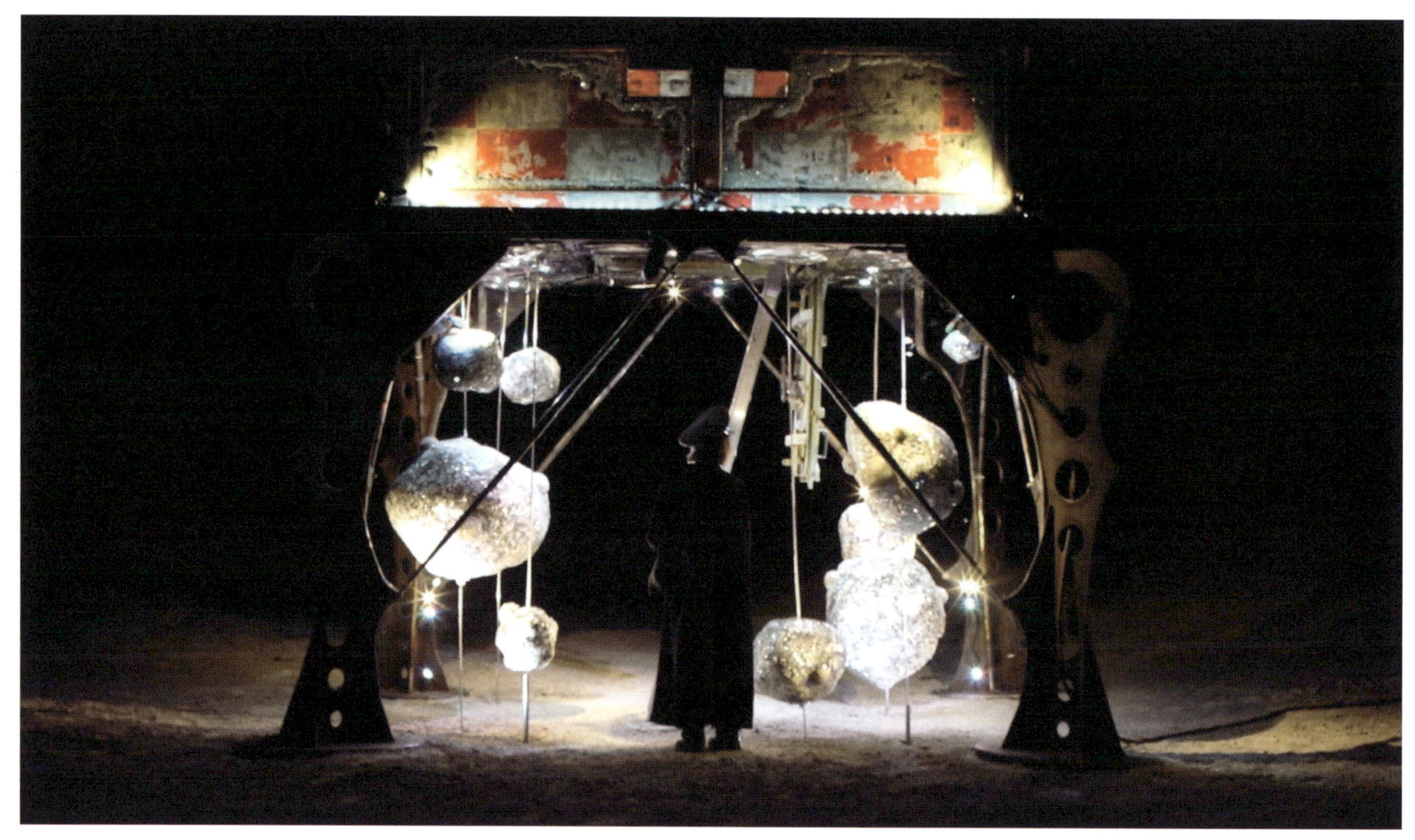

Bombay Beach

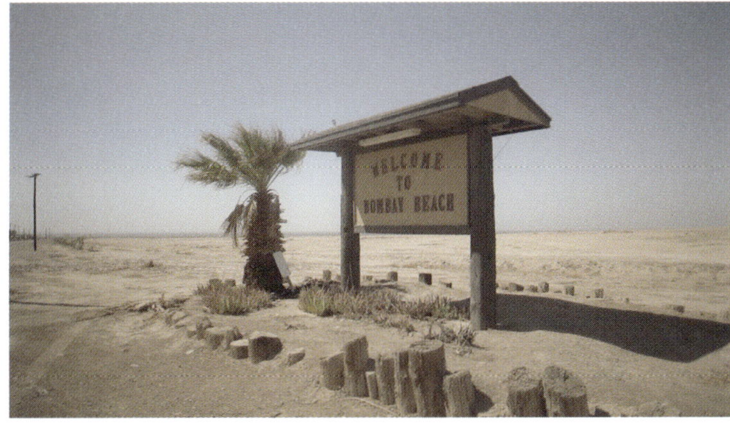
WELCOME
TO
BOMBAY BEACH

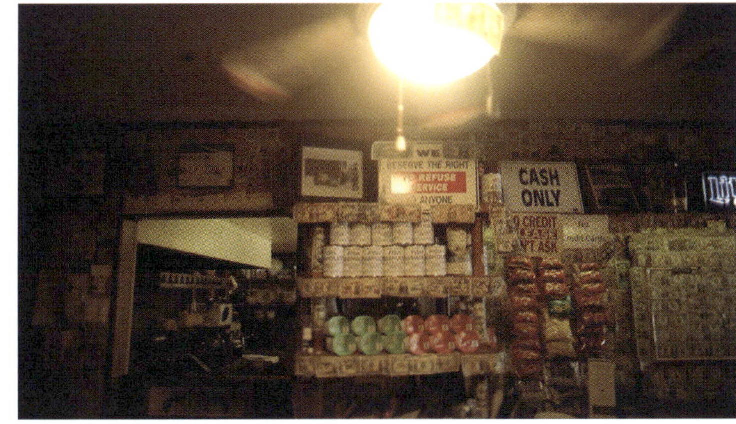
WE
RESERVE THE RIGHT
REFUSE
SERVICE
ANYONE
CASH
ONLY
No
Credit Cards

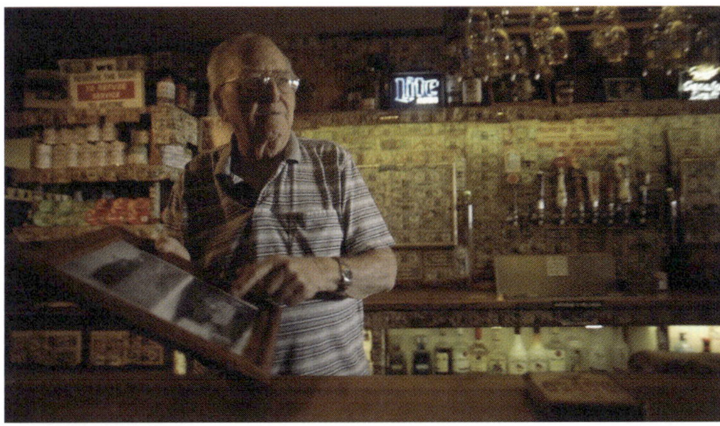

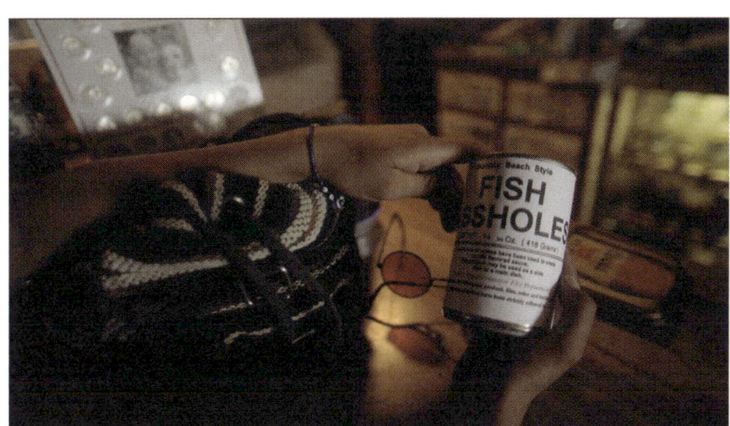
FISH
SSHOLES

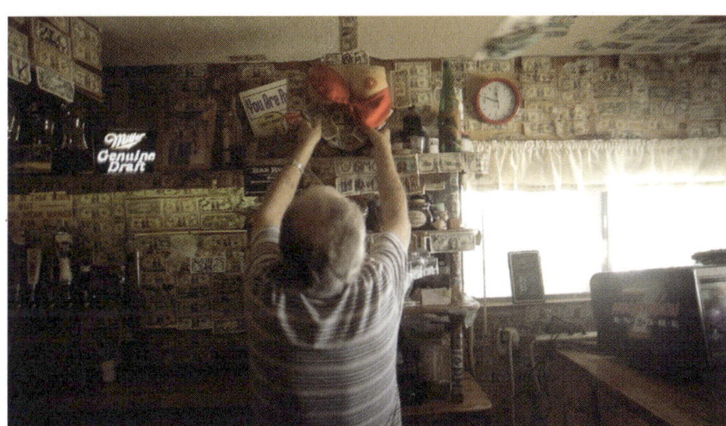
Miller
Genuine Draft
You Are

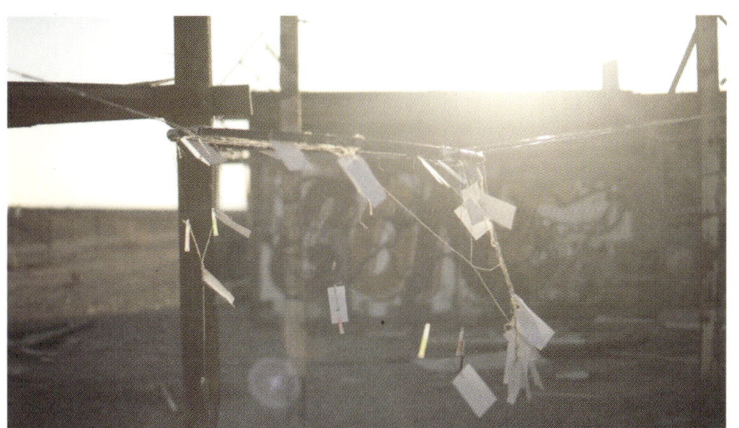

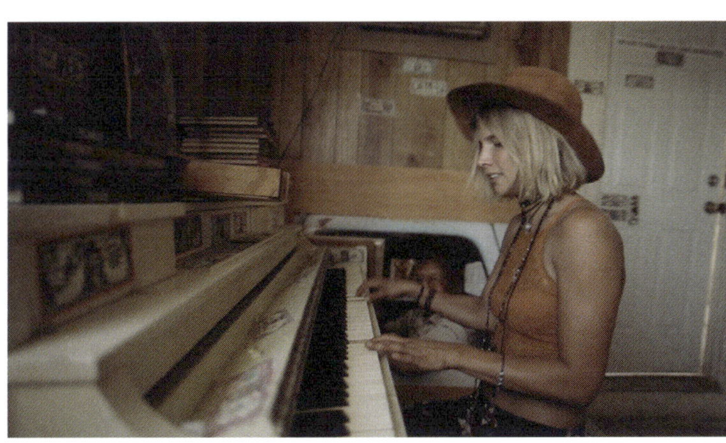

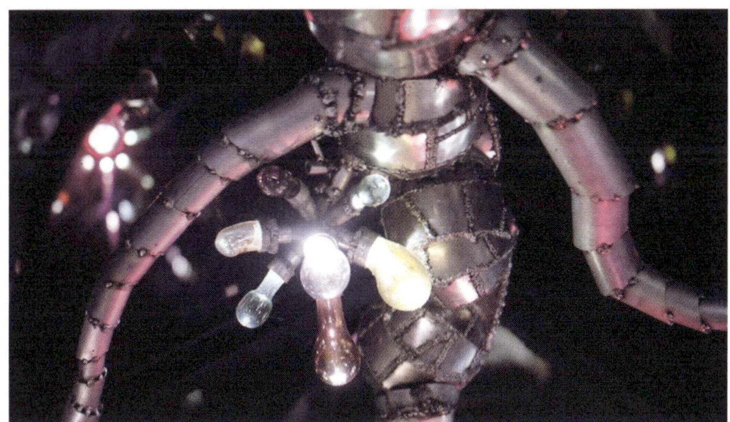

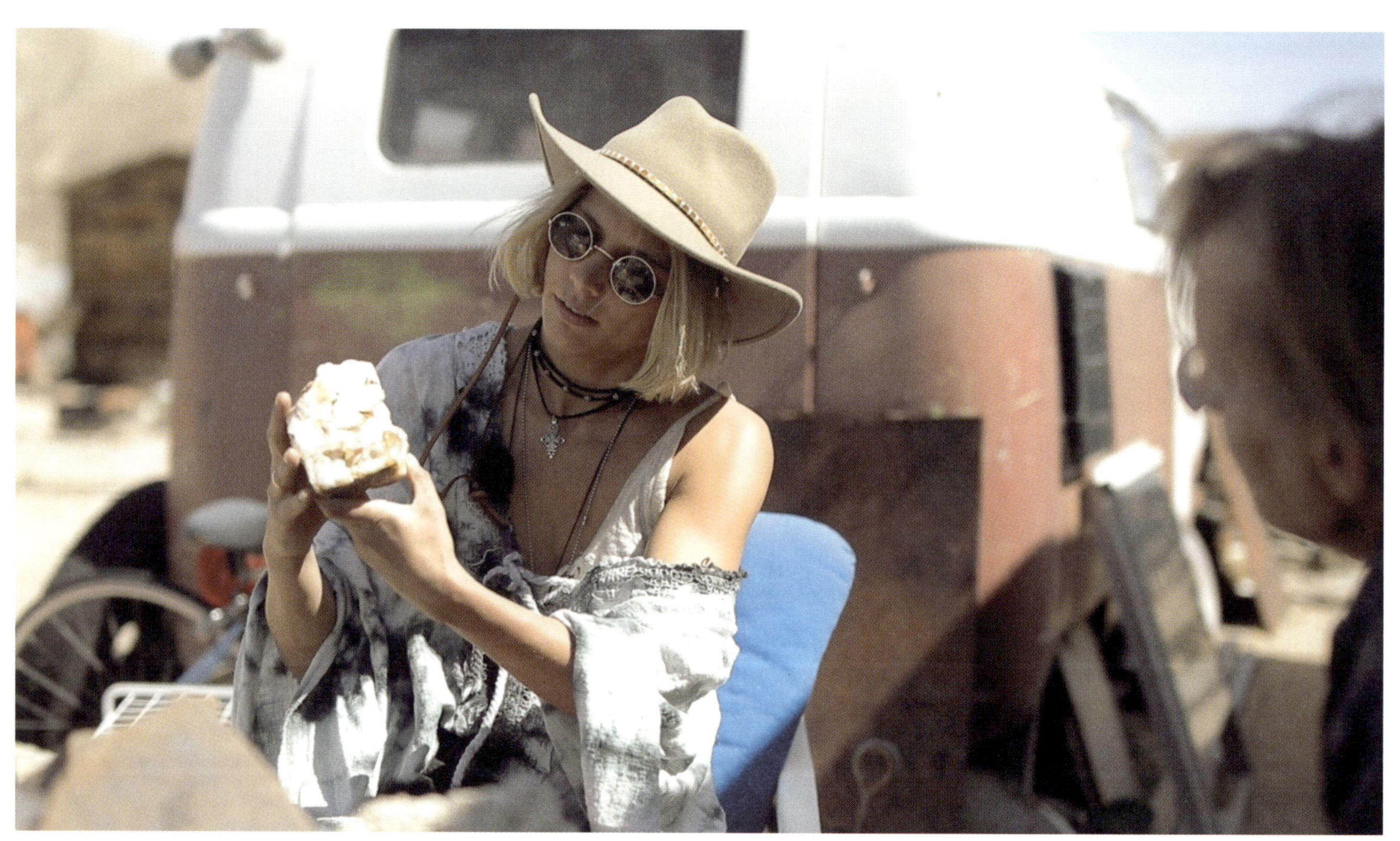

Darwin

Still of video by Kris Lathouwers, 2017

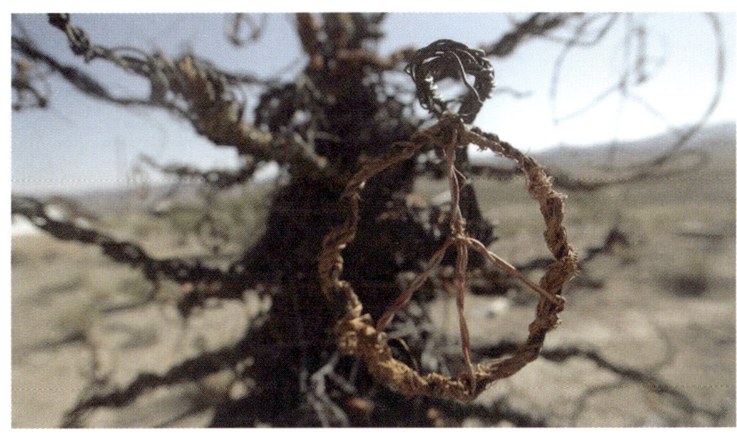
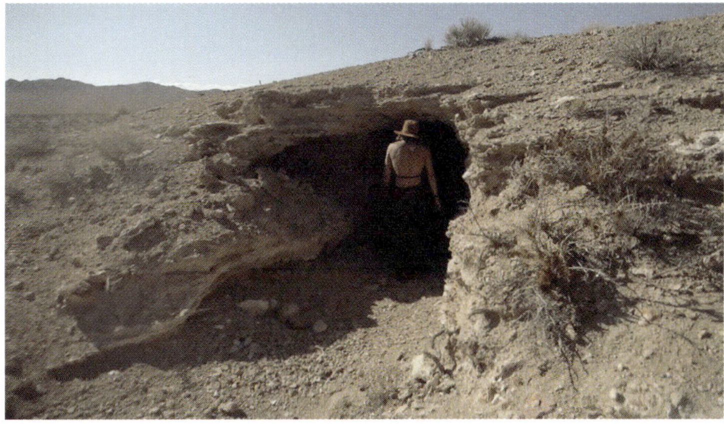
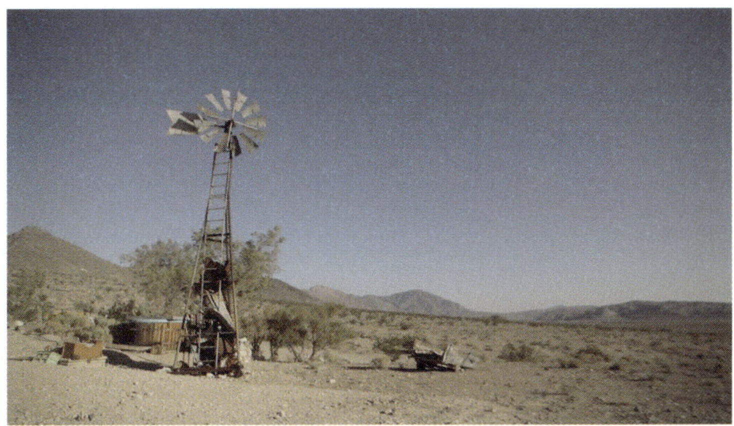
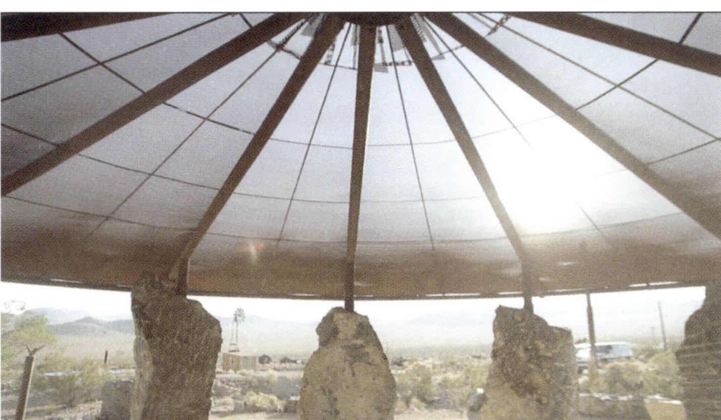

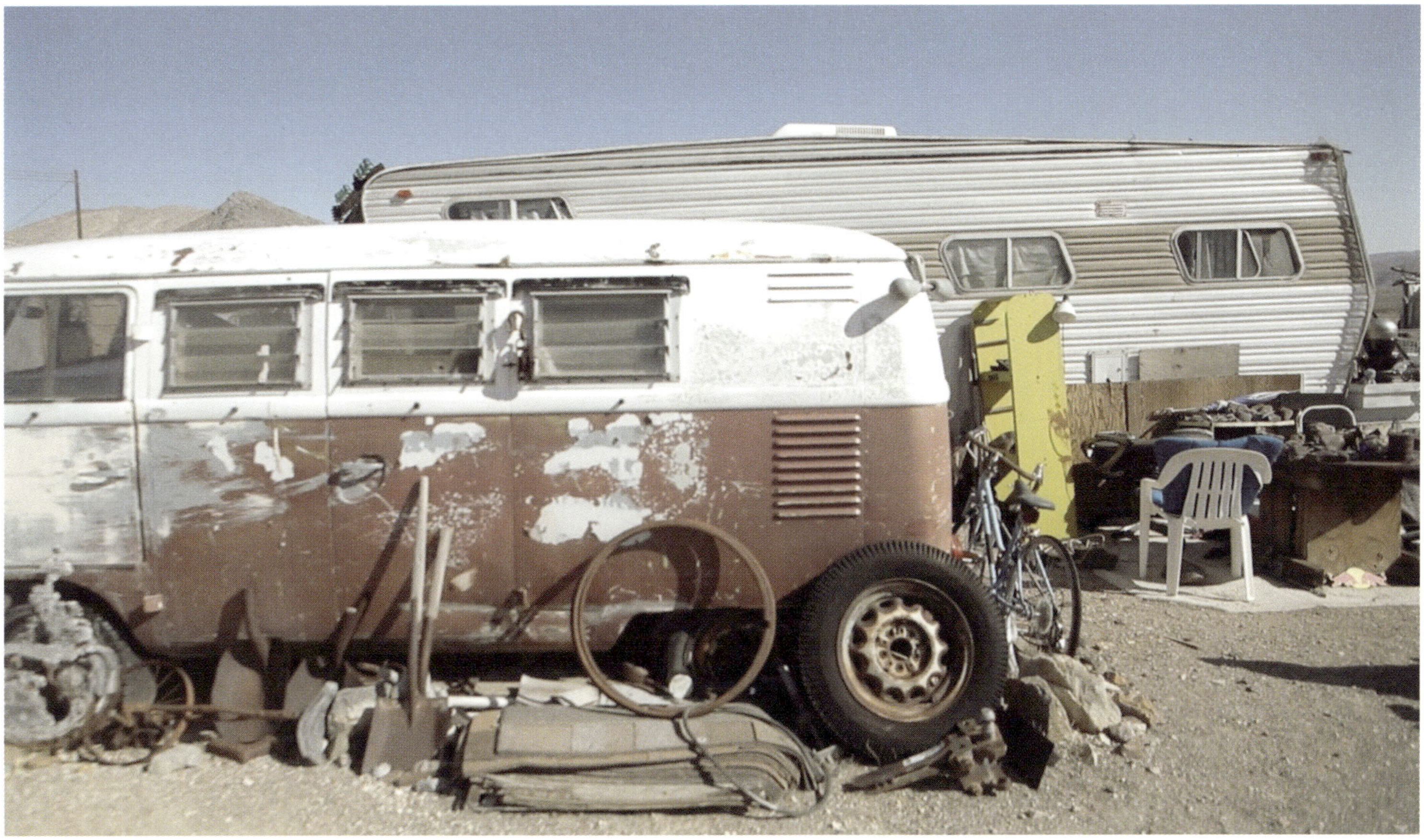

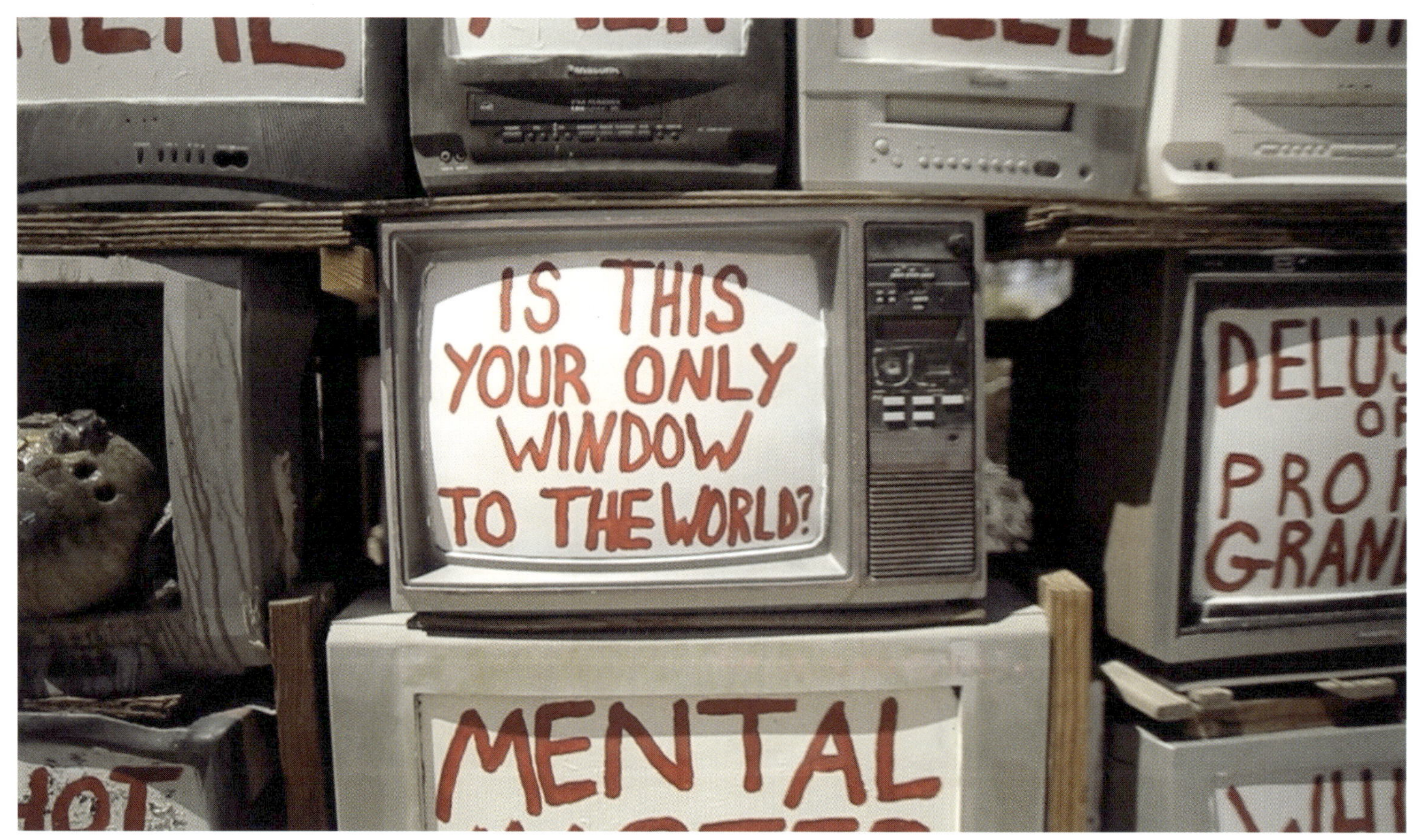

Slab City

3. MY CALIFORNIA: DOCUMENTARY

Still of video by Kris Lathouwers, 2017

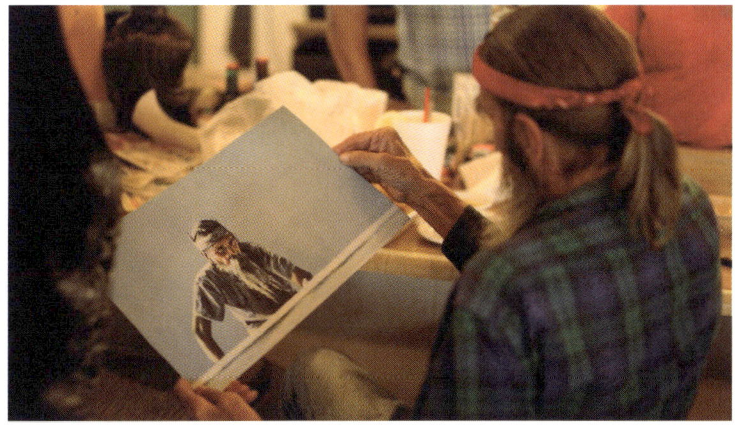 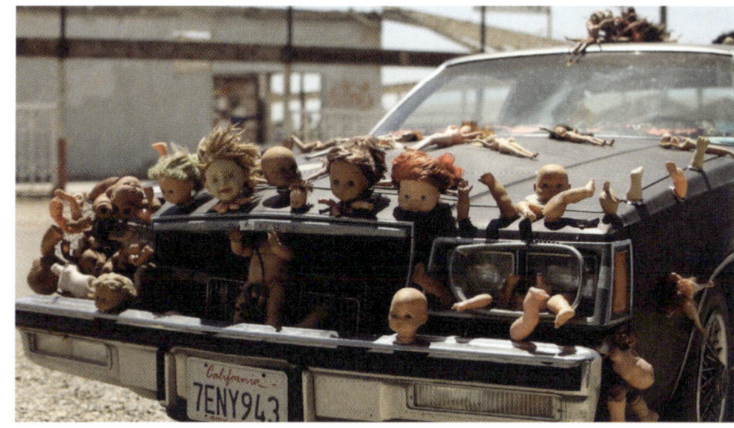

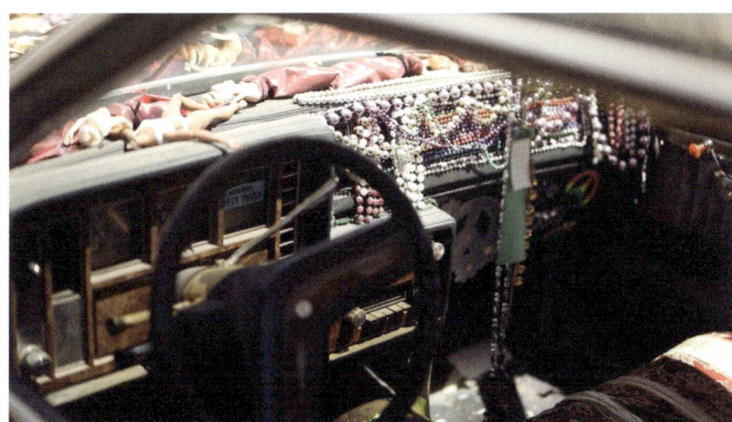 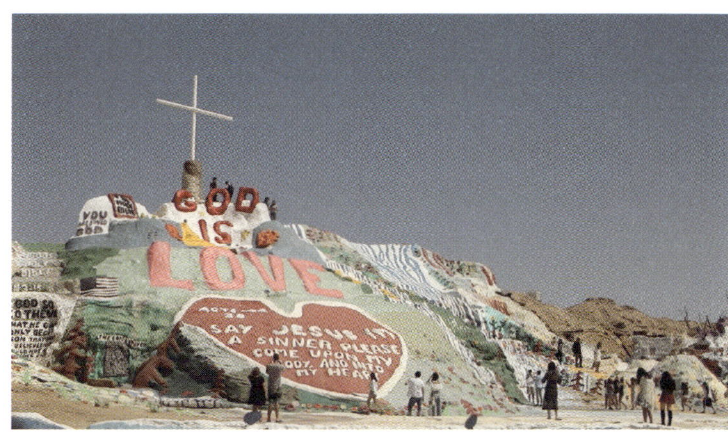

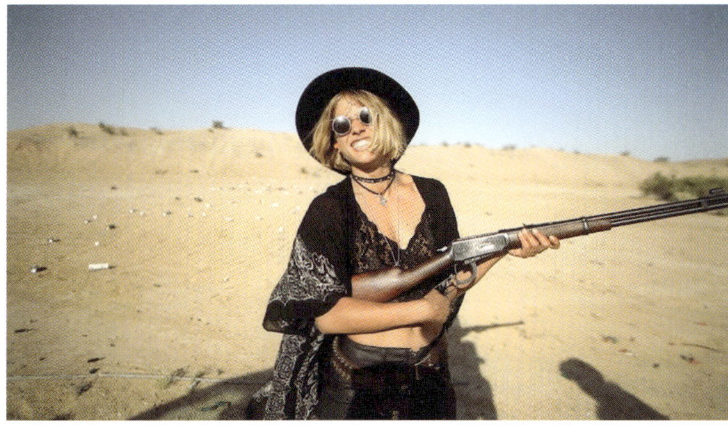 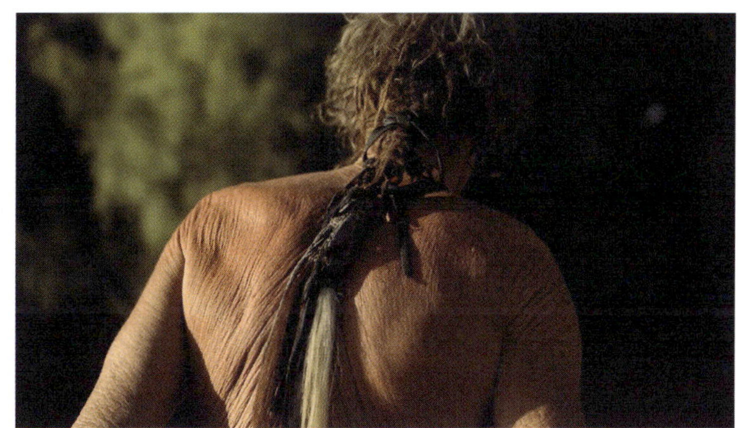

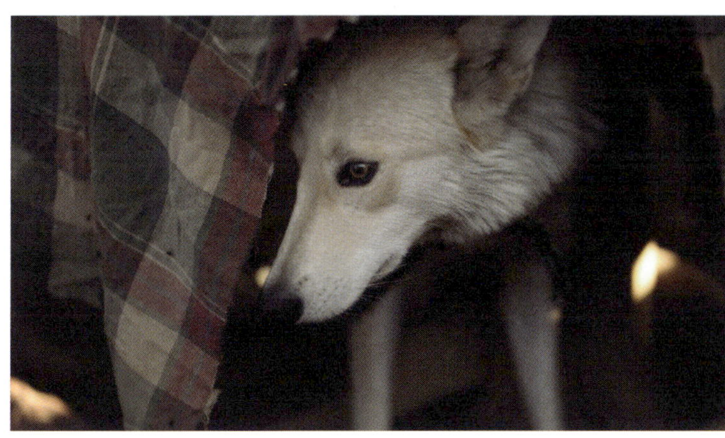 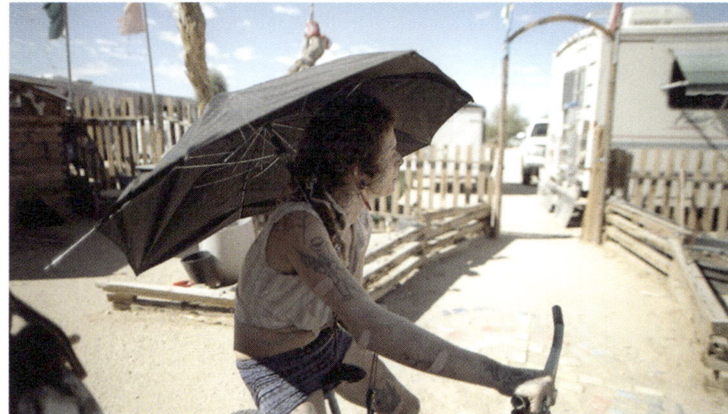

My California

Paintings Pt. 2

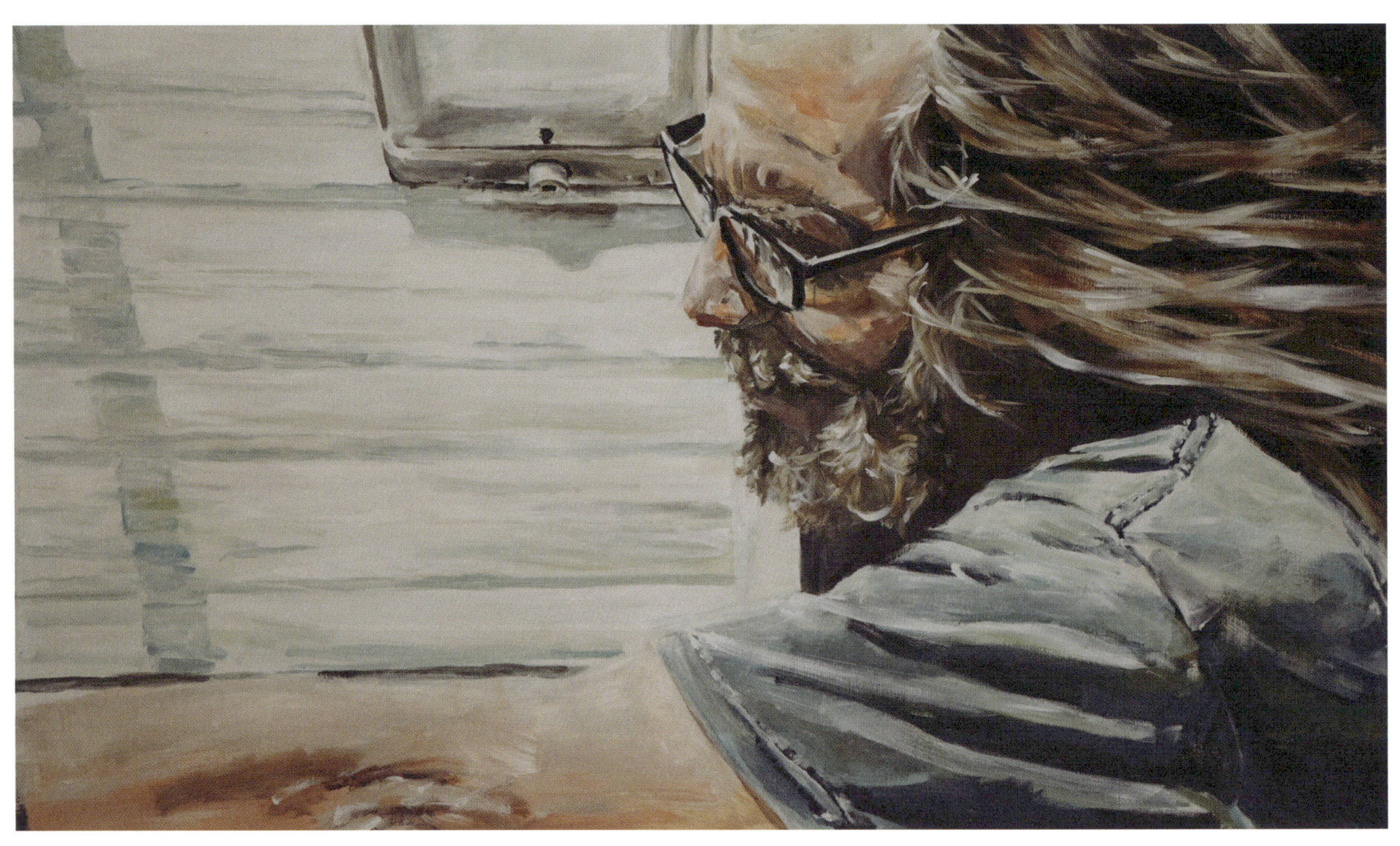

3. MY CALIFORNIA: PAINTINGS PT. 2

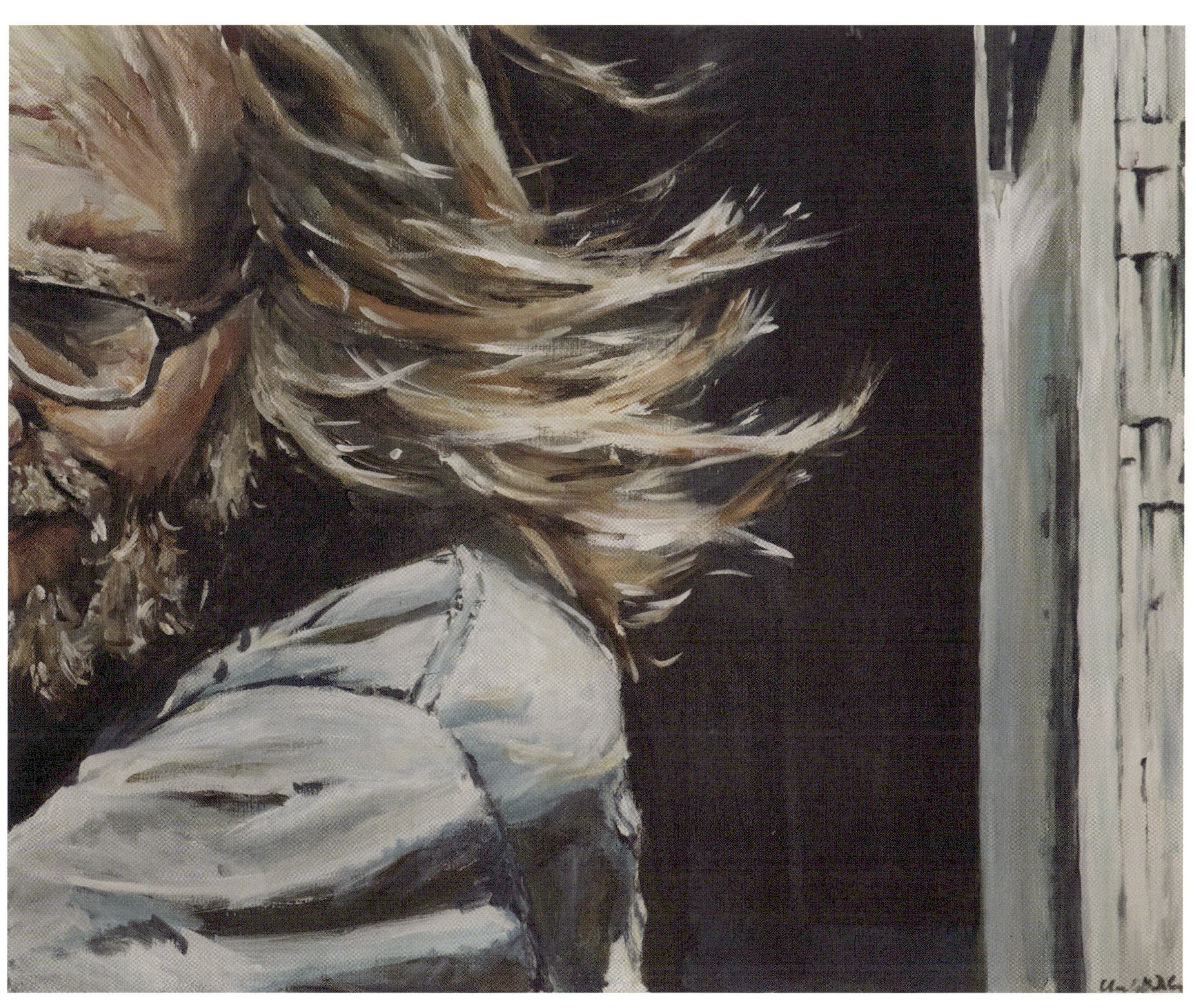

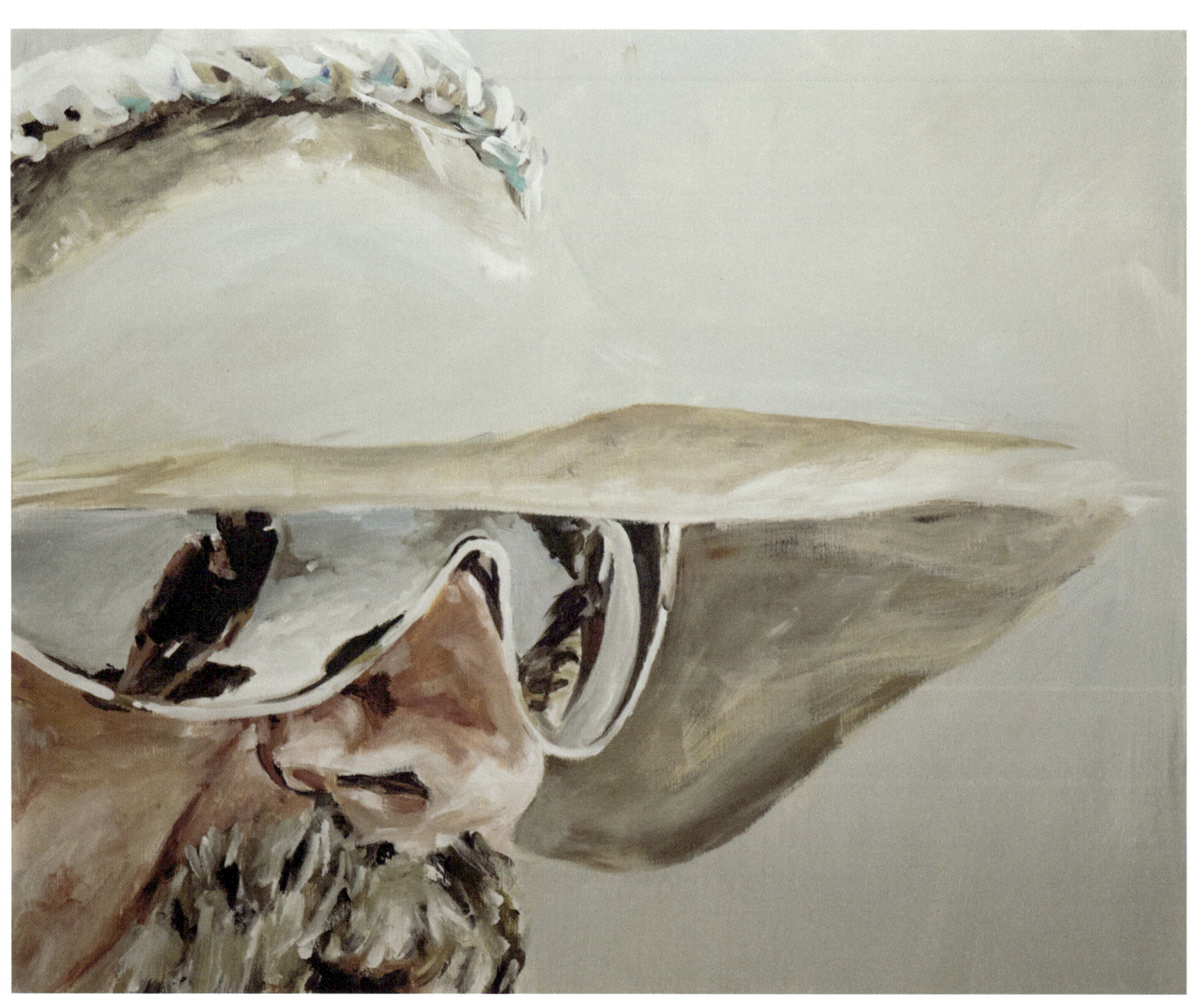

3. MY CALIFORNIA: PAINTINGS PT. 2

Dramatic Theme,
My California series,
acrylic on canvas, 120 x 100 cm, 2018

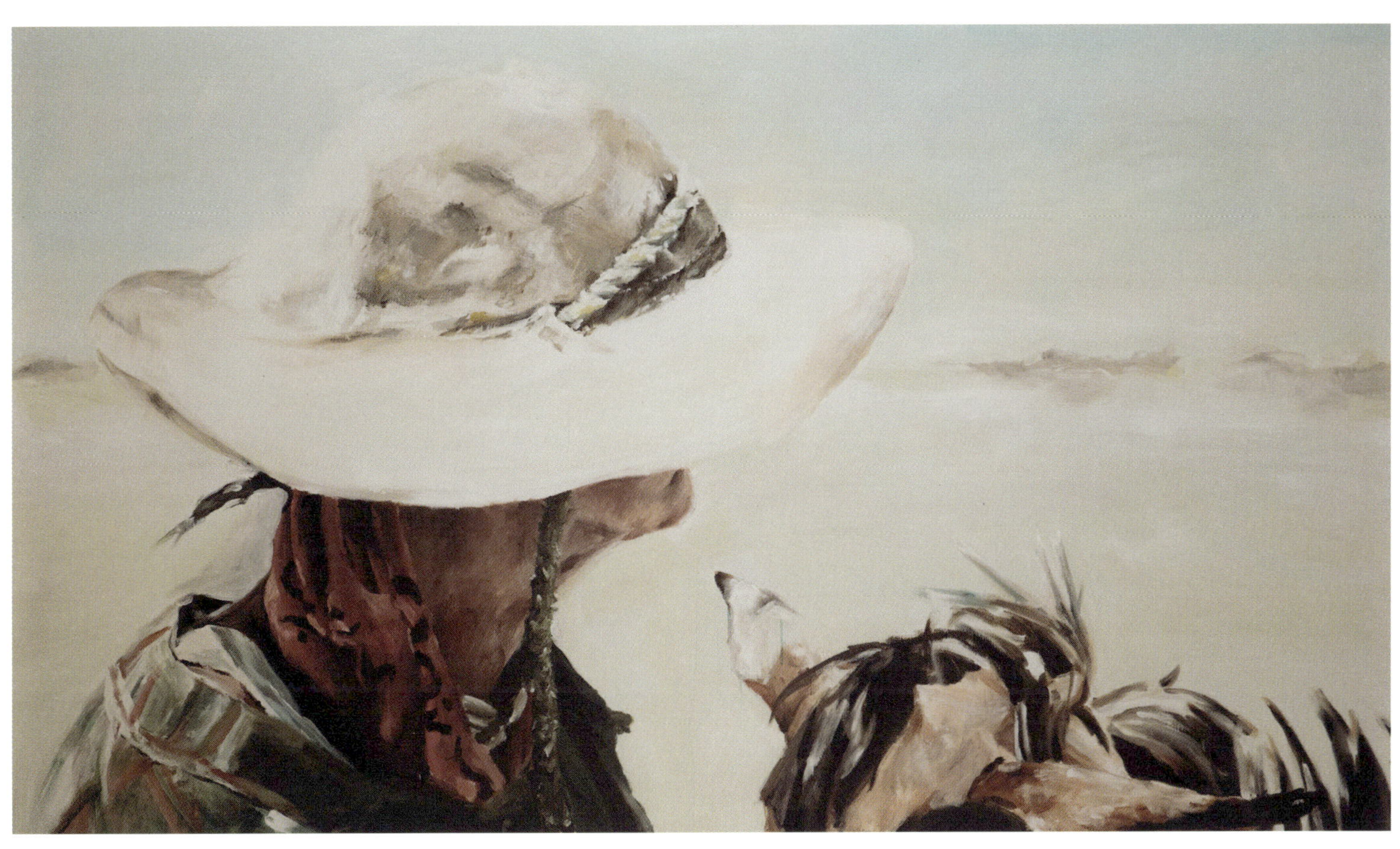

Main Theme,
My California series,
acrylic on canvas, 250 x 150 cm, 2018

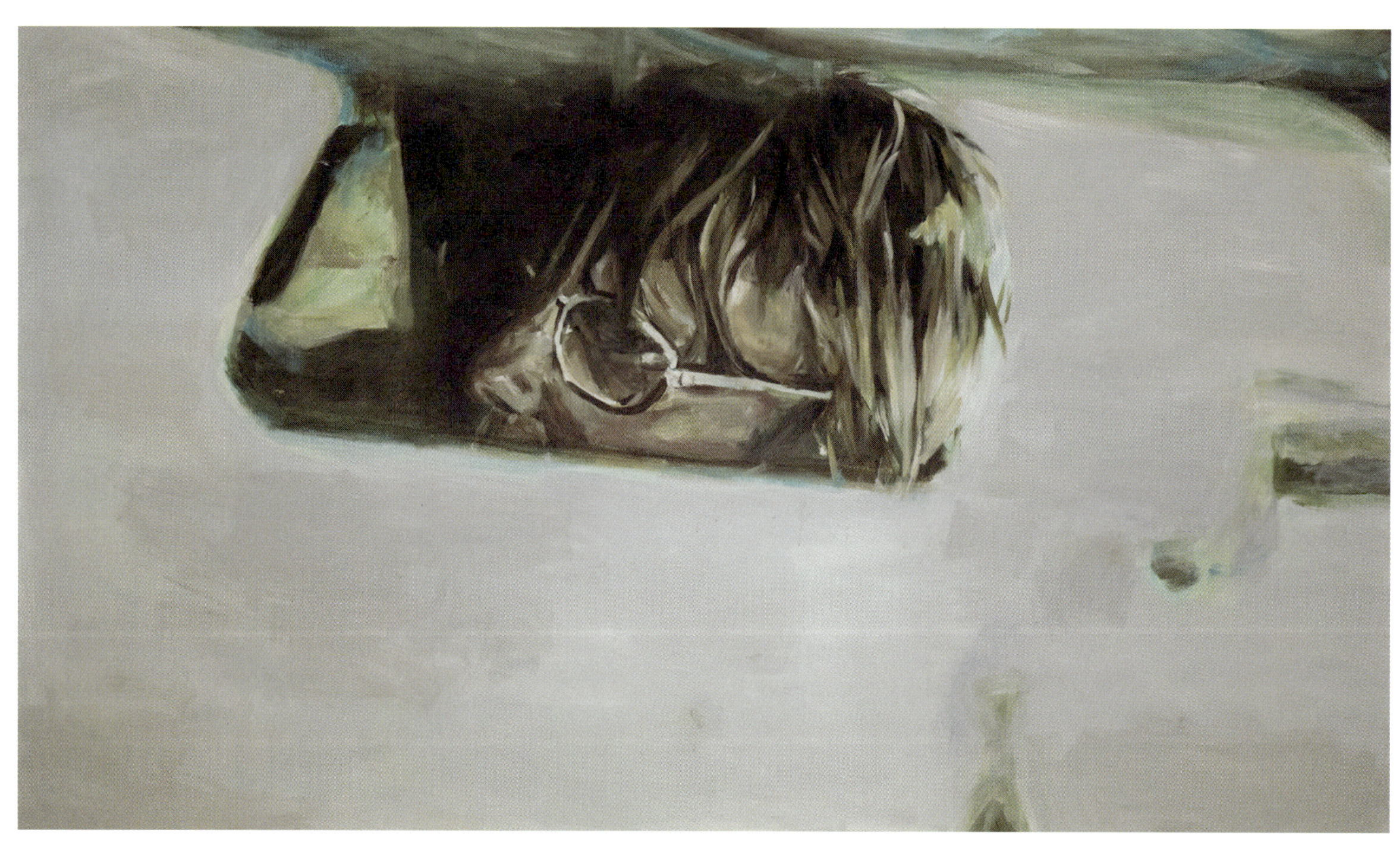

3. MY CALIFORNIA: PAINTINGS PT. 2

Breathe (In the Air),
My California series,
acrylic on canvas, 250 x 150 cm, 2018

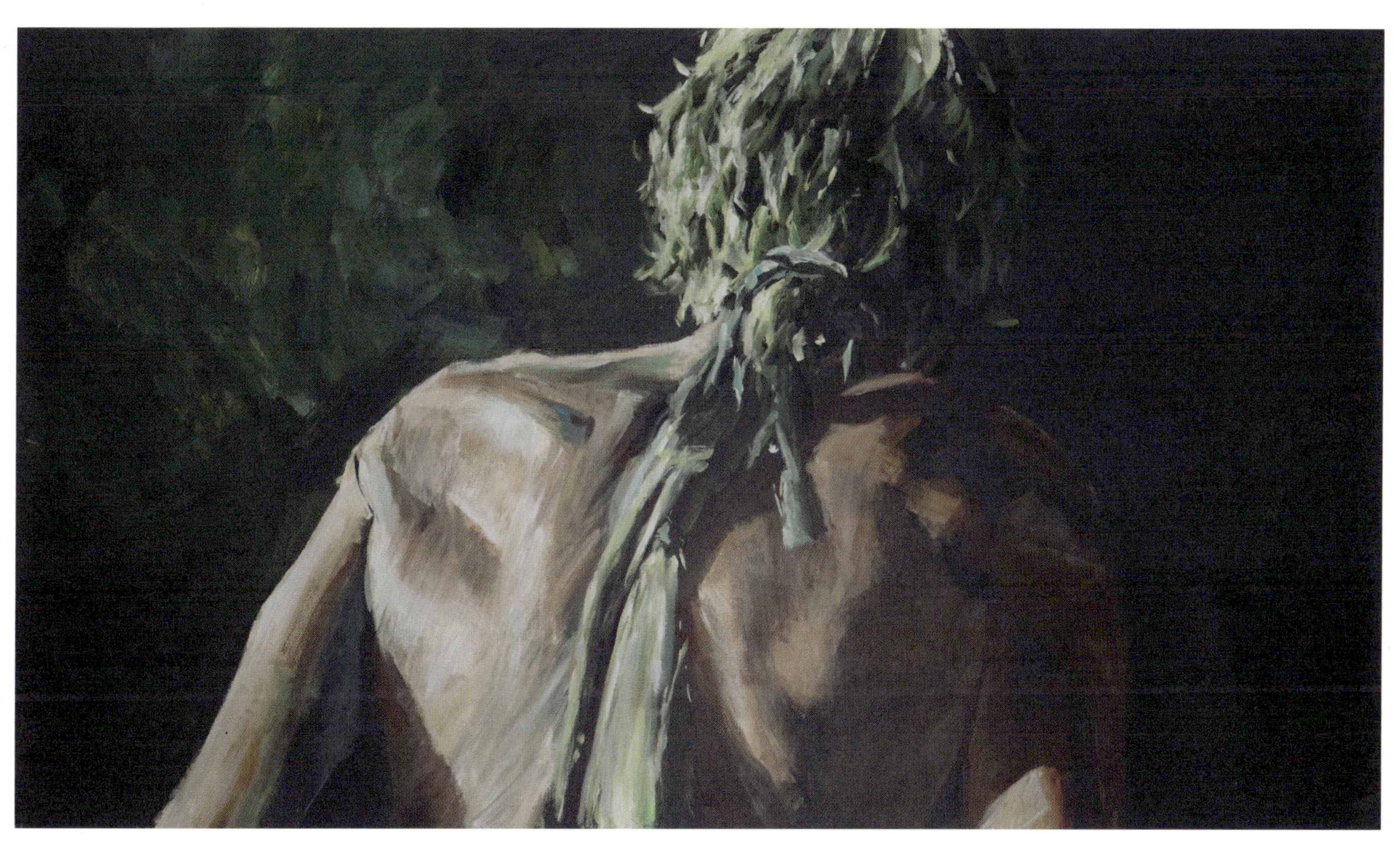

Little Wing,
My California series,
acrylic on canvas, 250 x 150 cm, 2018

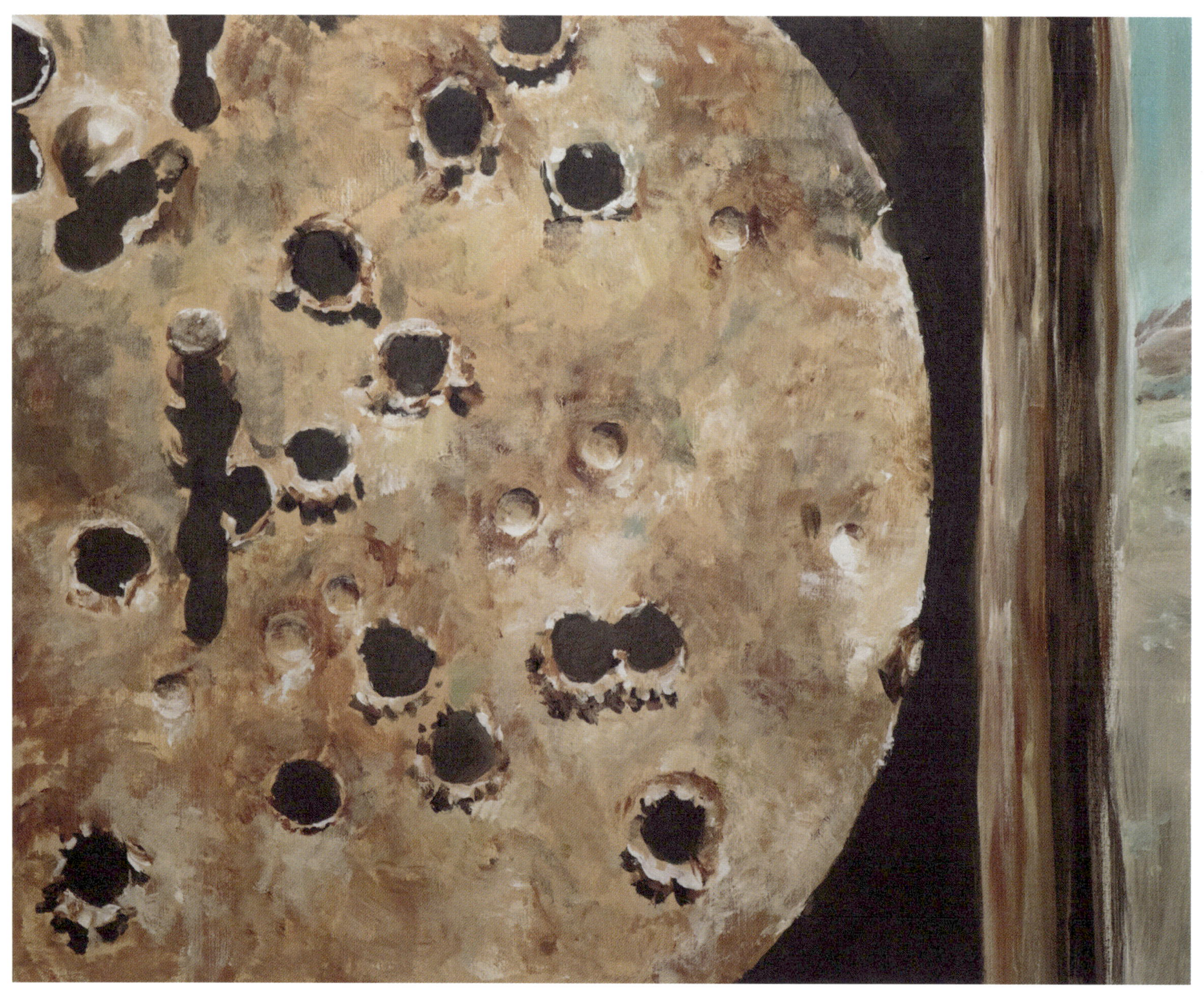

3. MY CALIFORNIA: PAINTINGS PT. 2

The End,
My California series,
acrylic on canvas, 120 x 100 cm, 2018

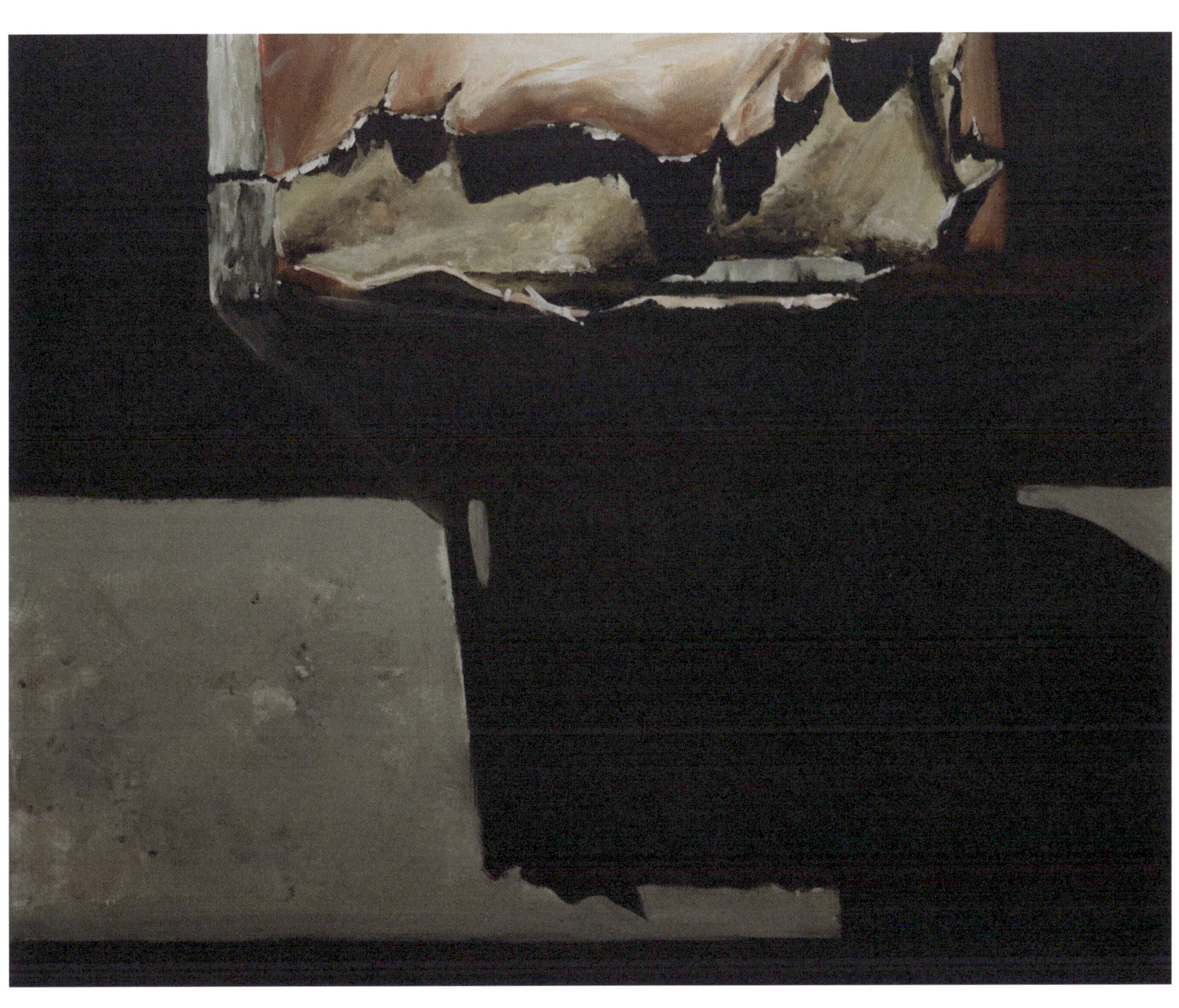

No Quarter,
My California series,
acrylic on canvas, 120 x 100 cm, 2018

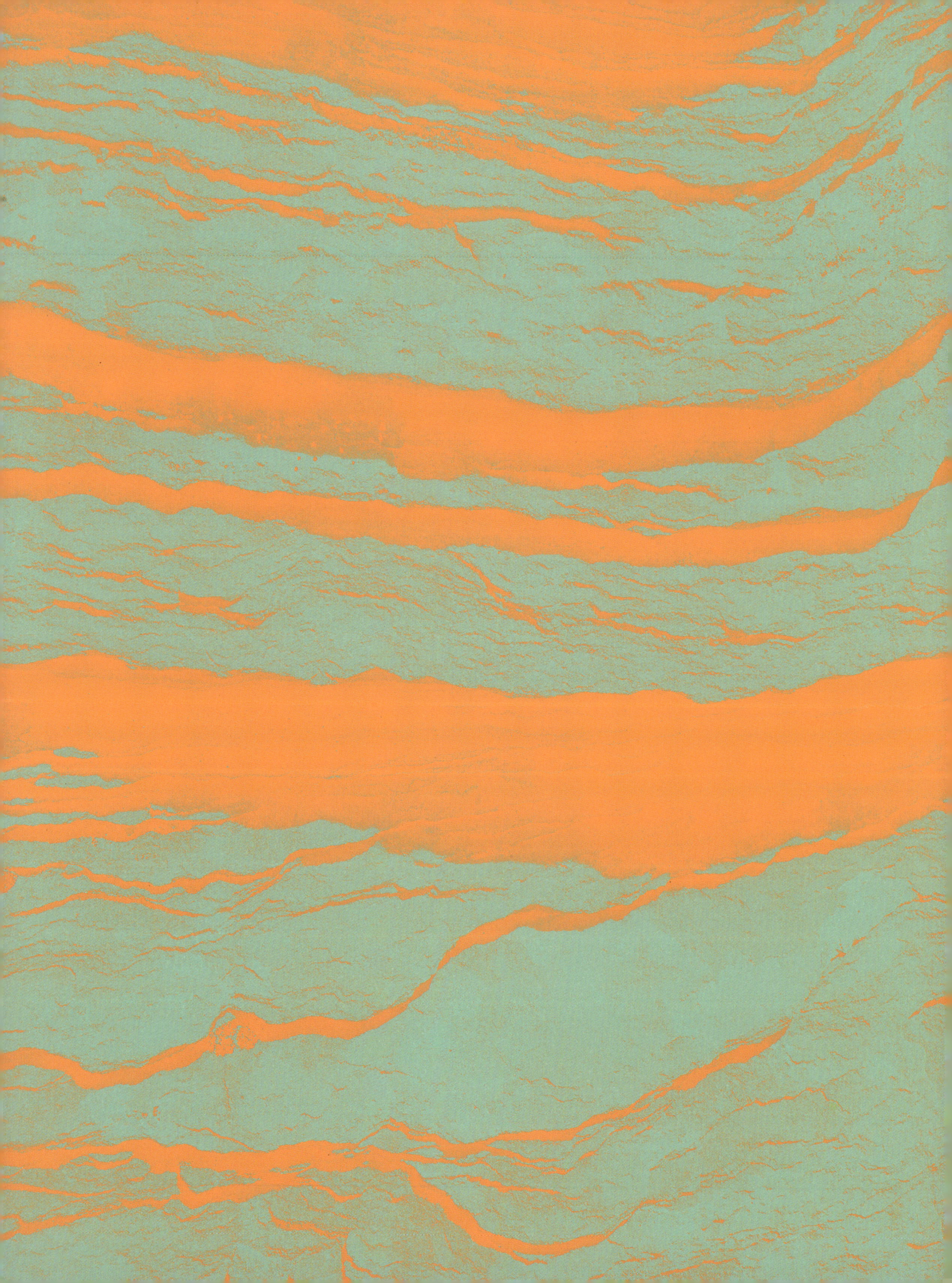

Barefoot Festival

"Barefoot was an experience, not just another party. A truly magical moment of music, arts, food, drinks, fashion and more... You could call it an event with a very big heart and eye for detail. It grew rapidly, not in a commercial way, but in a creative, artsy underground way, which was exactly the plan. After 4 years unfortunately it came to an end, due to lack of funding."

"It was a place of love and peace inspired by the philosophy of the Burning Man Festival: a green and naturally beautiful location, a "leave no trace"- policy and love for nature. Arts and music were central. The stage and all other art and installations were created out of recuperated material and wood. No plastic, all handmade. This in combination with the 'Barefooters' dressed as crazy as can be, and an amazing line-up created the perfect summer vibe."
(CHARLOTTE DE COCK)

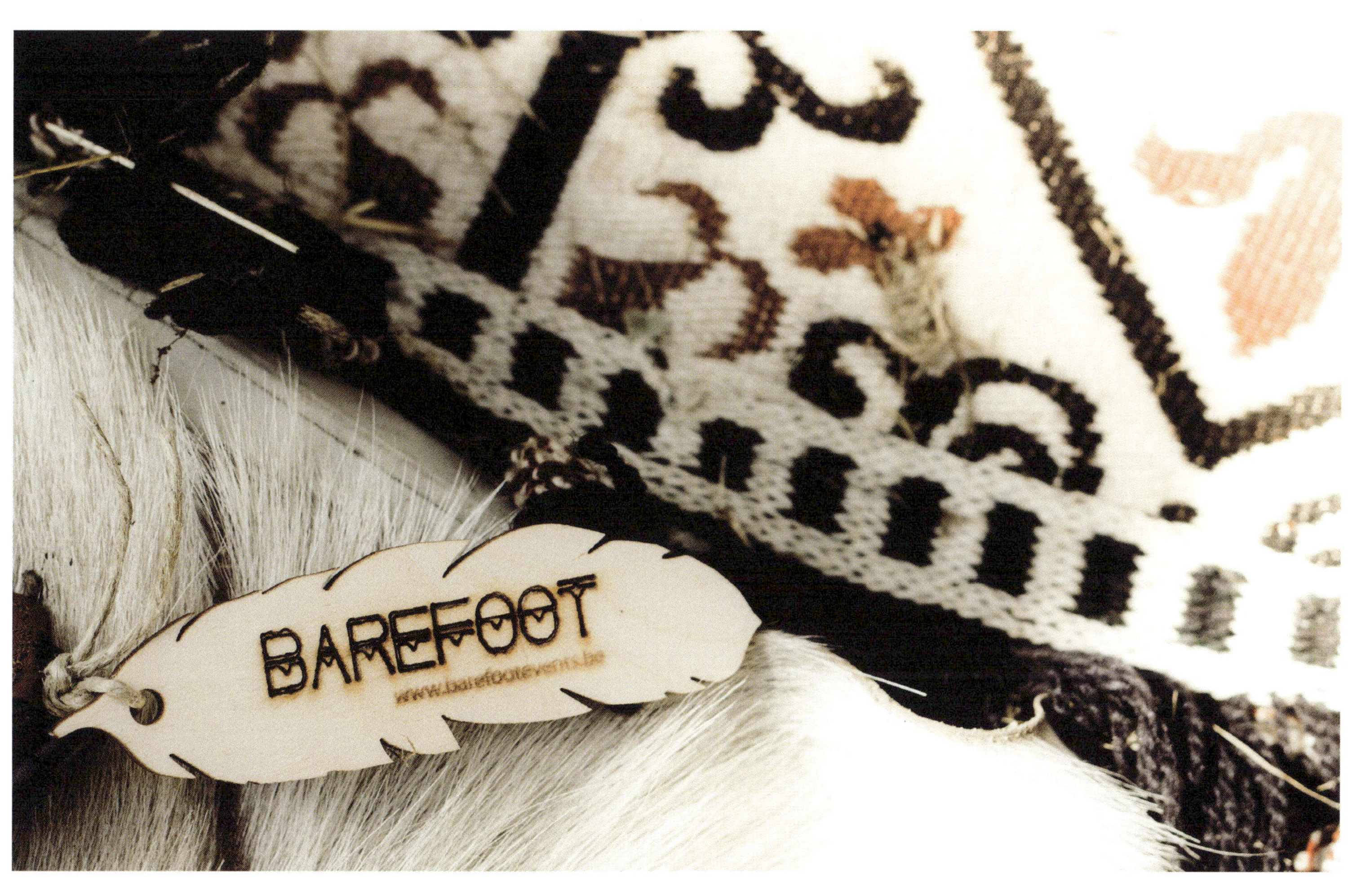
BAREFOOT
www.barefootevents.be

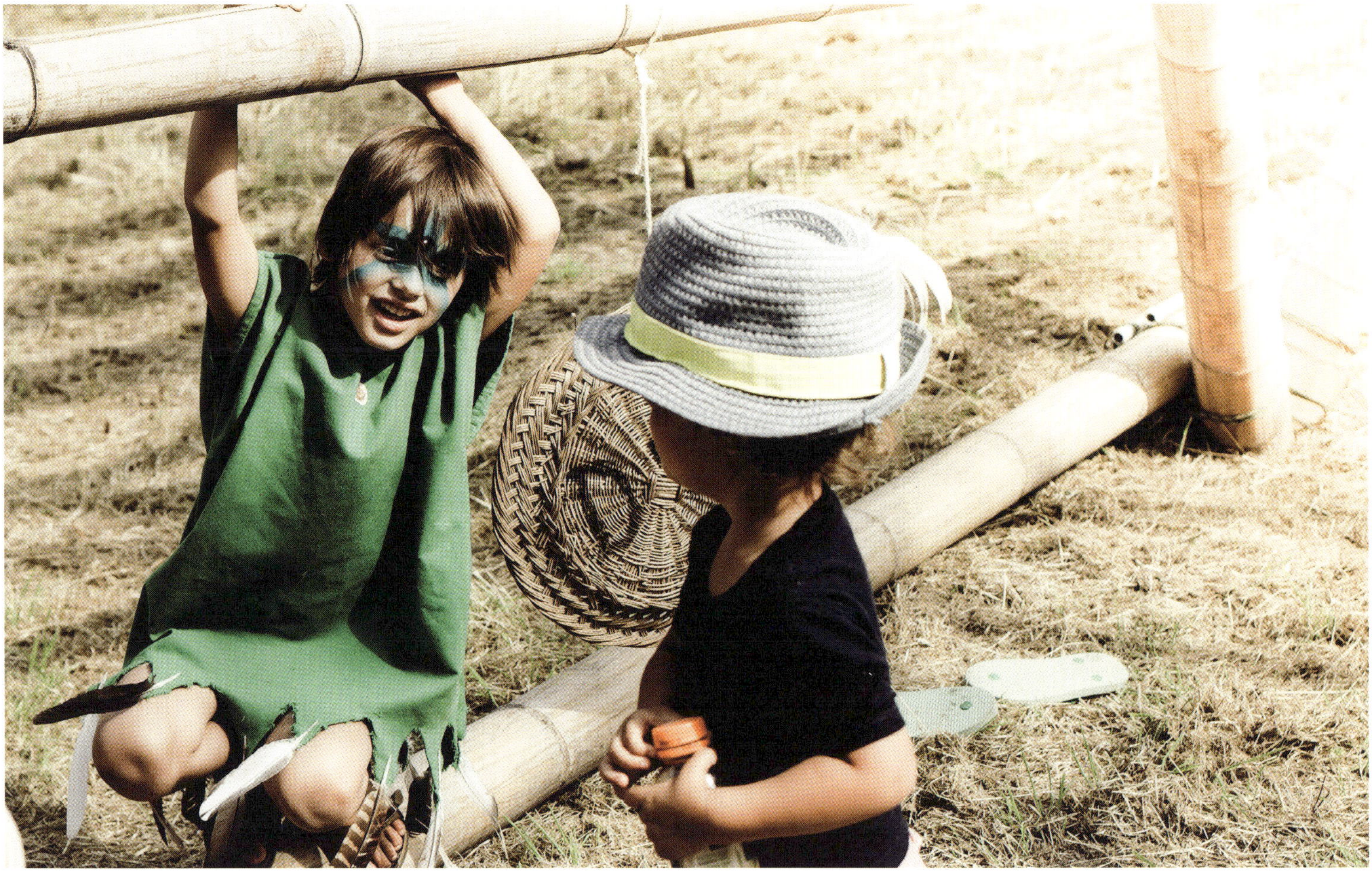

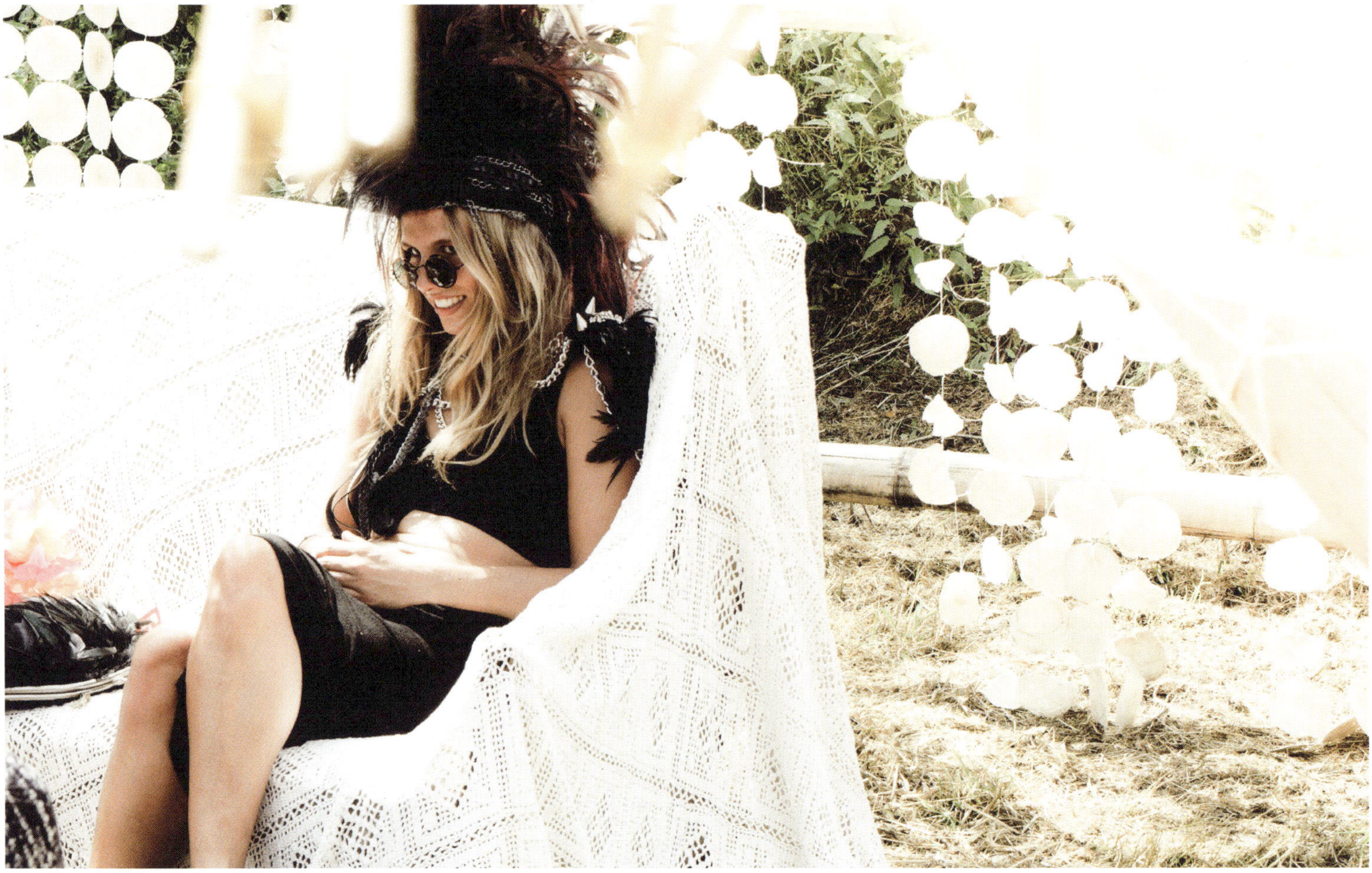

     4. BAREFOOT FESTIVAL   © OOGILLES

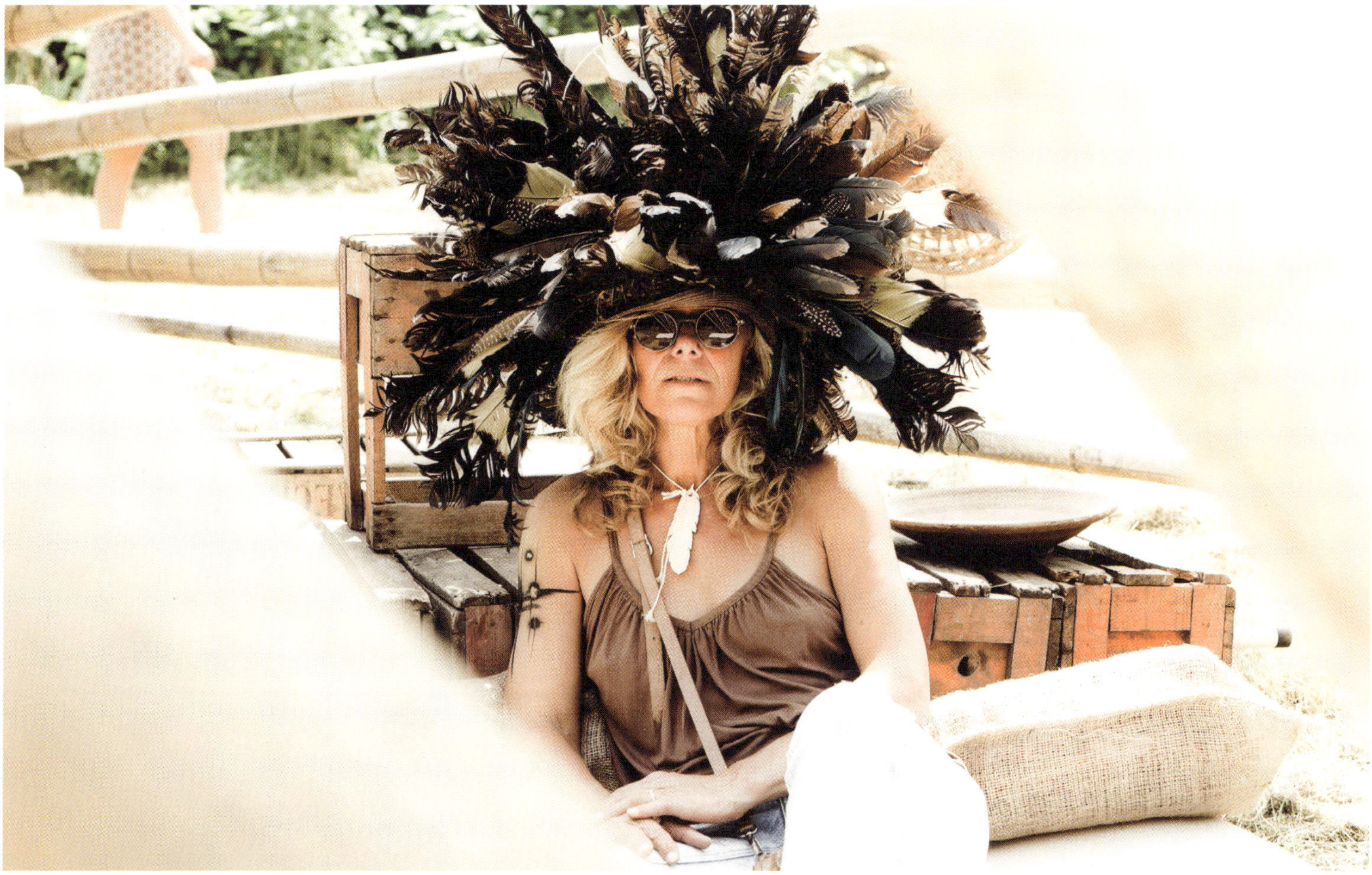

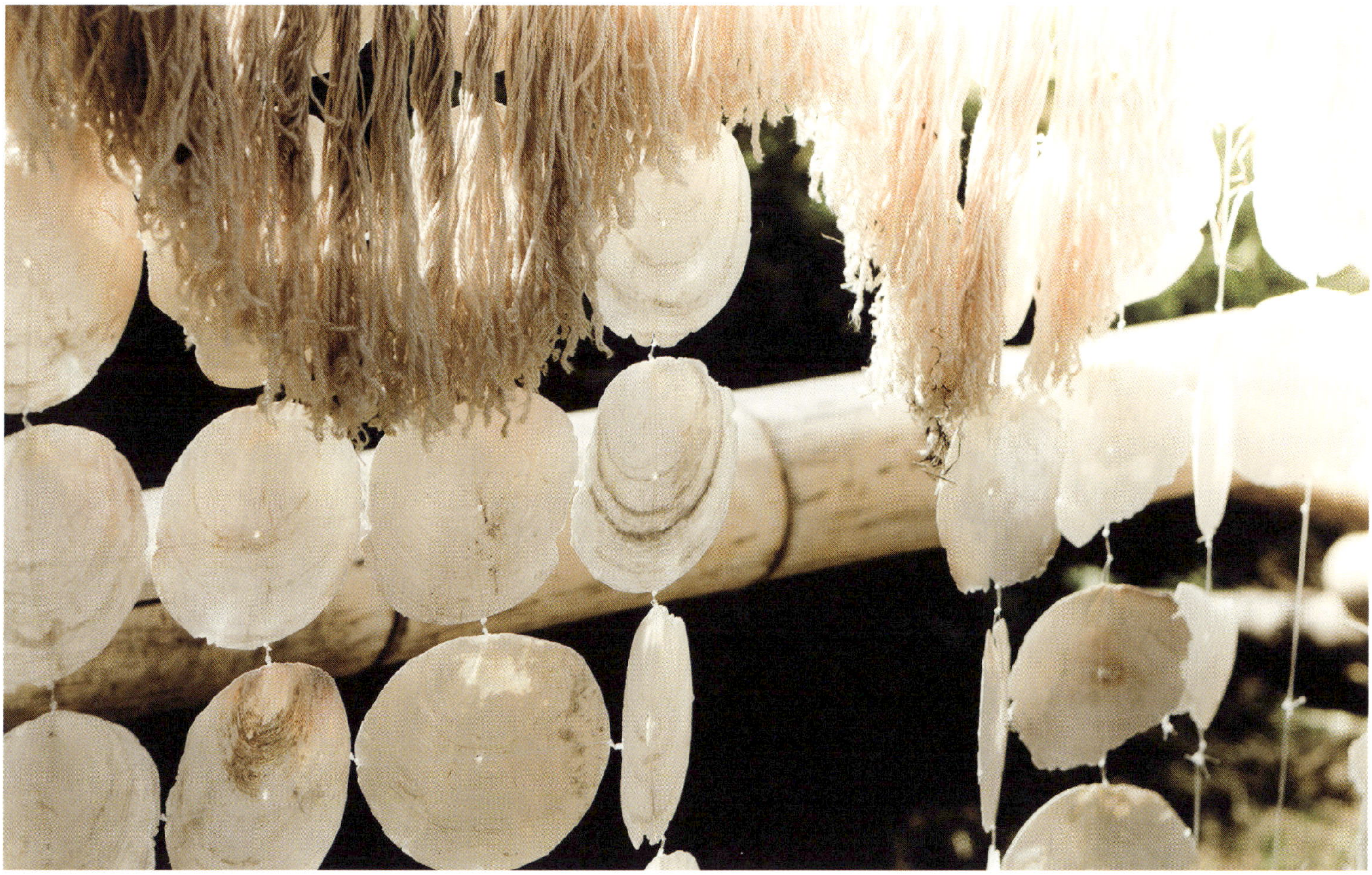

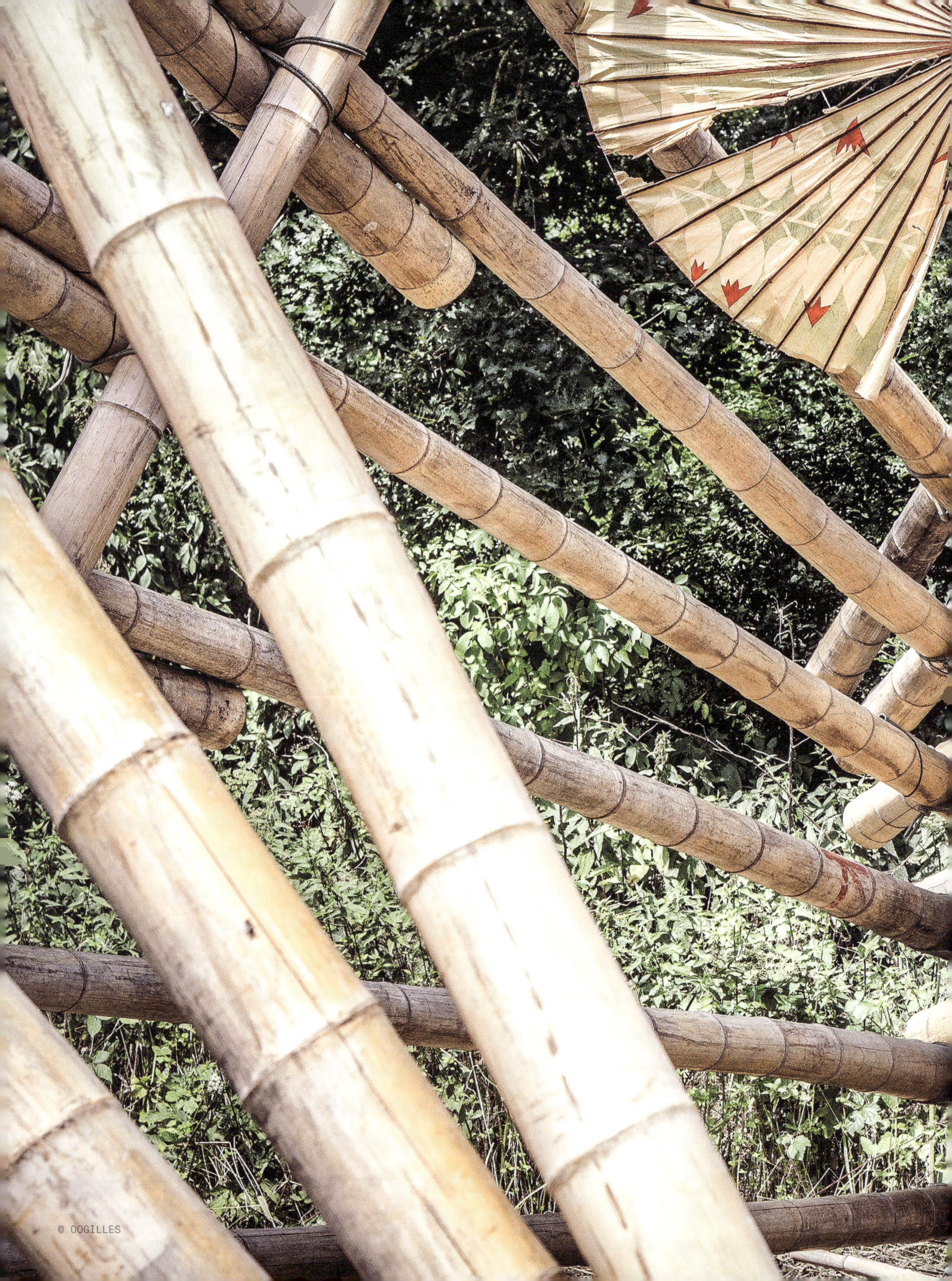
© OOGILLES

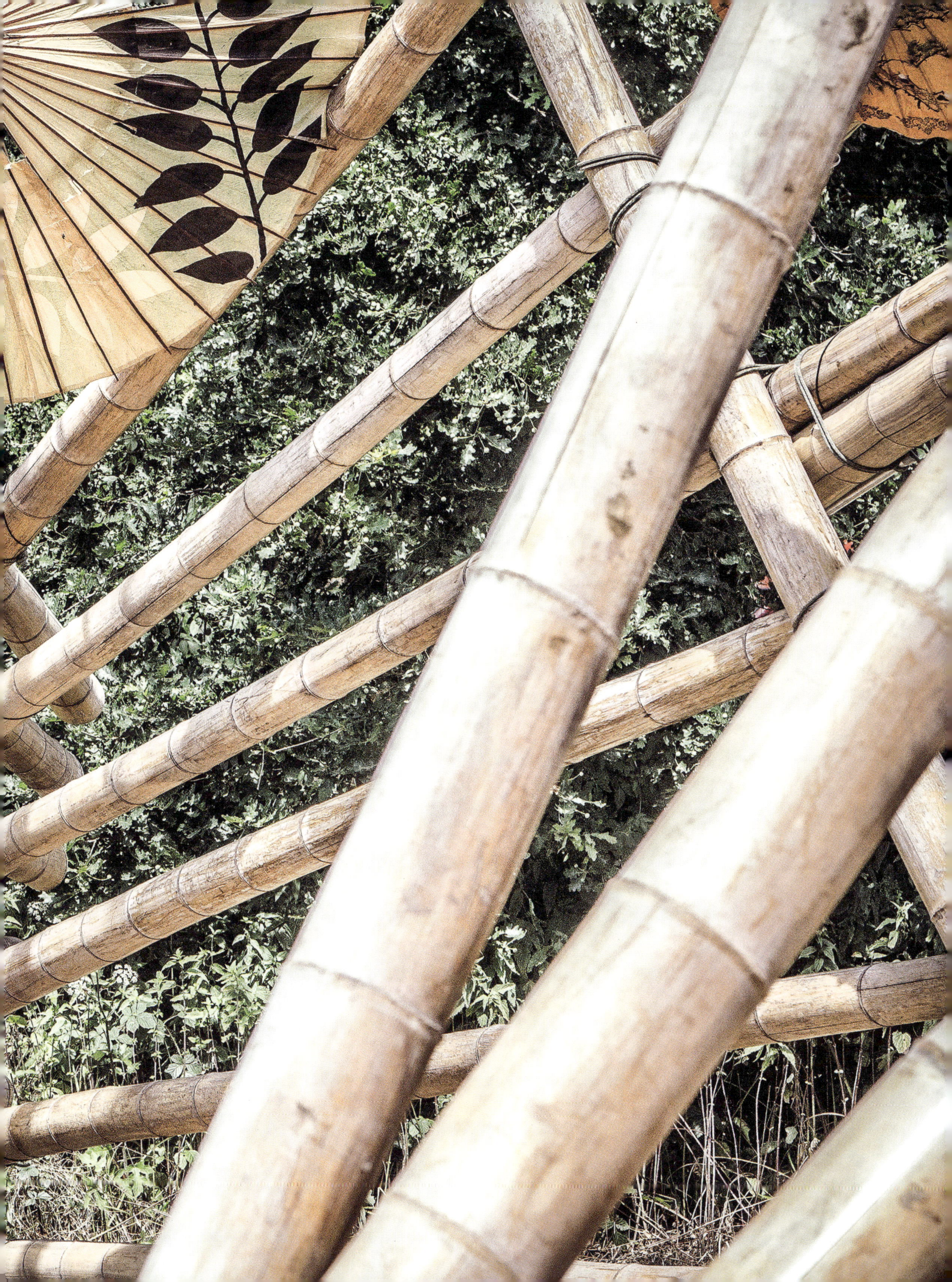

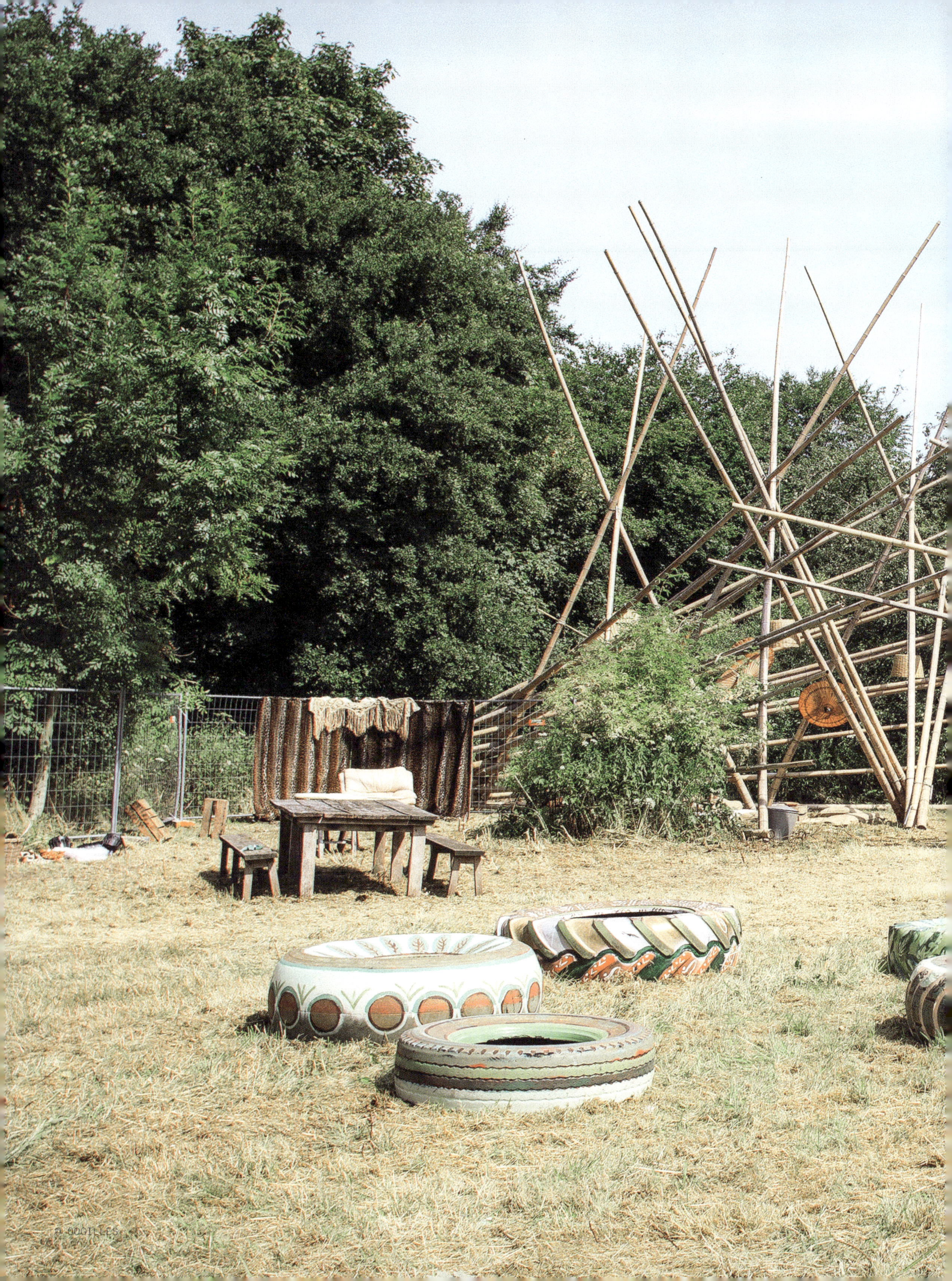
© OOGILLES

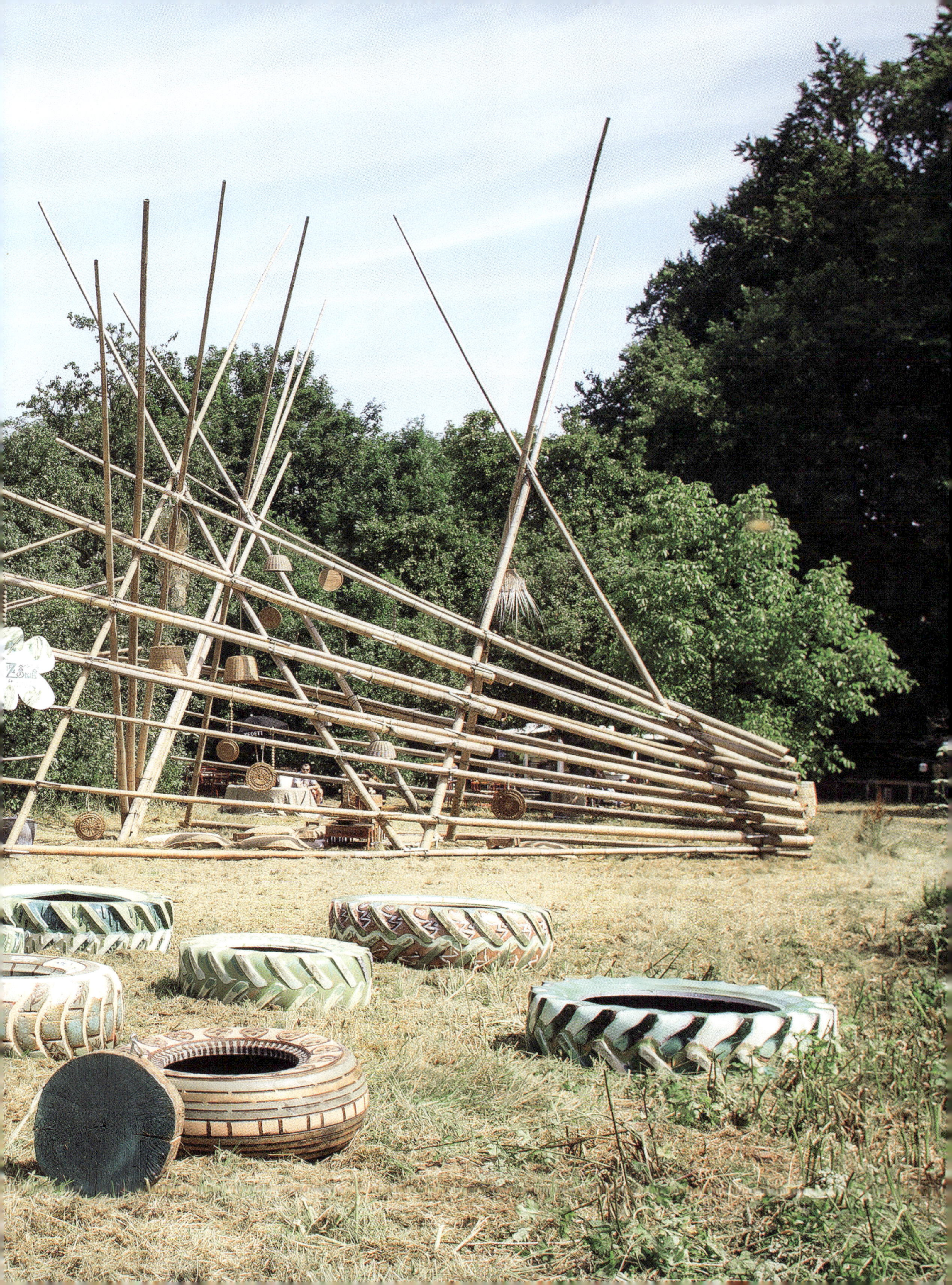

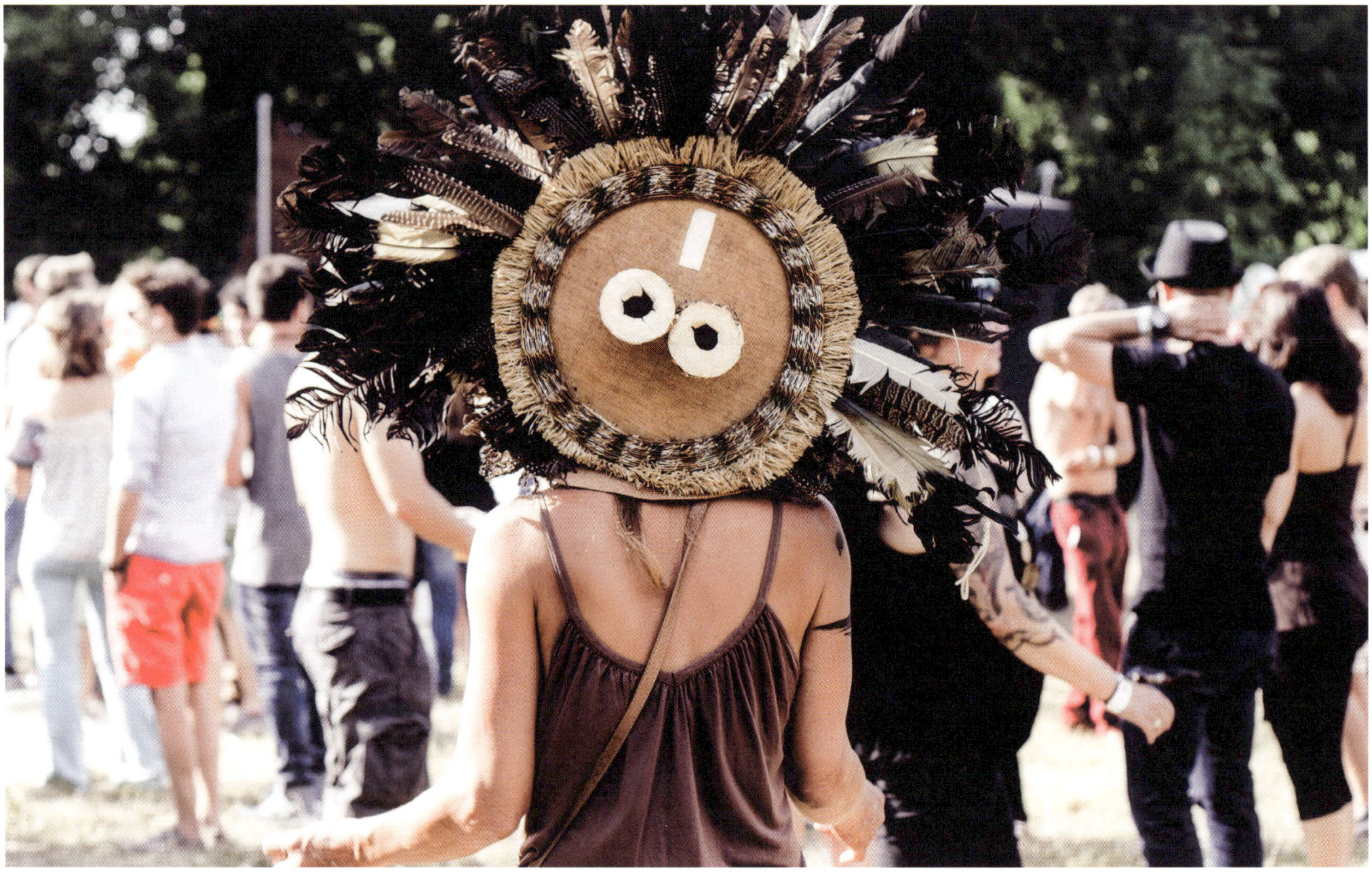

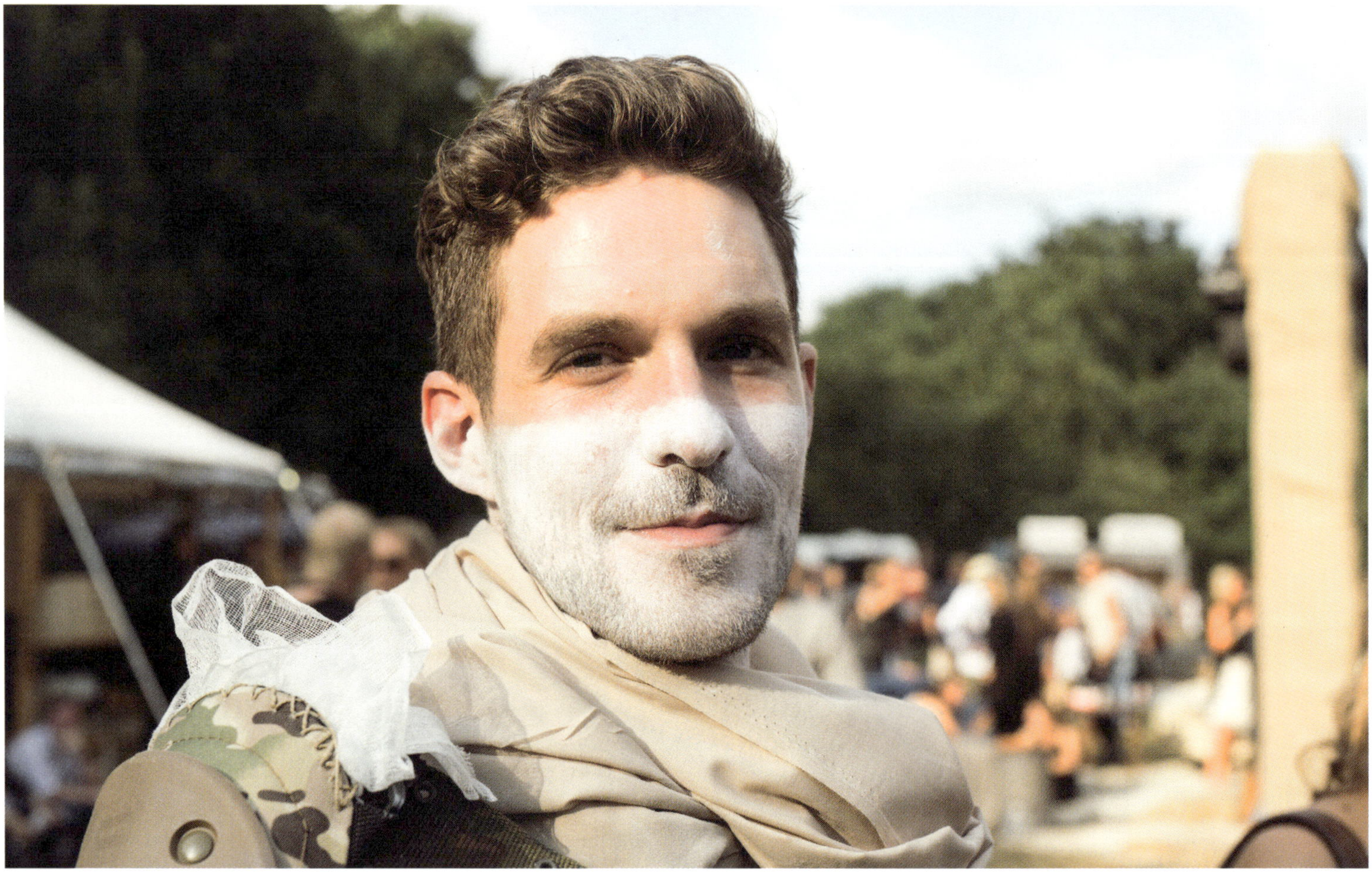

     4. BAREFOOT FESTIVAL

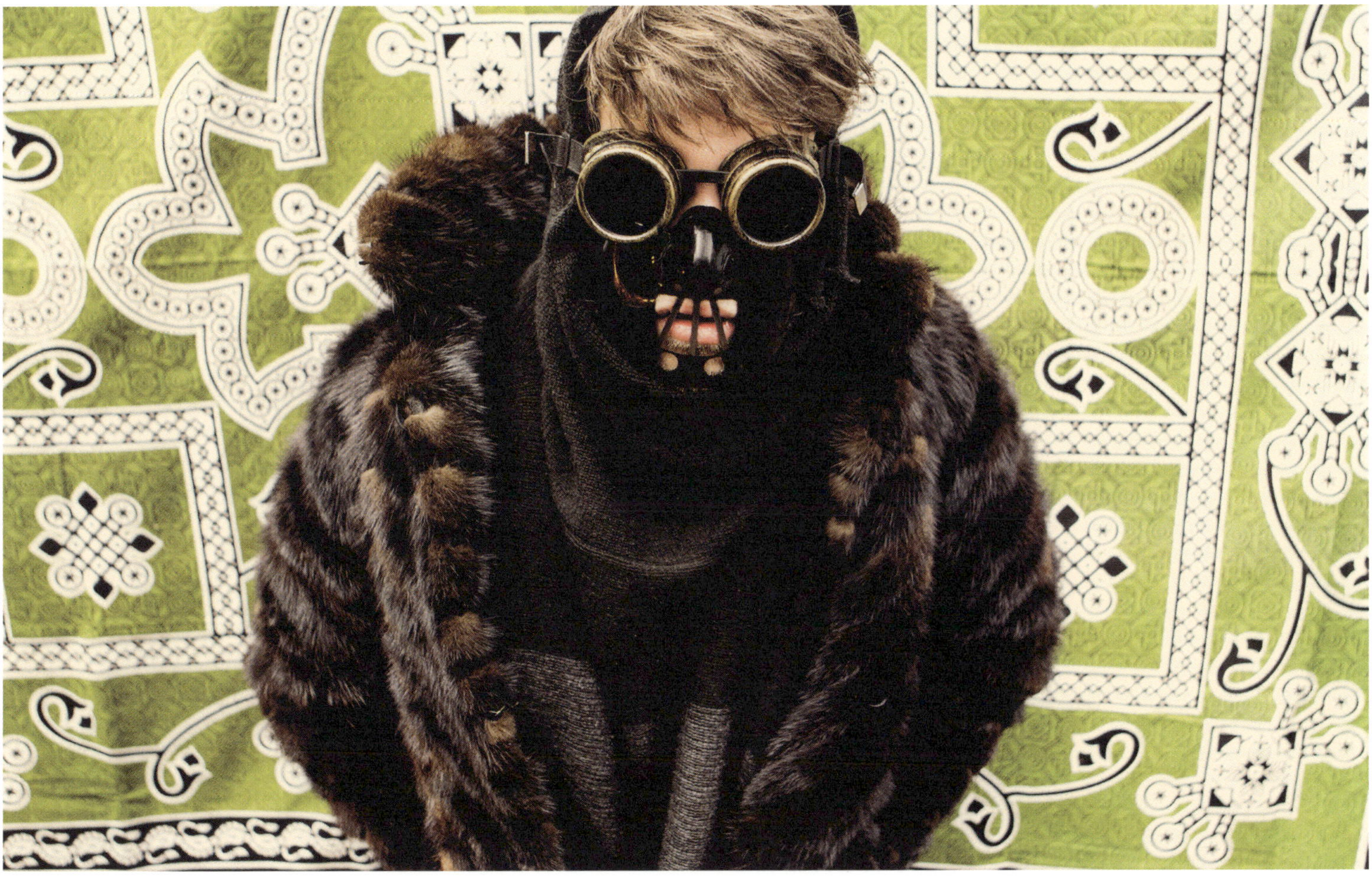

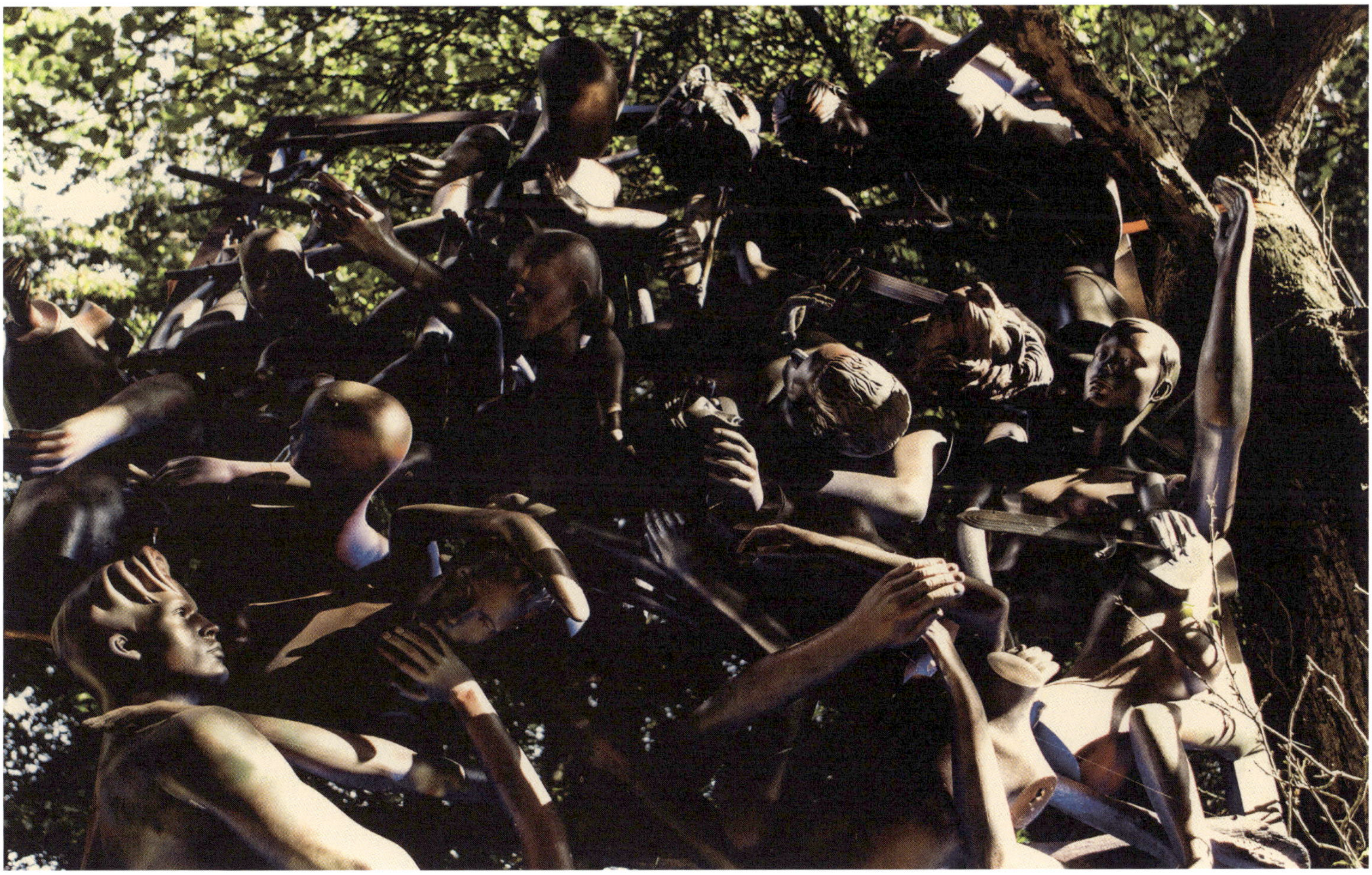

TOP © Sara De Graeve
BOTTOM © Sara De Graeve

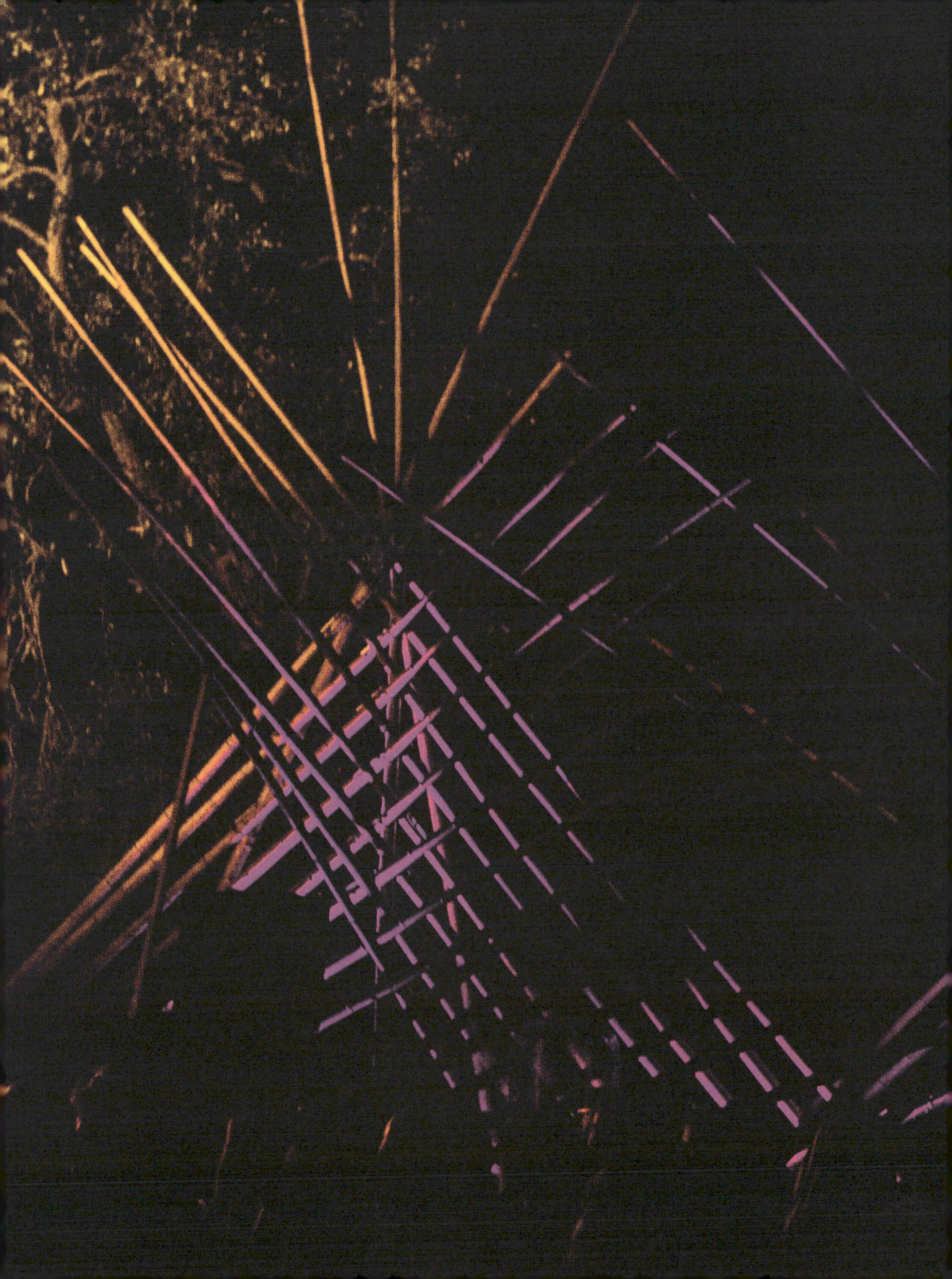

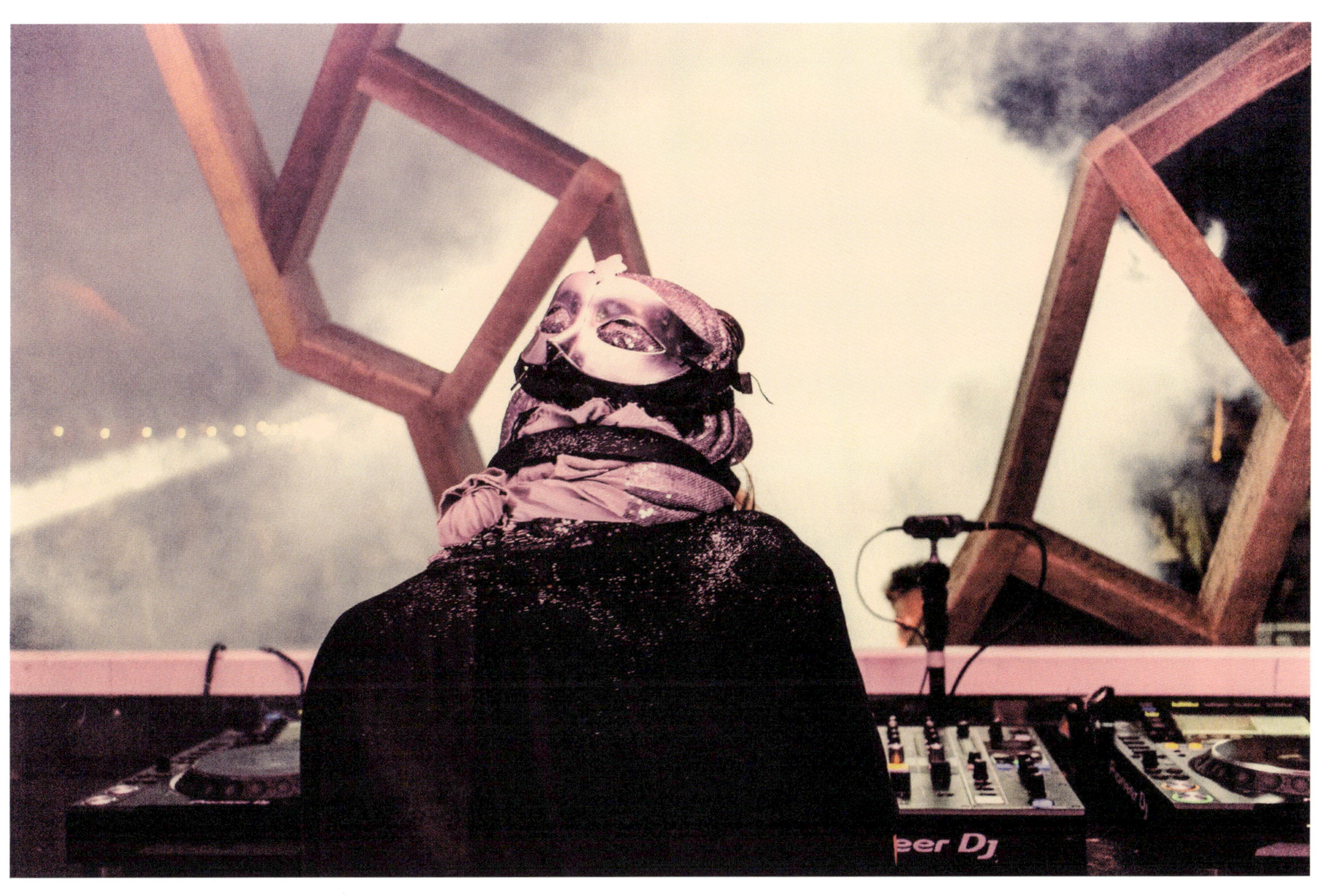

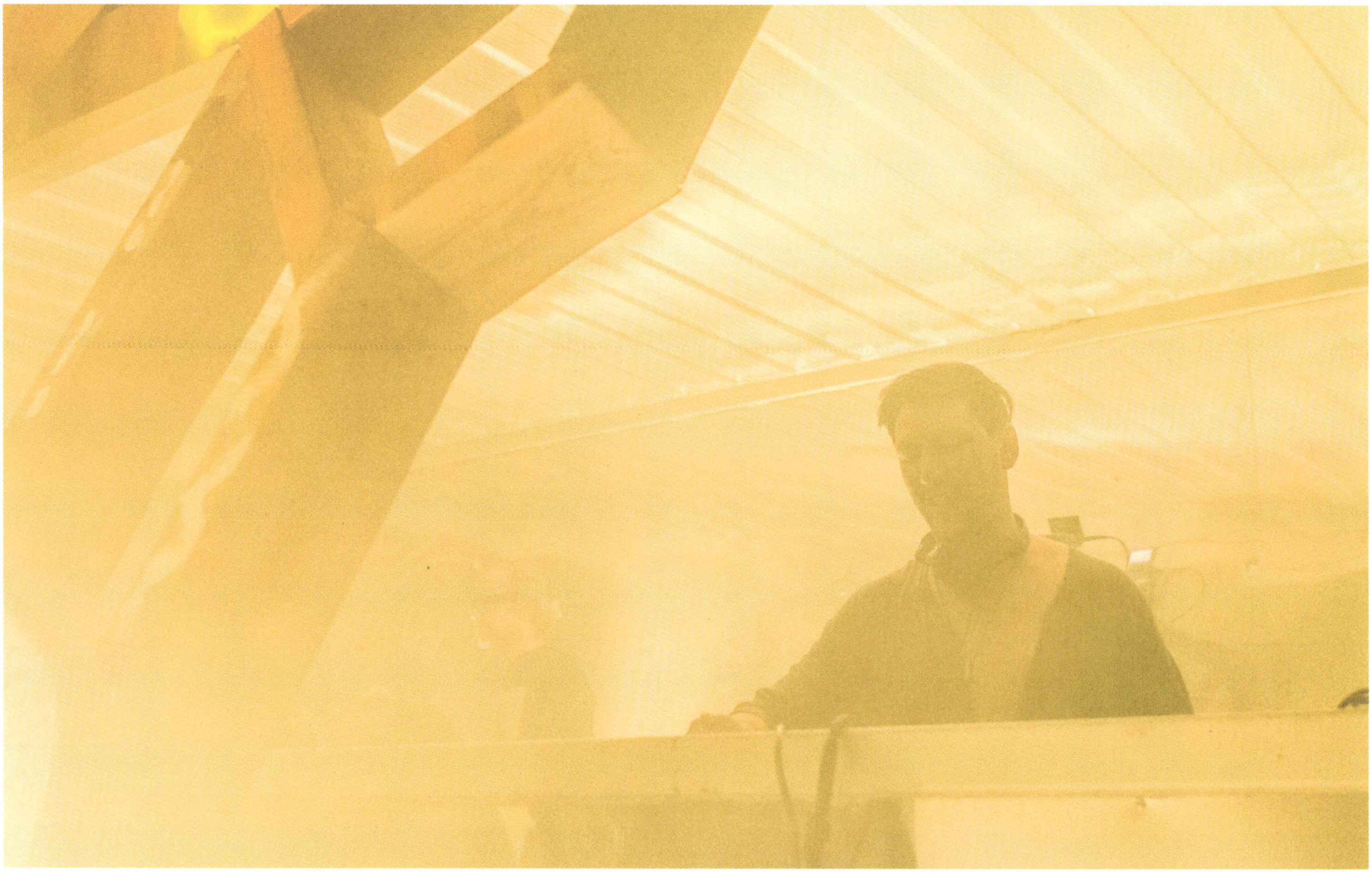

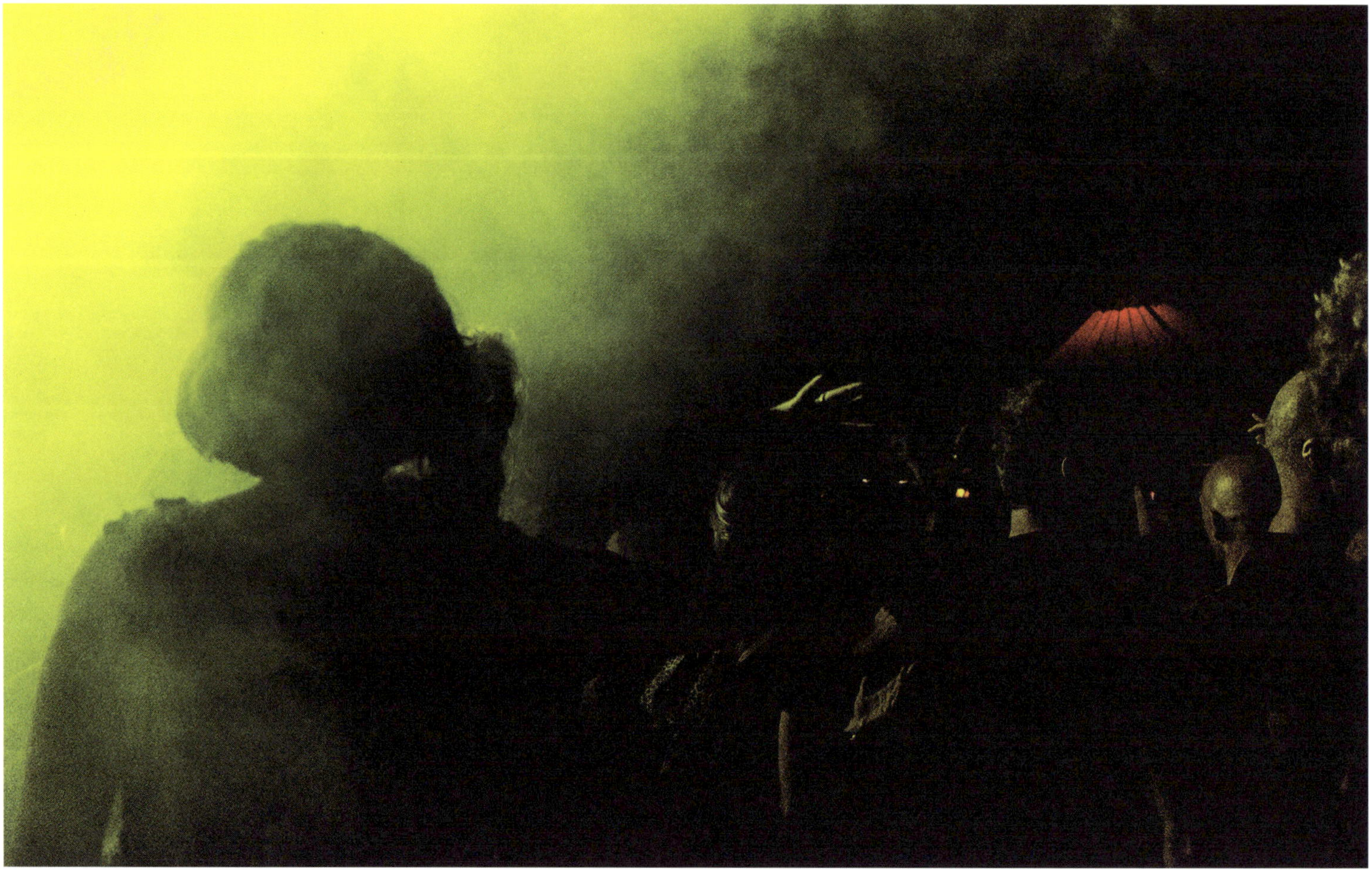

4. BAREFOOT FESTIVAL

© Sara De Graeve

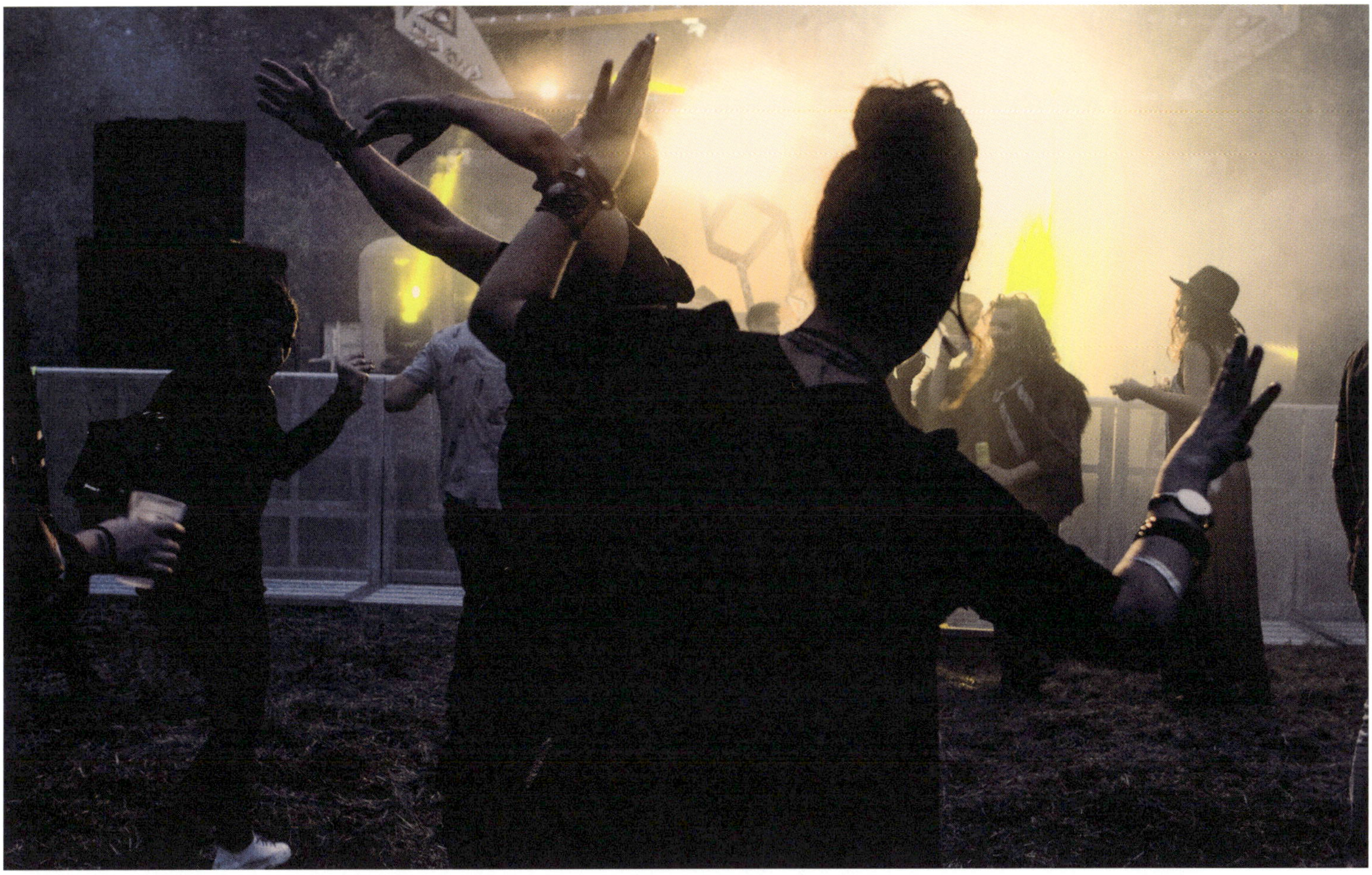

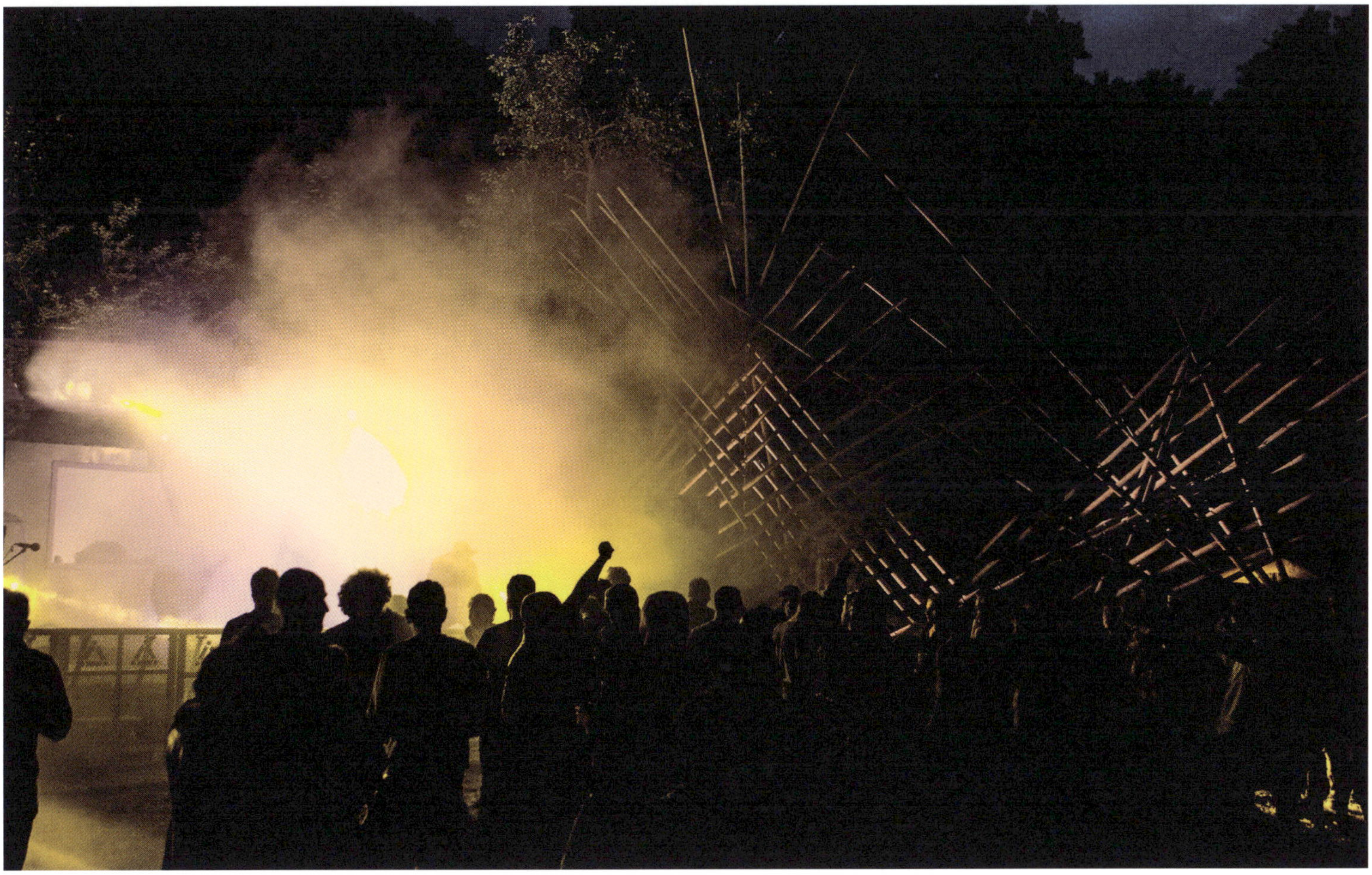

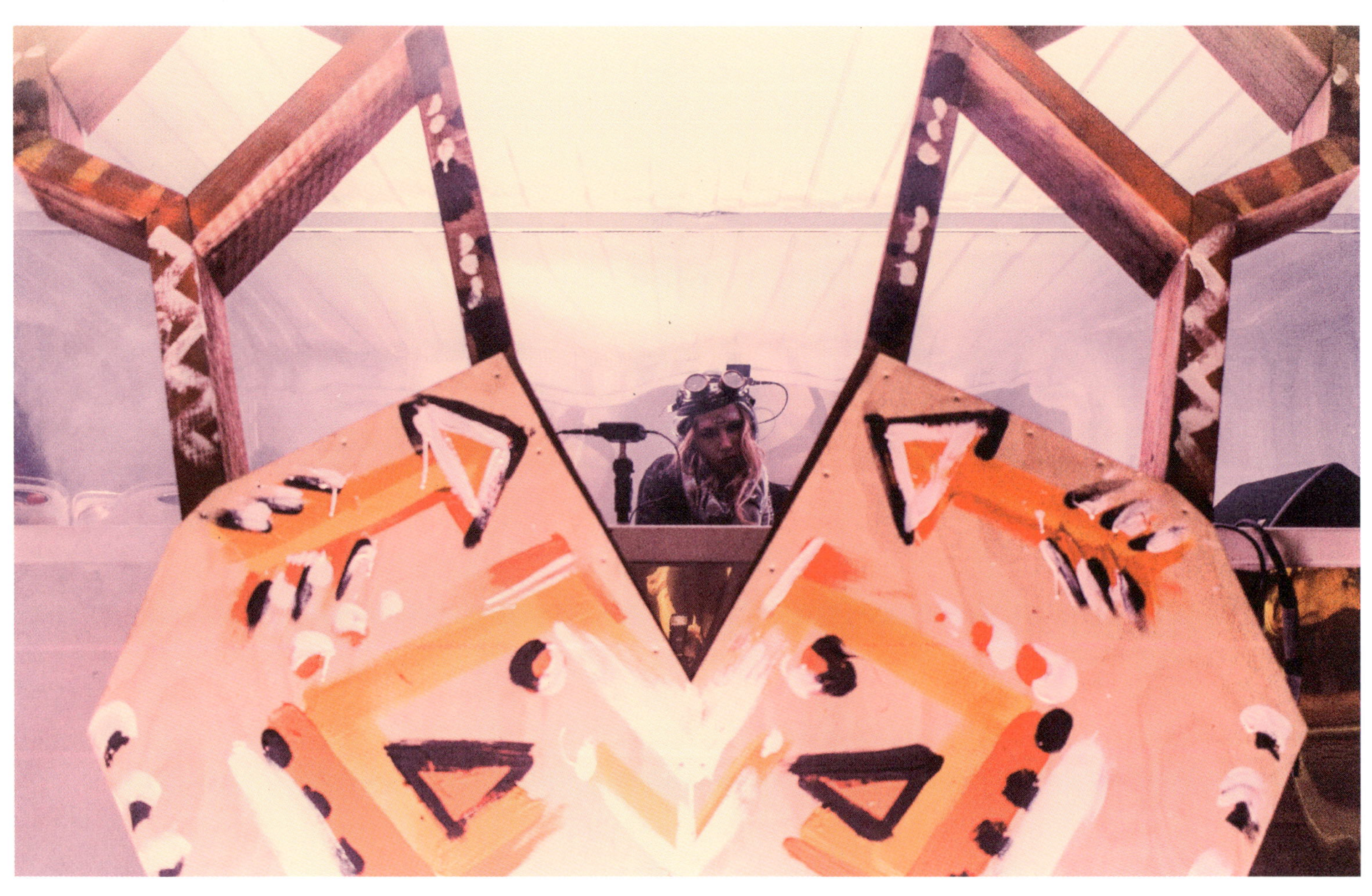

4. BAREFOOT FESTIVAL

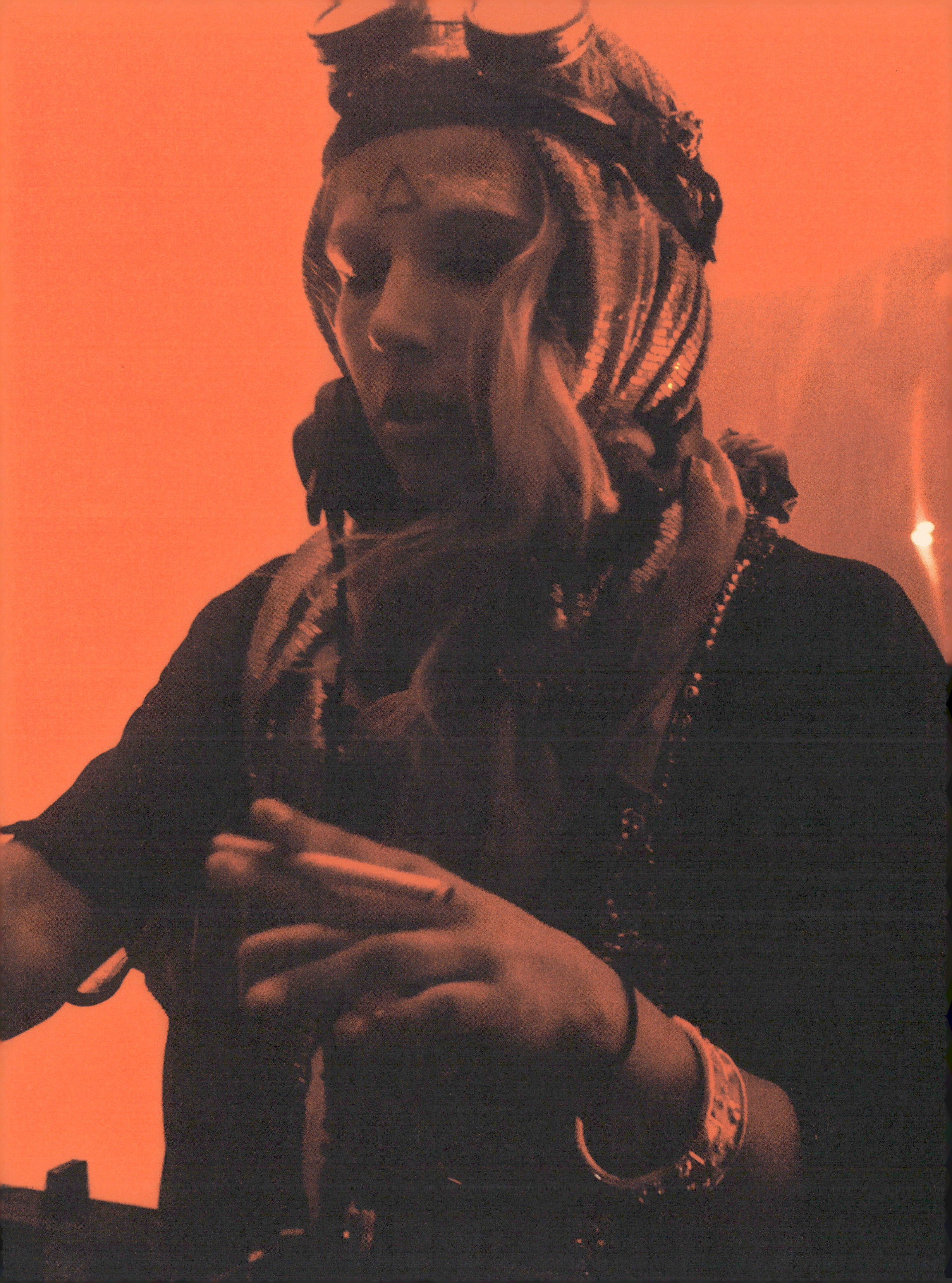

Daze Trilogy

In this Vimeo, including a series of time-lapses and hyper-lapses, with over 20,000 photos, Charlotte is seen in the process of painting from blank canvas to finished artwork, including her drawings and preparatory sketches for her dance performance as well.

Even though we are watching a smartly accelerated paste-up of these photos, we still are able to witness, step by step, be it a quick-step—Charlotte's pace—how the painting develops, how she finishes it, as always, with her brilliant white strokes.

This first part of a new trilogy, called DAZE, was shot and performed in The Jane, voted the world's most beautiful restaurant, offering the most high-class dining experience in Antwerp, and according to De Cock, is "a very powerful place full of creativity and the name screams femininity, passion and strength".

Watching her dance-performance, this fascinating duet with the white cloth—always that white!— carefully prepared in these drawings, and masterly executed thanks to her feline femininity, her passion and strength. There can be no doubt about her statement.

After all the masters, she has become a master herself. (LÉON LEMAHIEU)

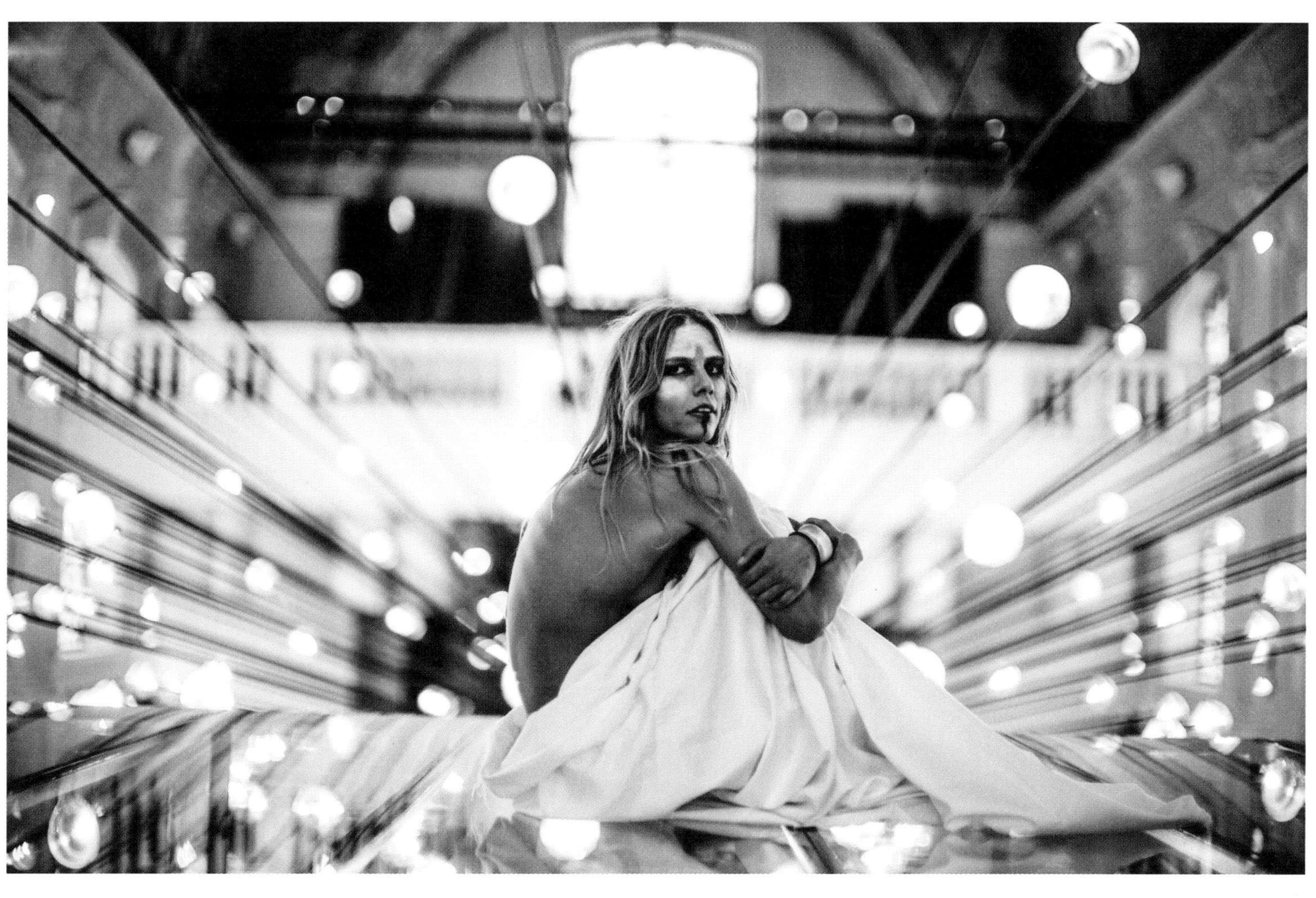

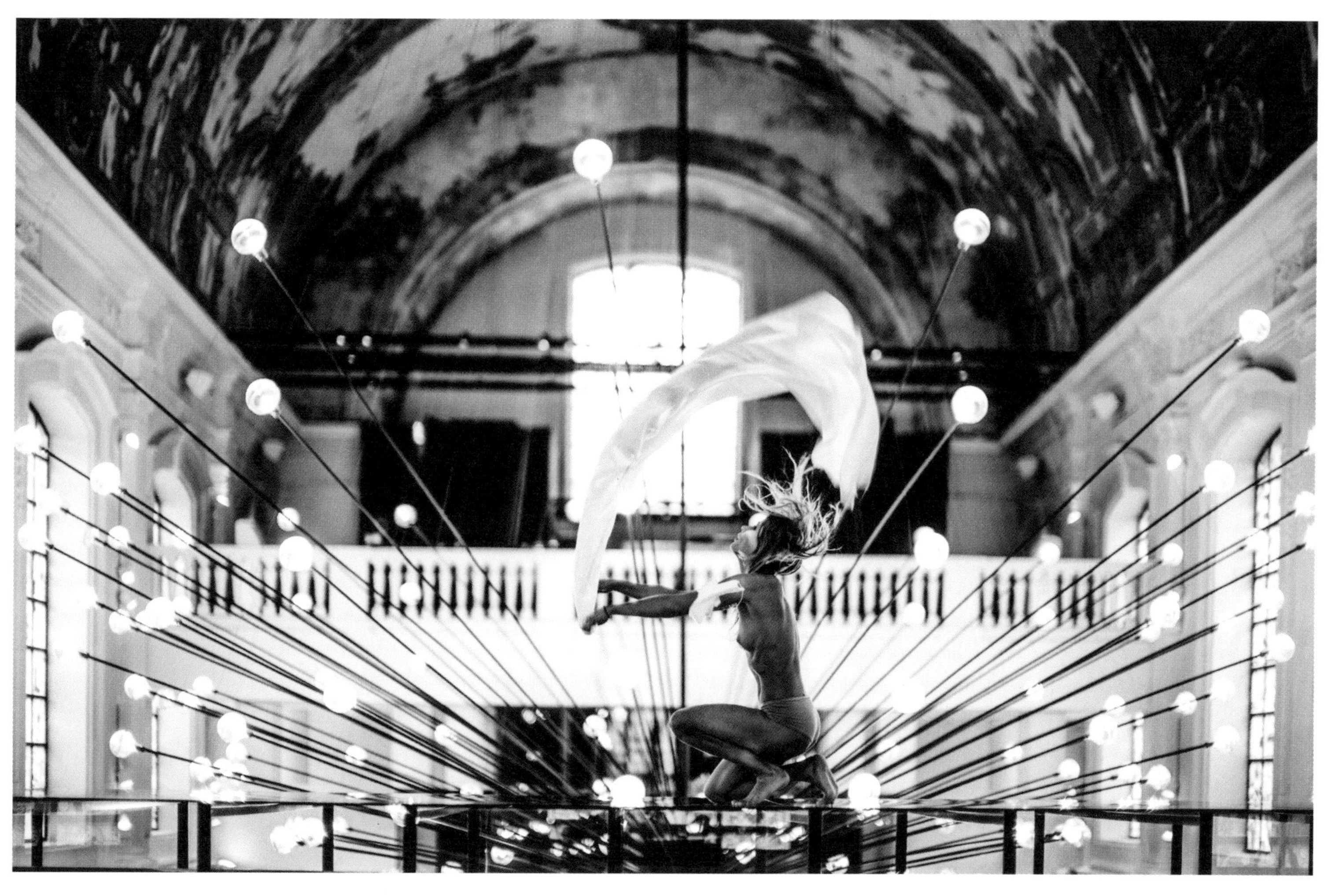

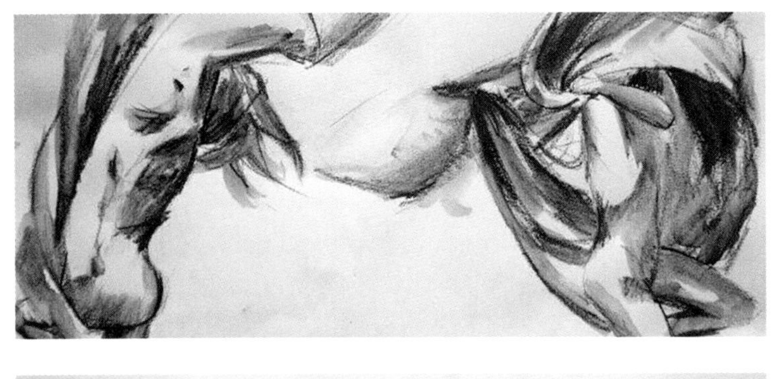 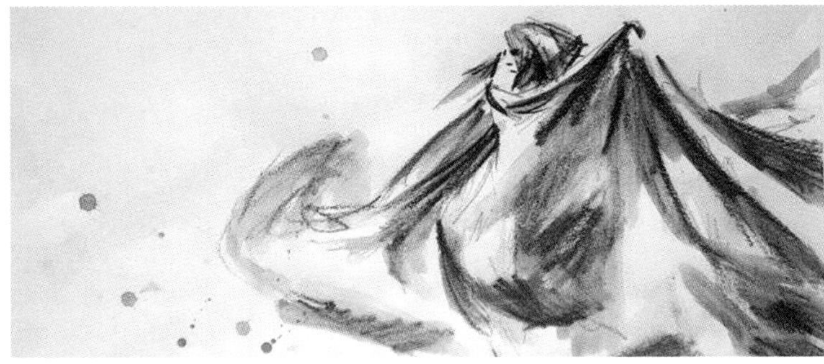

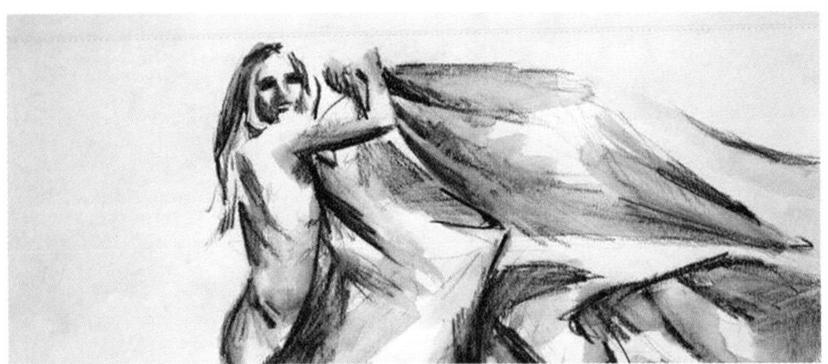 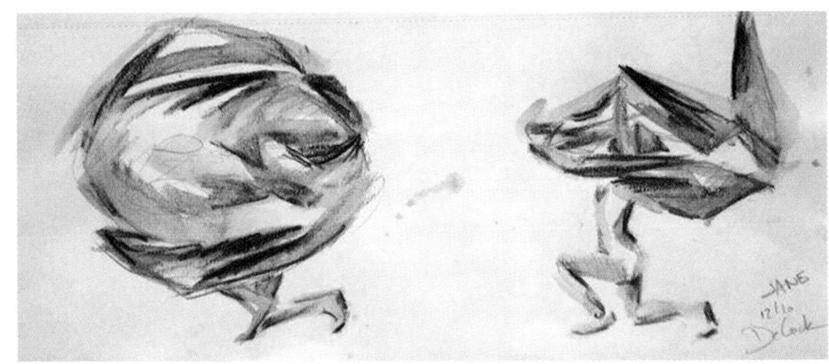

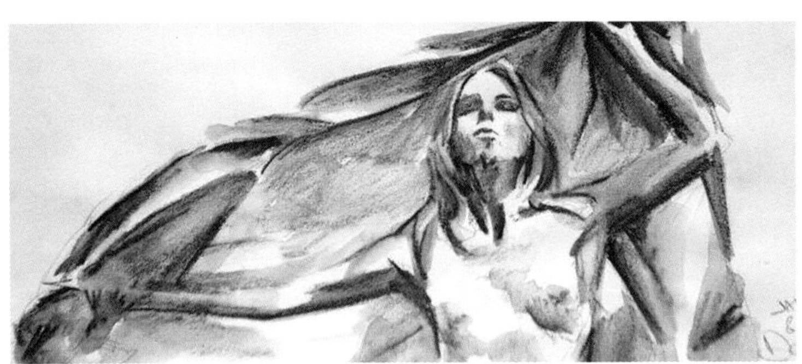 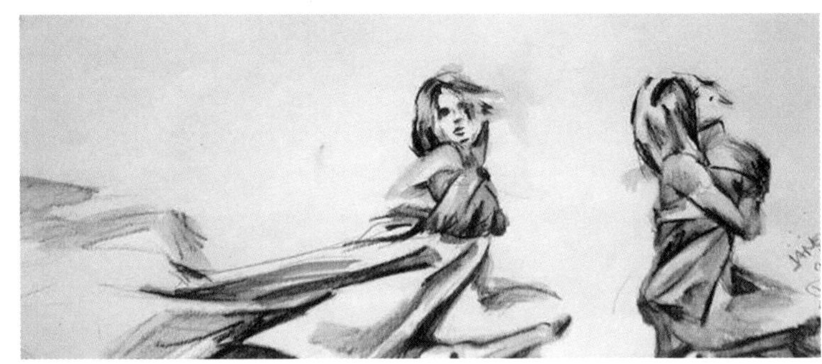

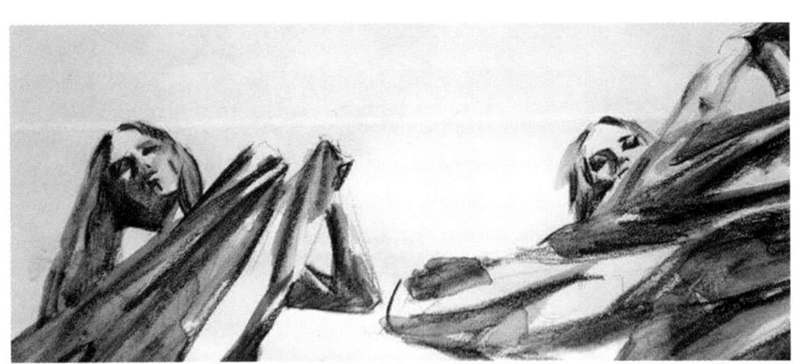 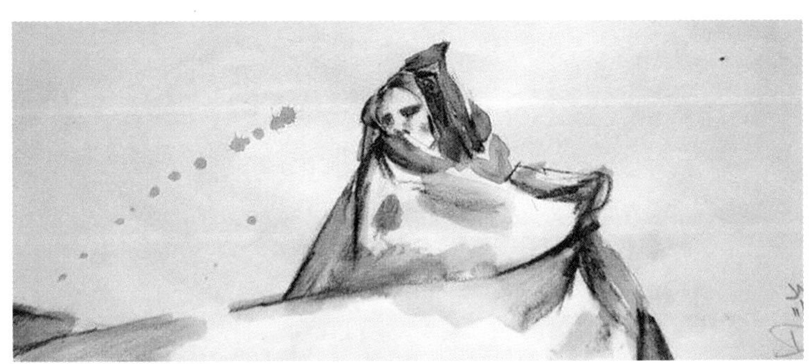

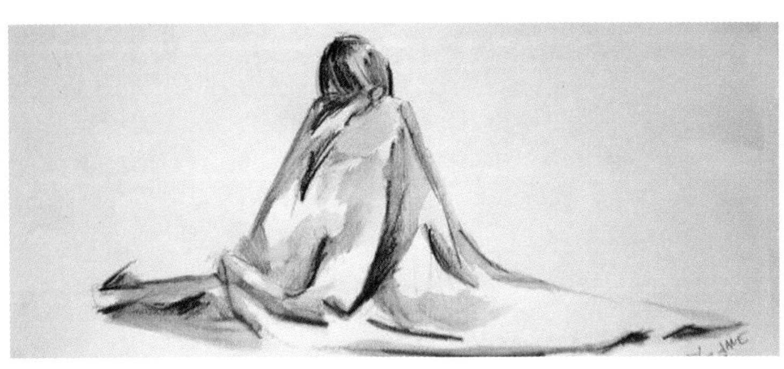 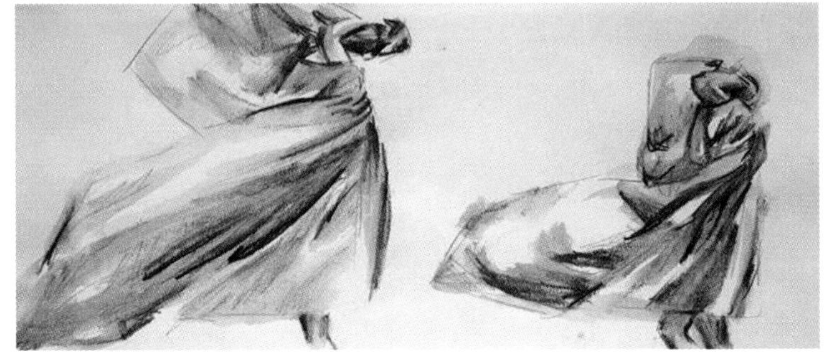

5. DAZE TRILOGY

Sketch Stack Daze,
pencil and watercolor, 2015

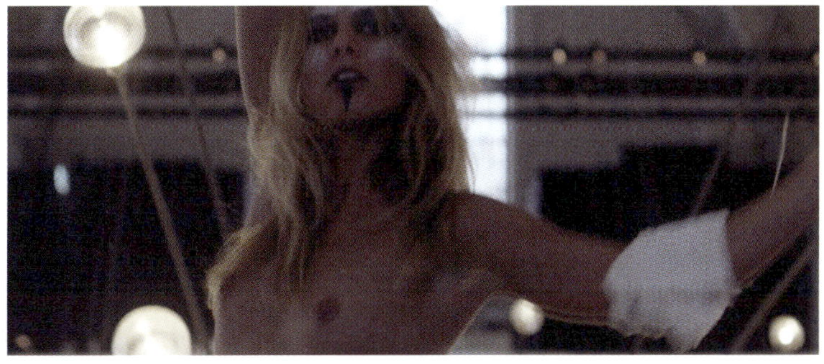
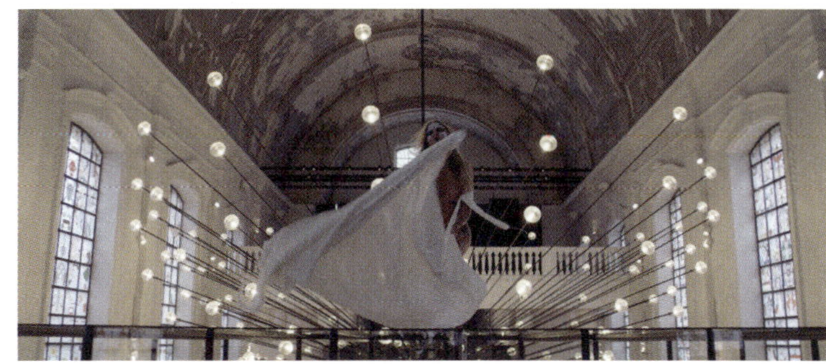
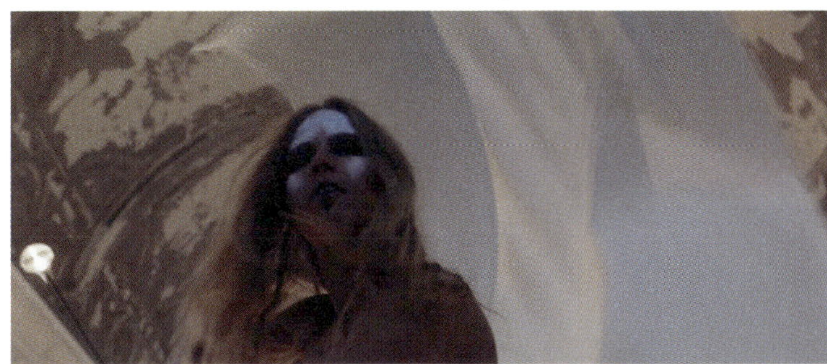
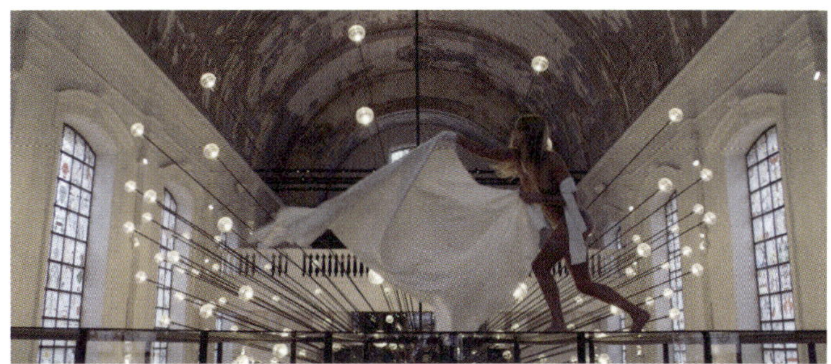
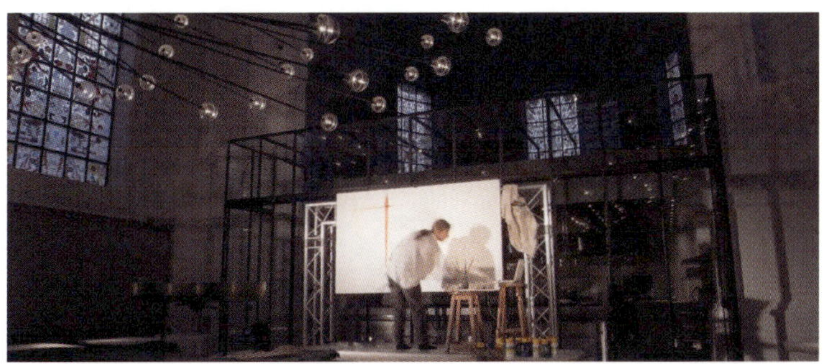
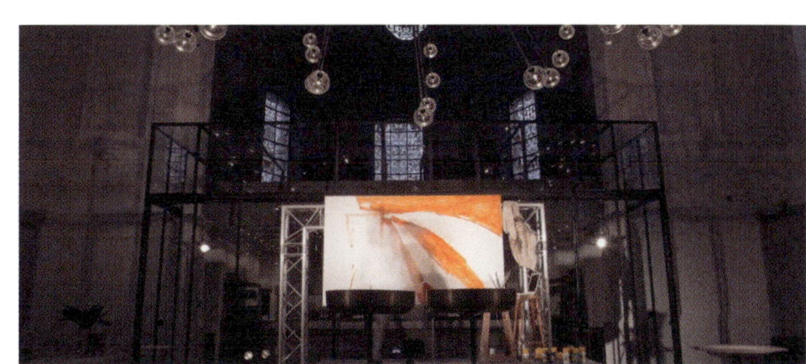
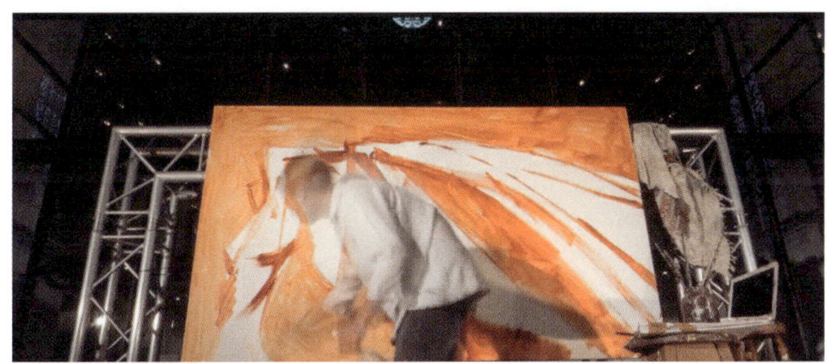
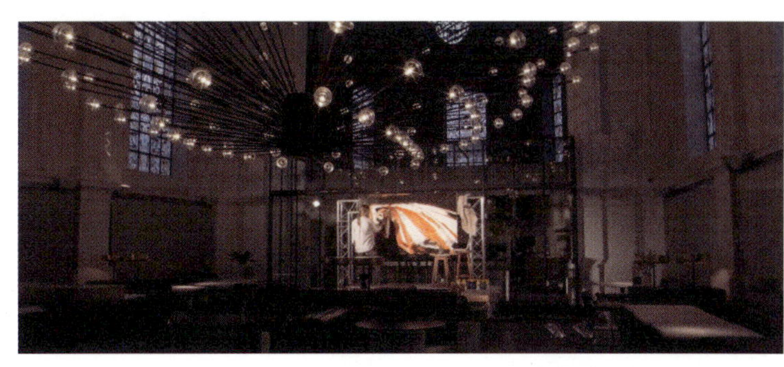
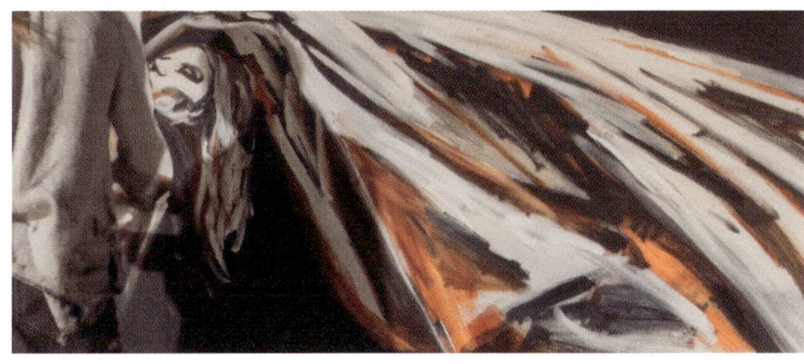
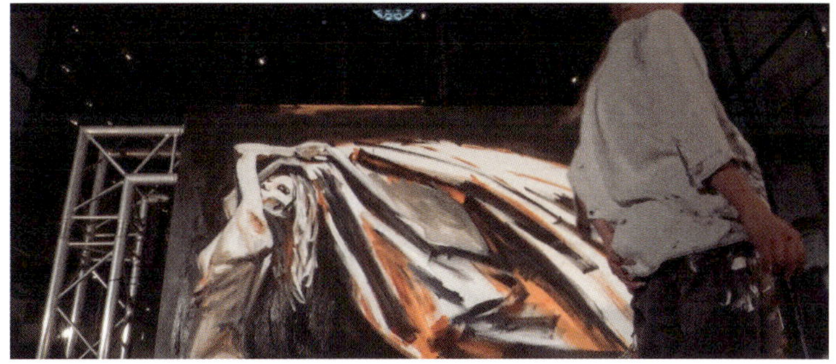

Stills from Daze video by
Richard Van der Vieren, 2015

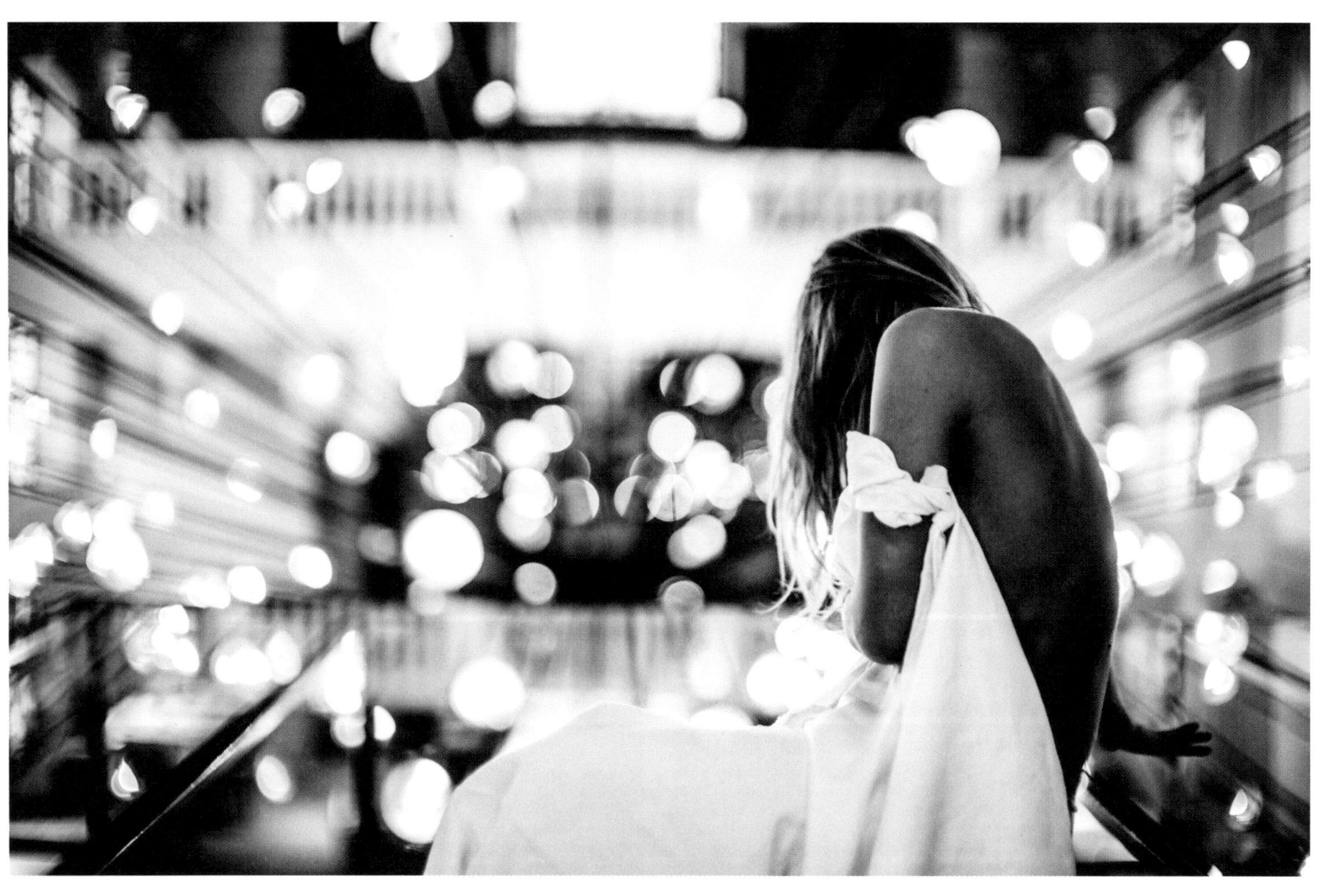

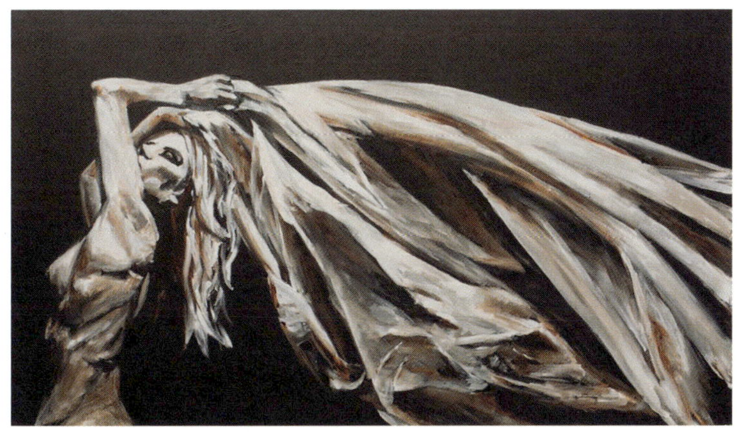

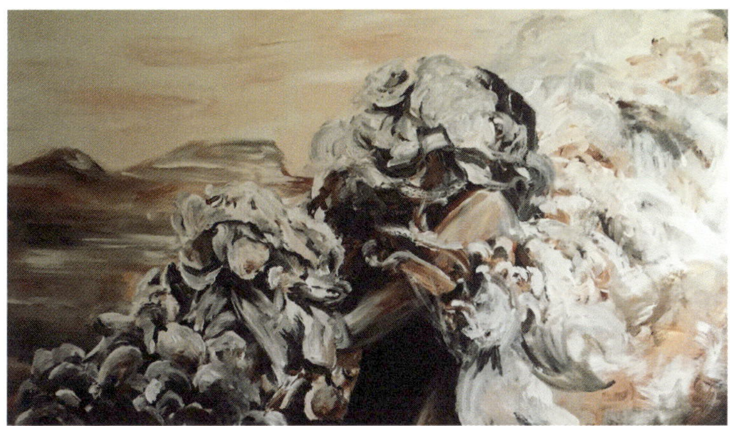

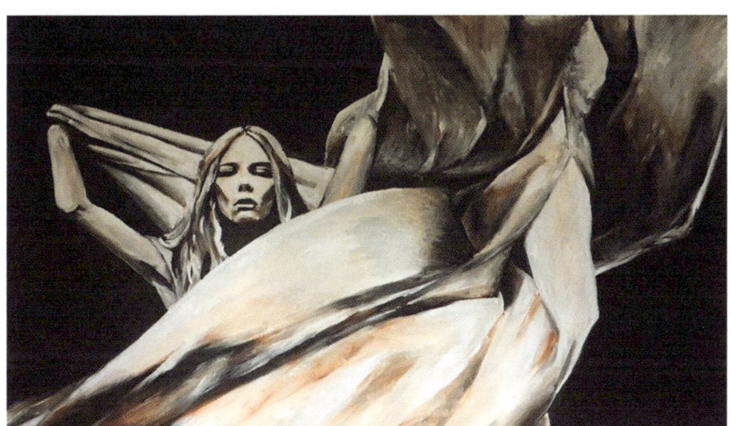

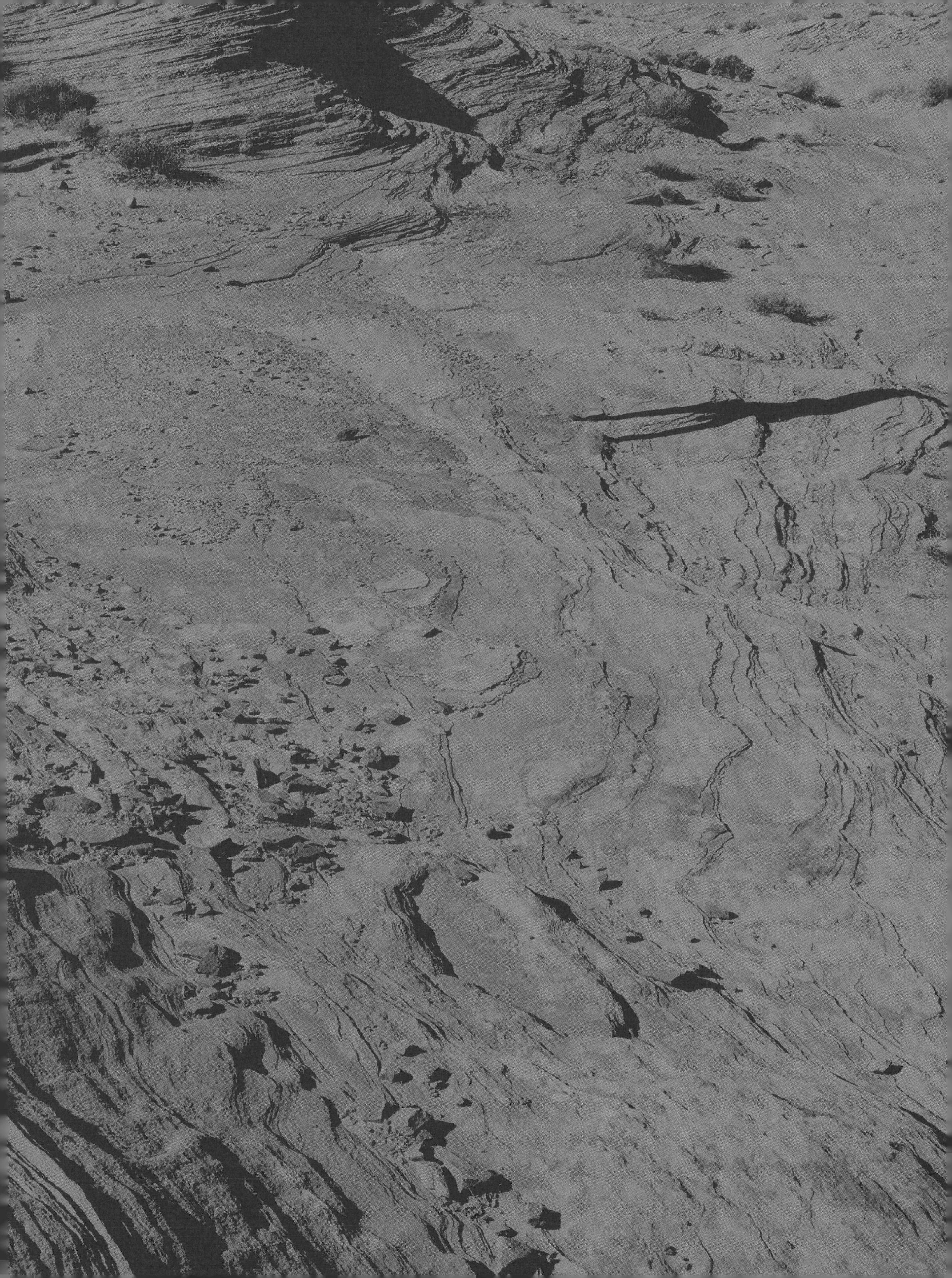

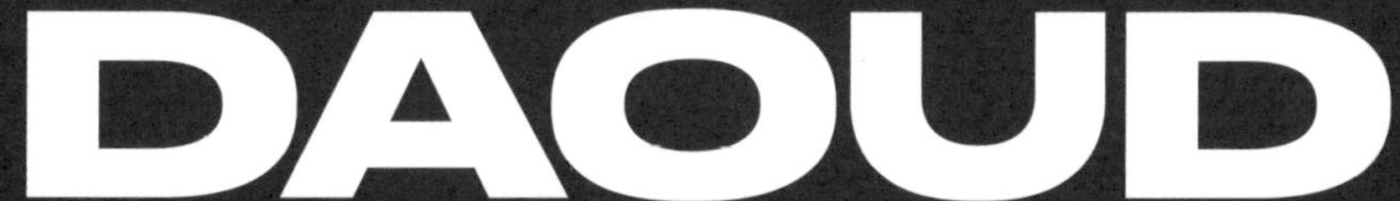

In *Daoud* we see Charlotte stepping in her with
seven-league strides, decisive and proud, wearing
a self-created, lace-like see-through dress
fluttering behind her, her face, chador-like,
wrapped in a silvery cloth, wearing a silver mask
as a cap at the back of her neck, adding to the
mystery. We see Queen Charlotte of Ithaca proudly
stepping through the mountains and valleys, hills
and dales of her newly claimed queendom, through
her Rockland, her Barockland, her Waste Lands,
her Badlands, her Dusklands, strengthened by
Kerouacs device, "Nothing behind me, everything
ahead of me, as if ever so on the road…" or
singing her Songline, like an aboriginal, her
new territory into life, creating a new past,
remembering Rimbaud, never halting because "when
I rest my feet my mind also ceases to function",
mapping out her new territory, her new *queen*dom,
collecting countries by walking through them,
this stepping trip starting from the water
of the lake, through a strip of desert, over
bare planes filled with the cadavers of fishes

sticking to her dress like if it were a dragnet,
collecting dust collecting stories, not halting
nor hesitating one single moment, keeping up that
stiff pace, committed to the hardships
of her odyssey, up to her beloved snow-white
planes, her Wild Wide Spaces, and again over
rocks and ridges back to the water: the circle
is completed.

In this video DAOUD presents *A Dust Odyssey*:
the debut album that includes 10 chapters, 10
wastelands, 10 stories, and a video inspired
by the Homeric epic poem, of ancient Greece,
relating the ten-year wanderings of Odysseus,
king of Ithaca, after the Trojan War. With a
hunger for new experience, DAOUD walks for 10
years, through the wastelands of the west, with
an air of universal longing. This is a human
adrift in a universe that she doesn't, that
she never will, understand. She discovers the
bittersweet ephemerality of everything, and the
idea that to "know time" is to know ourselves at
the mercy of time. (LÉON LEMAHIEU)

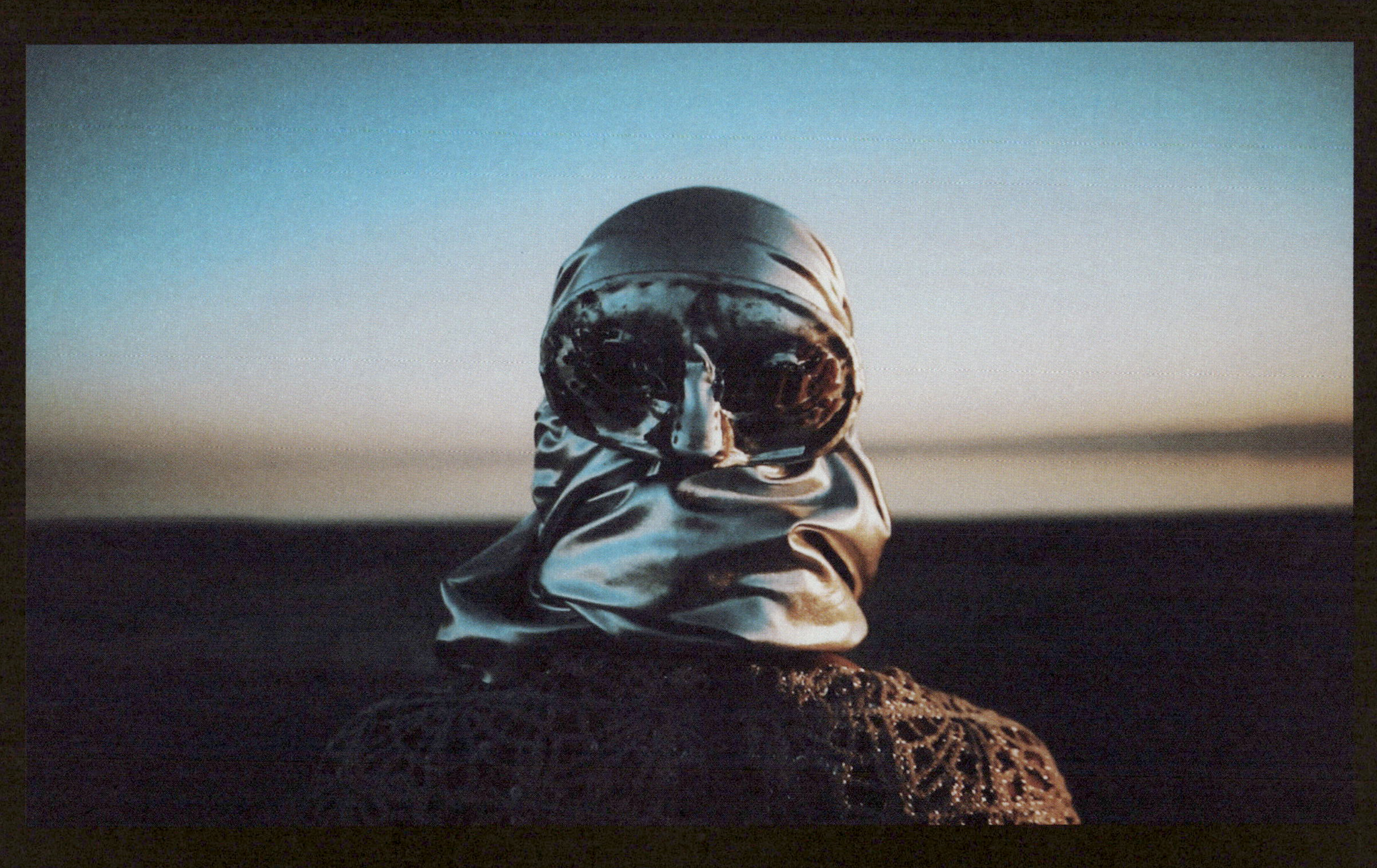

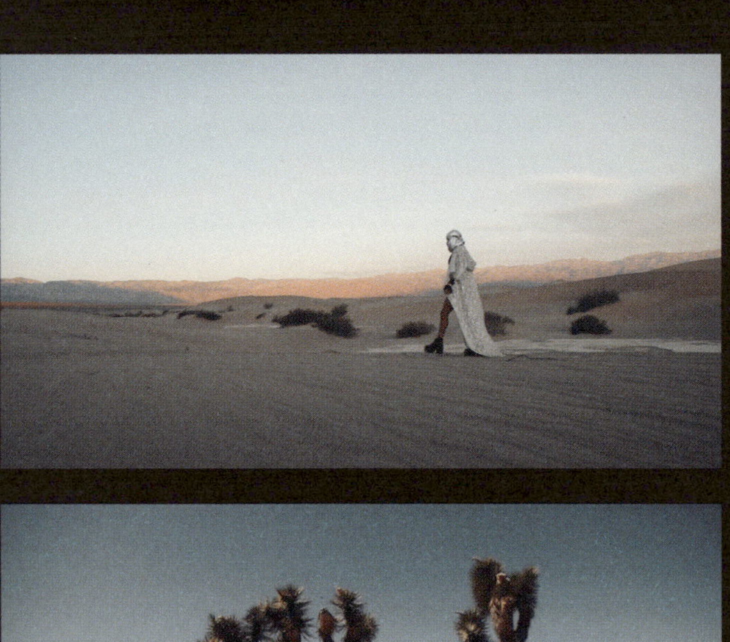
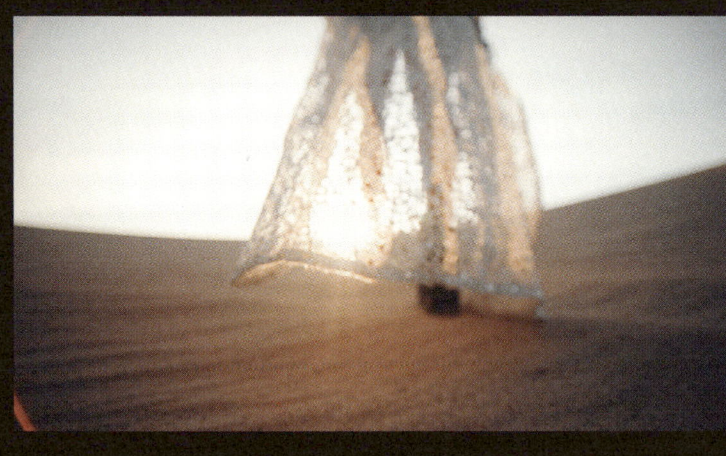
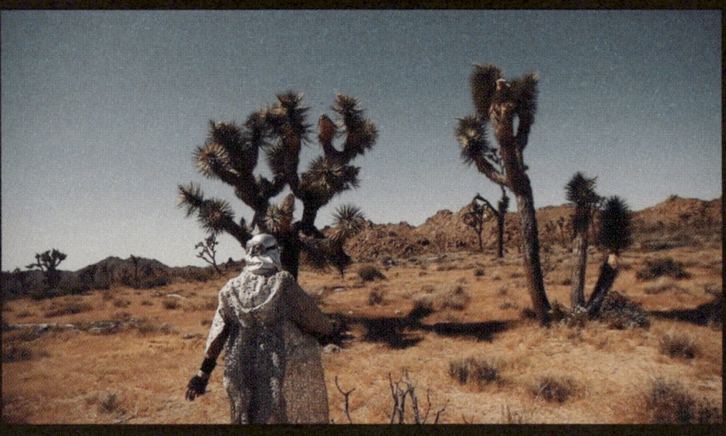
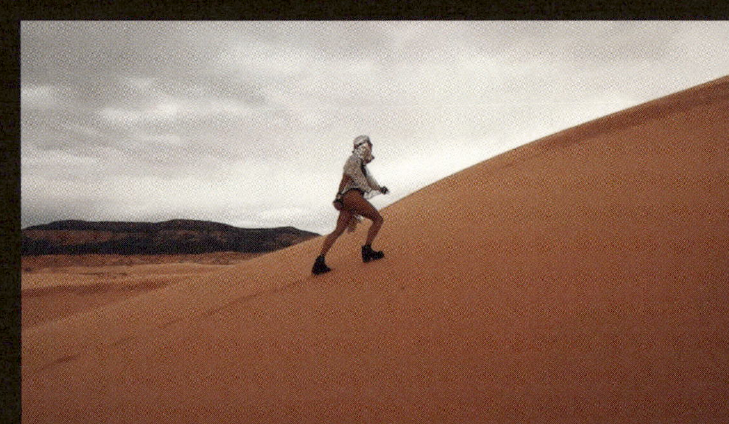
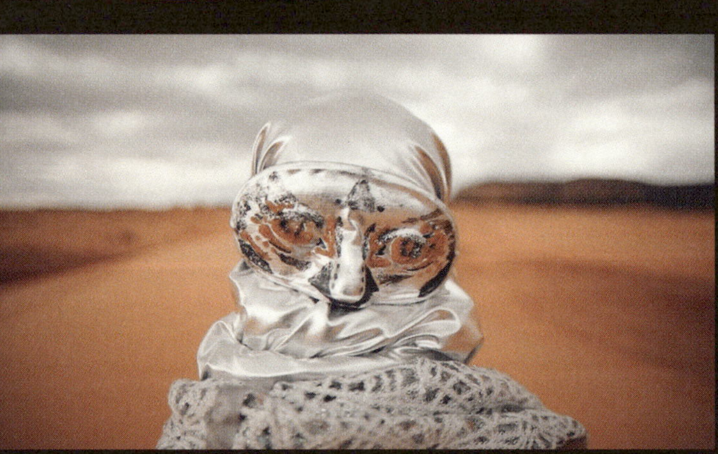
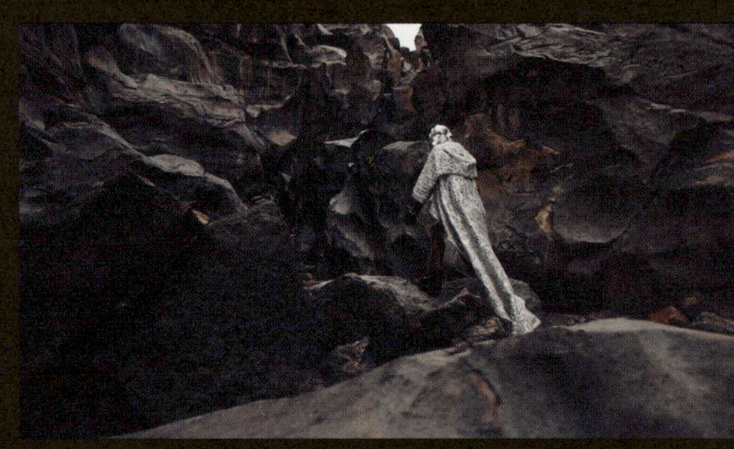
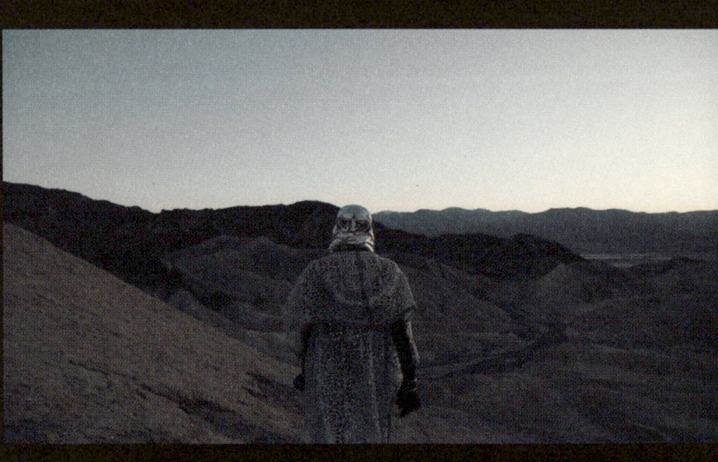
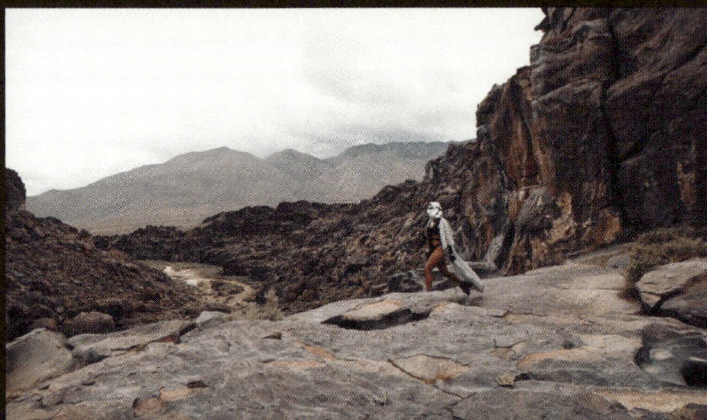

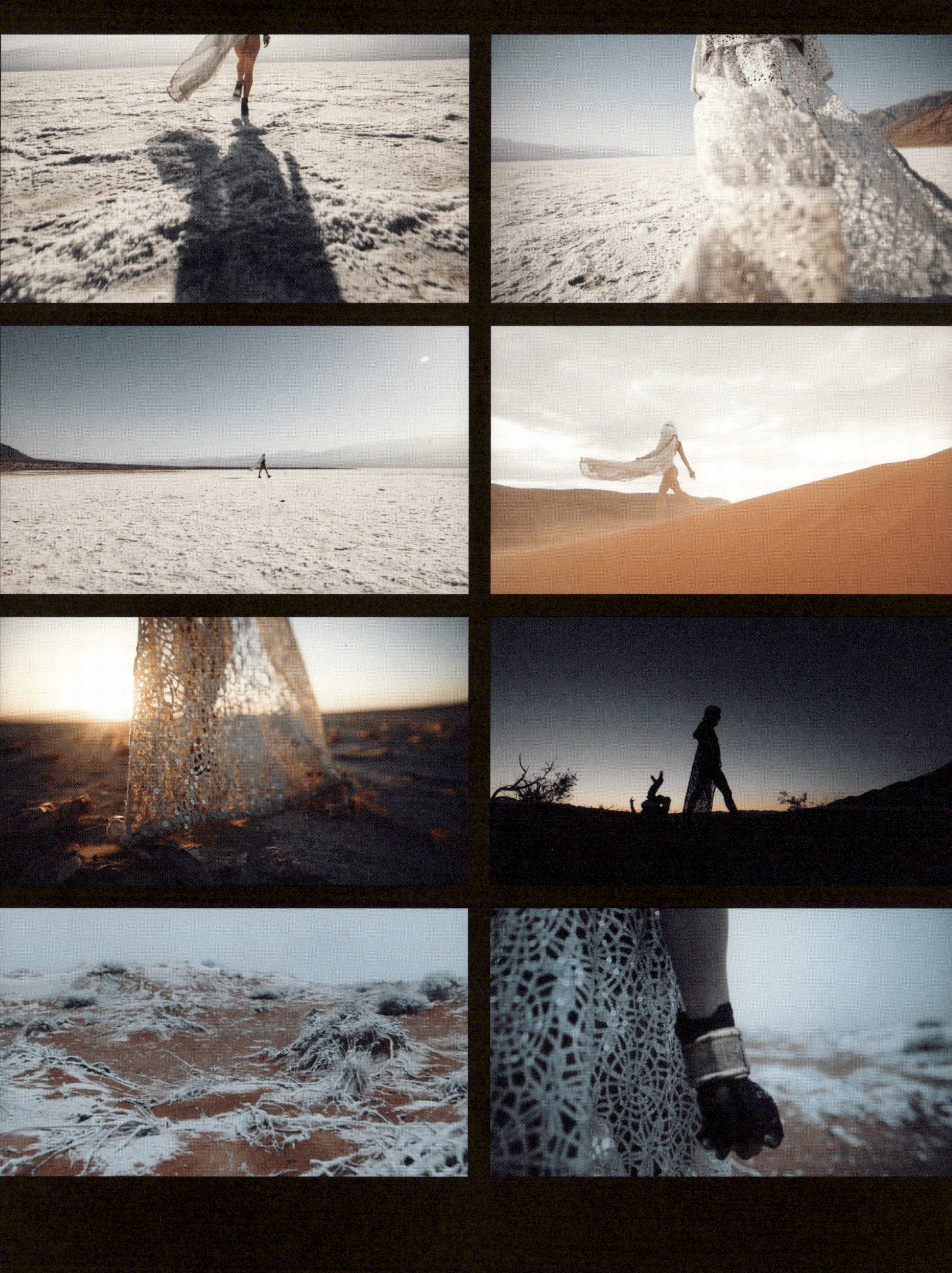

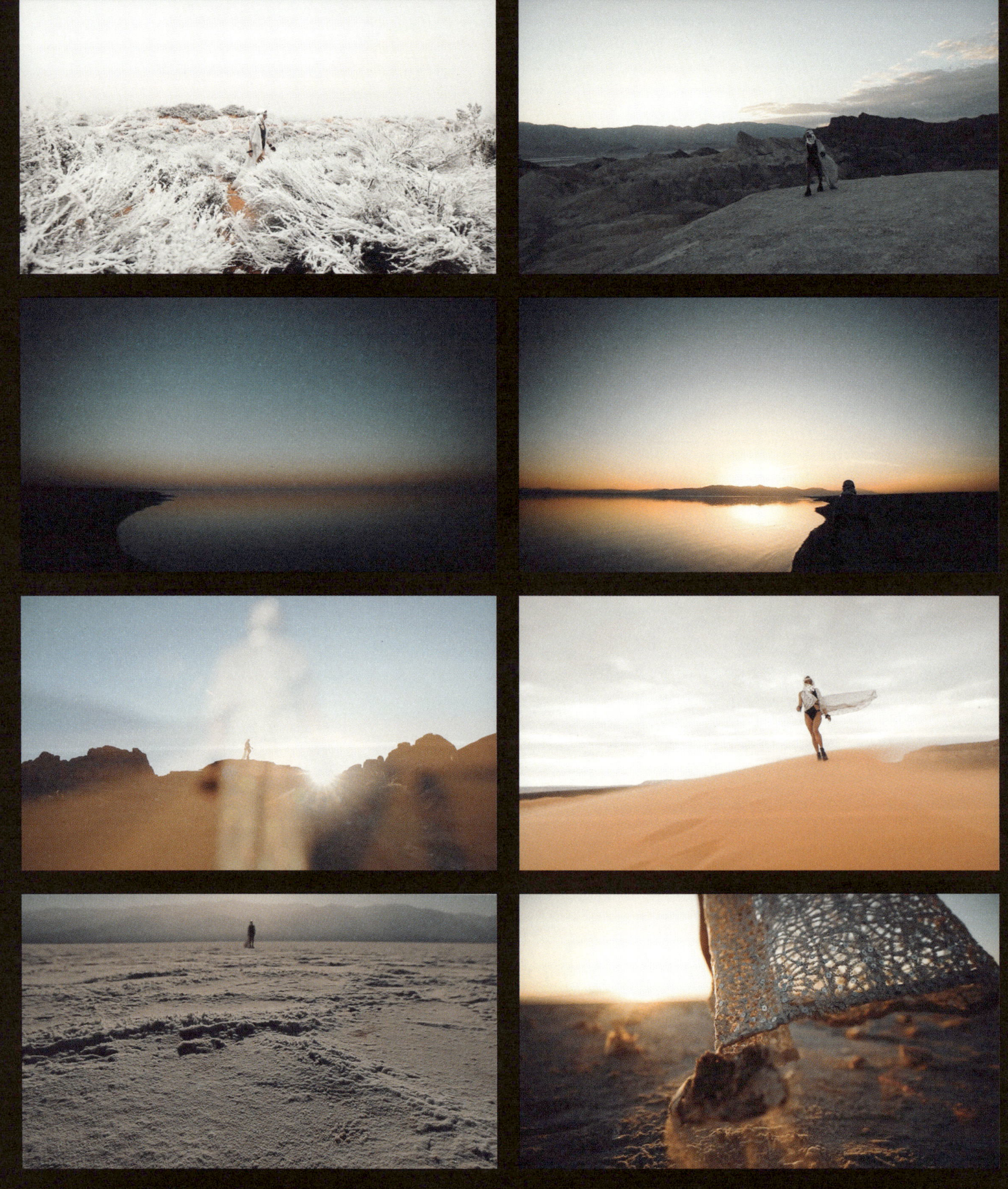

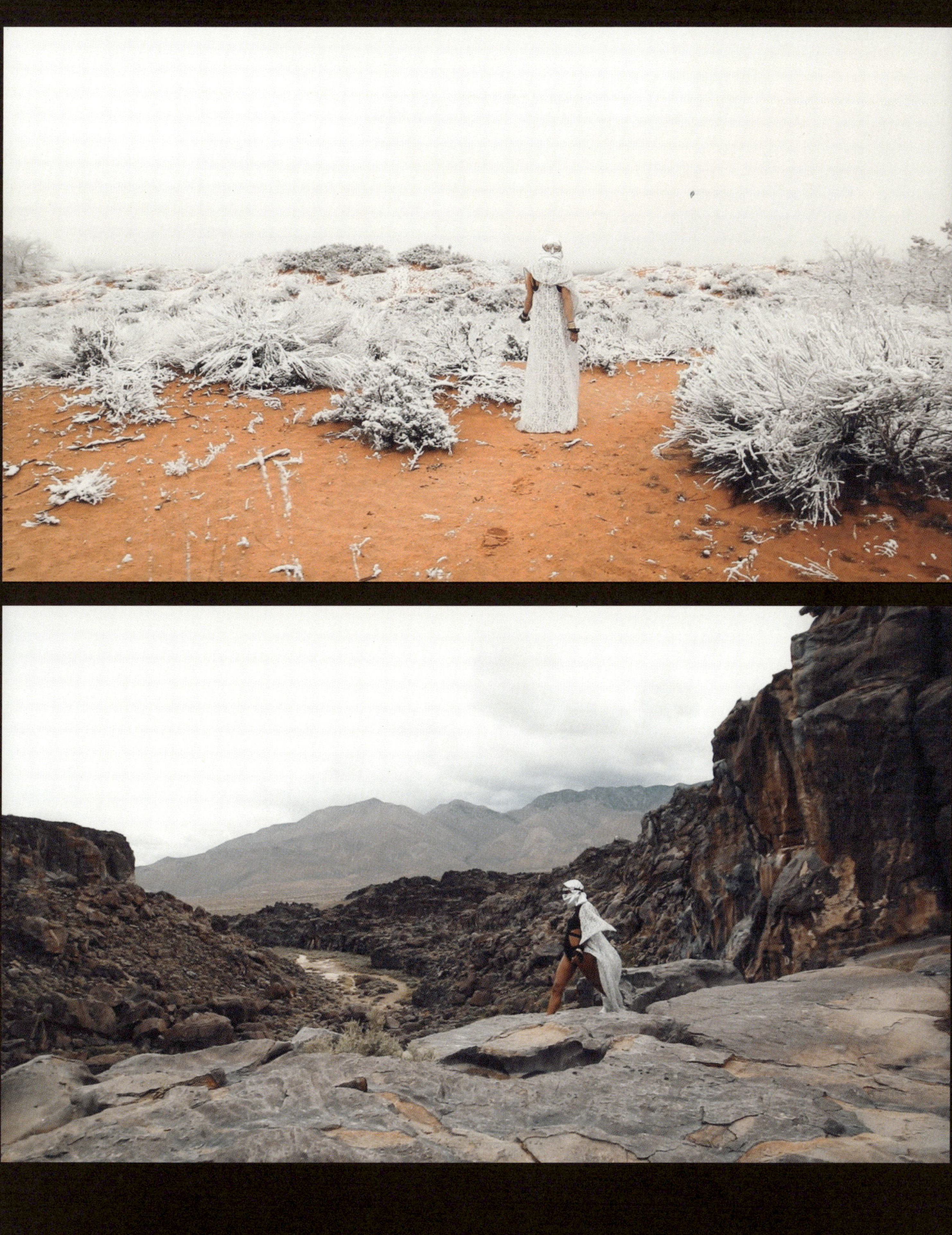

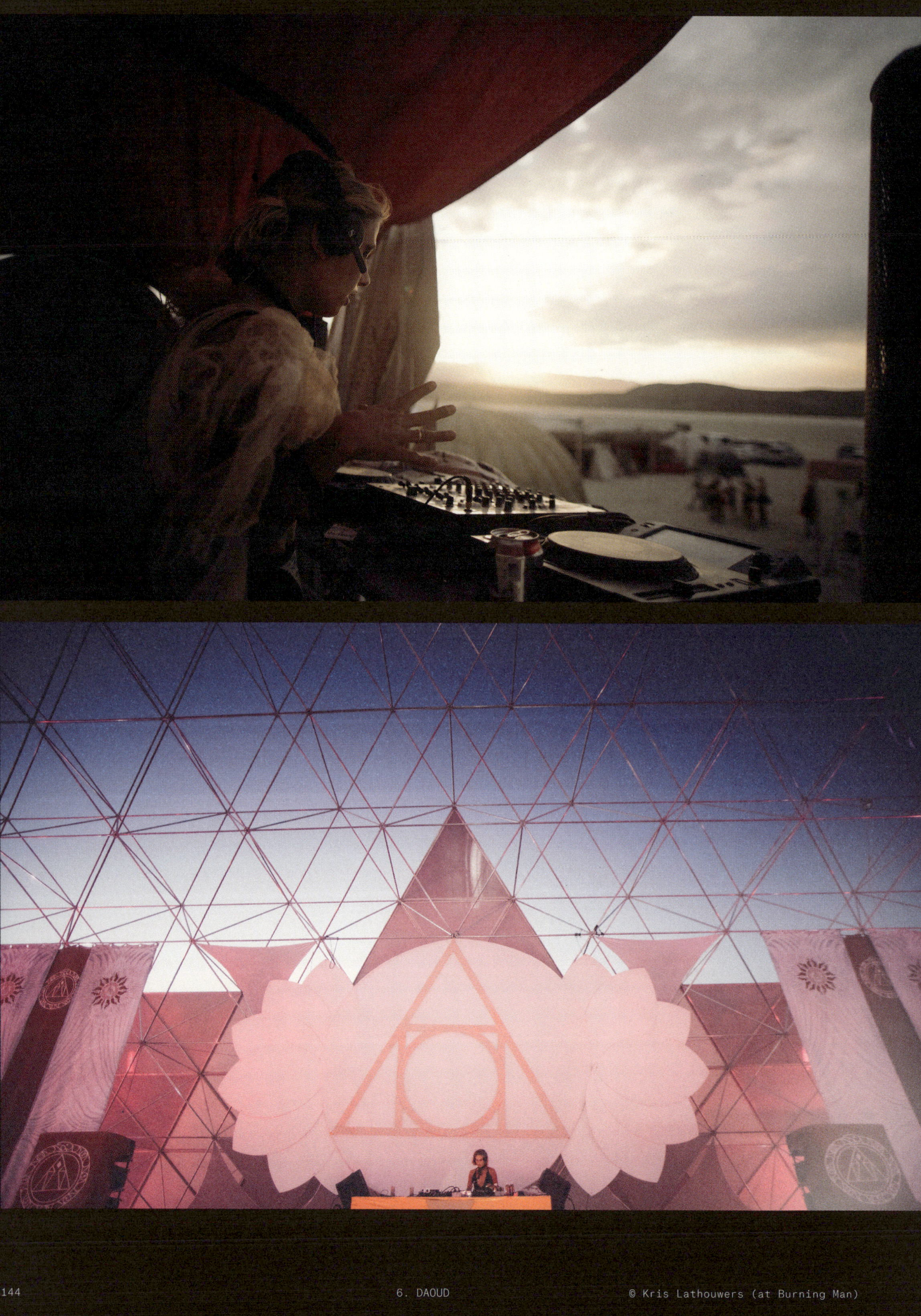

6. DAOUD

© Kris Lathouwers (at Burning Man)

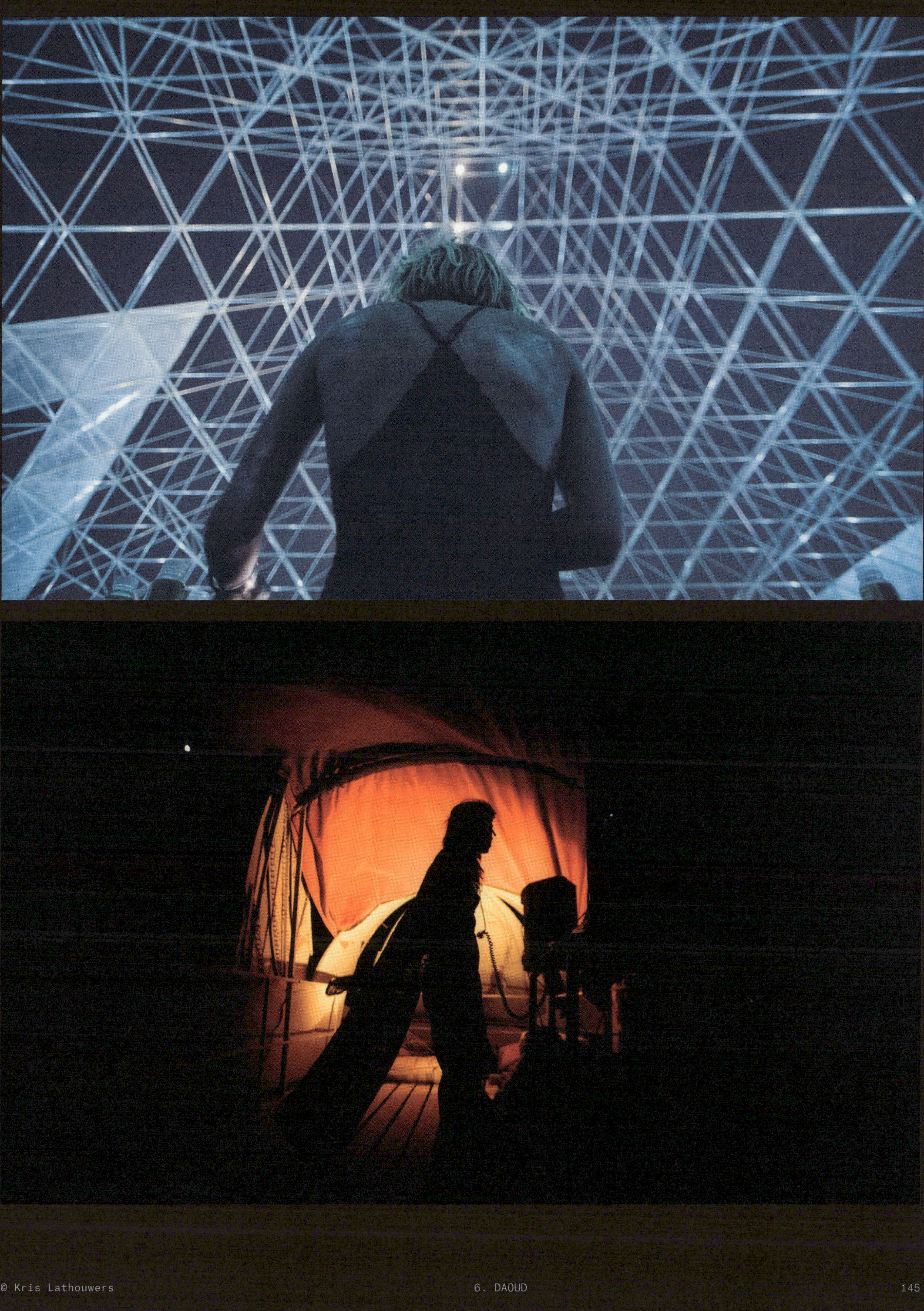

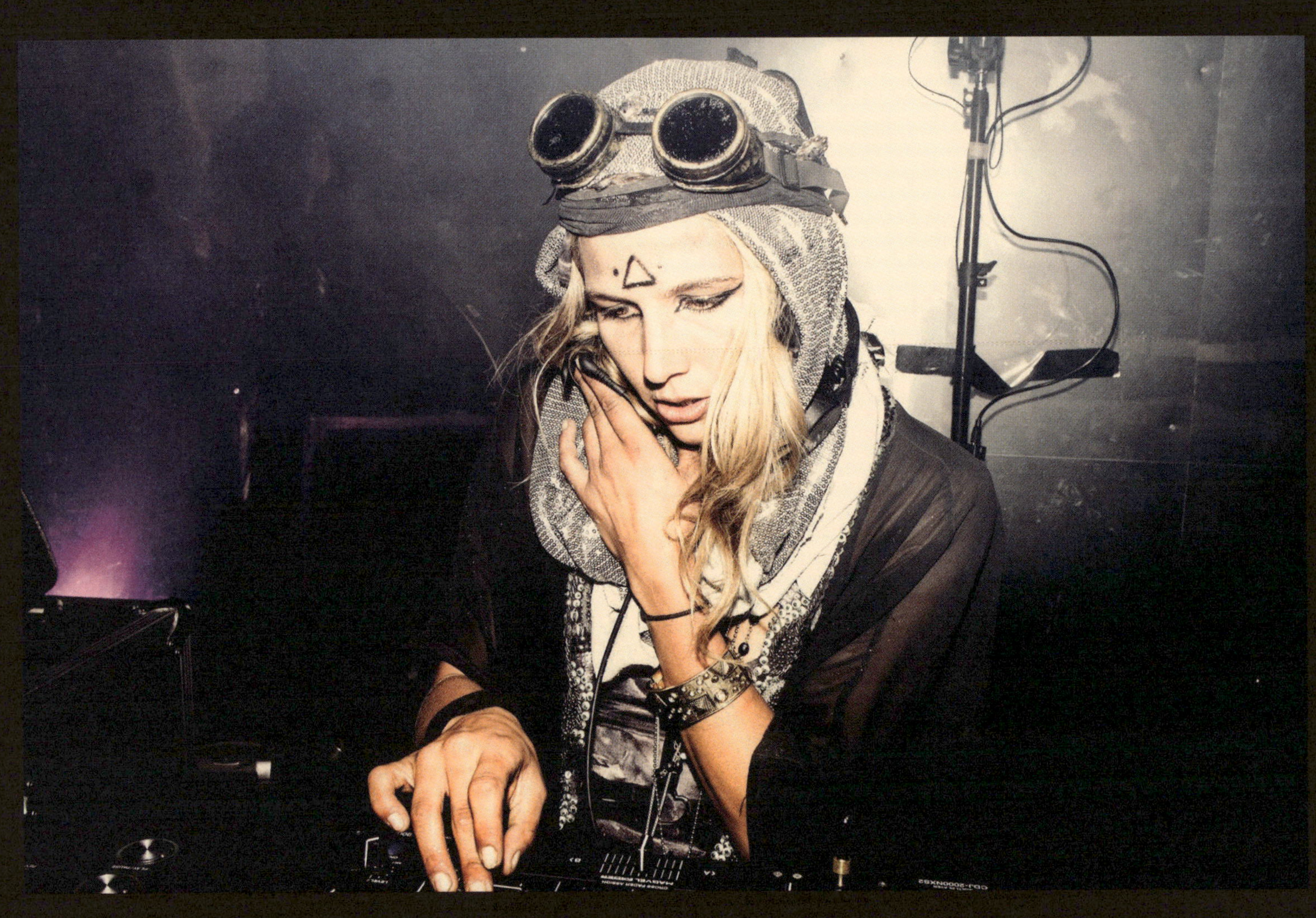

6. DAOUD

© Sara De Graeve

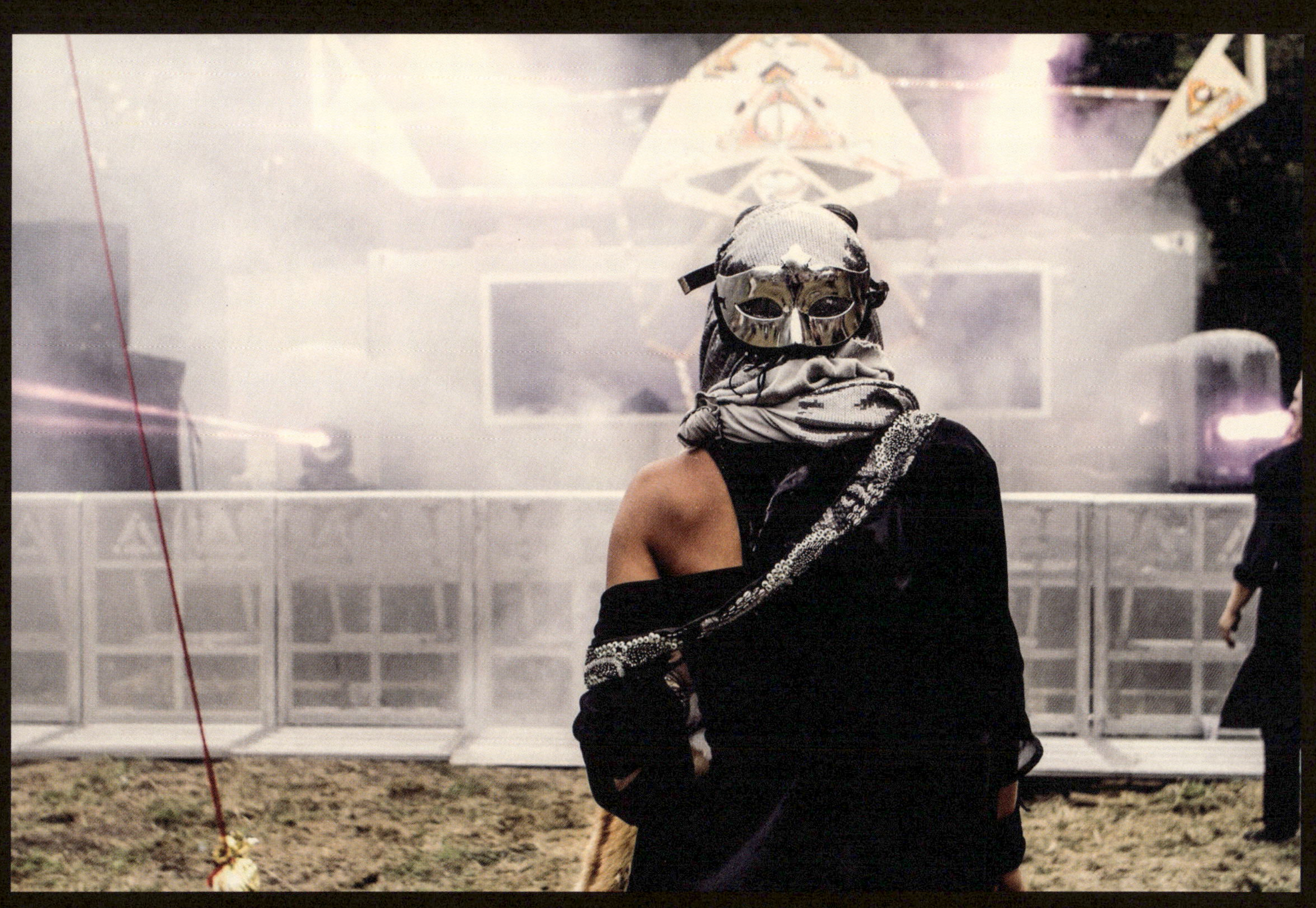

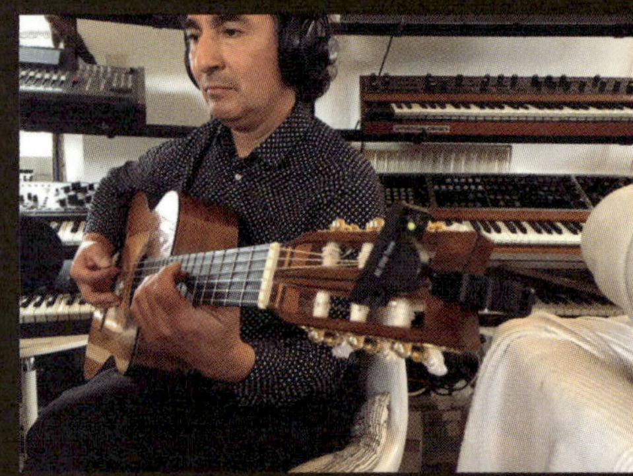
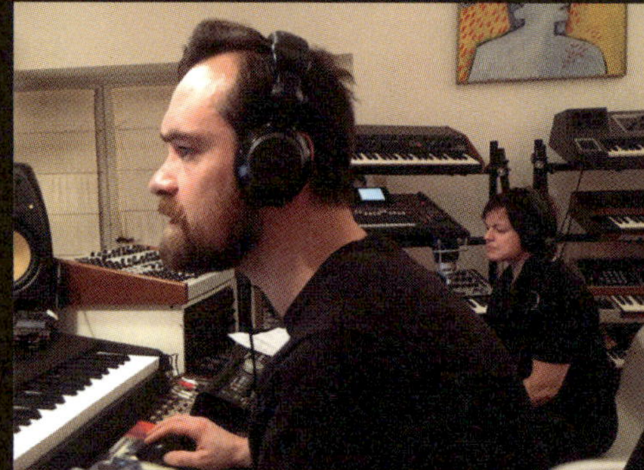
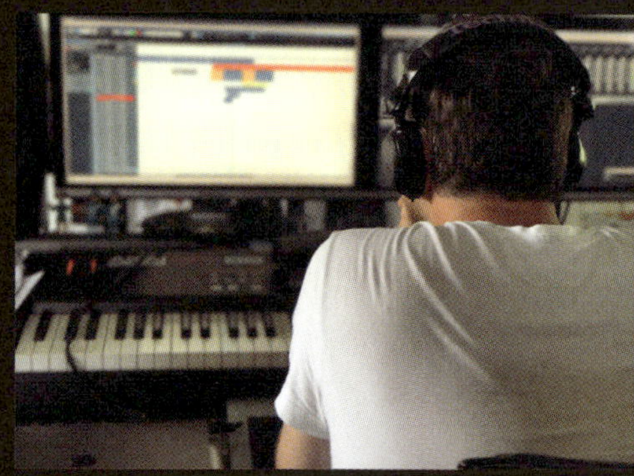
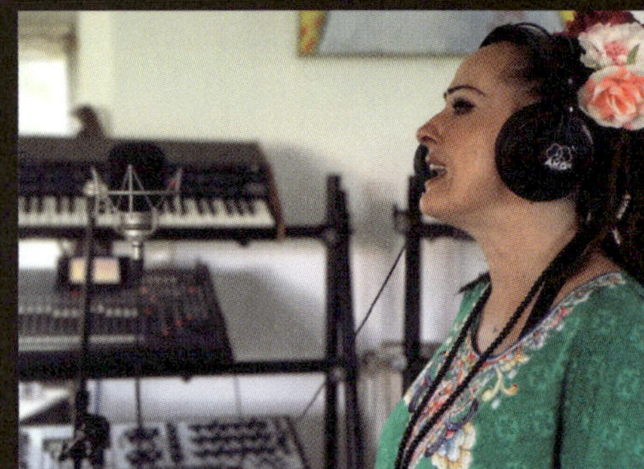
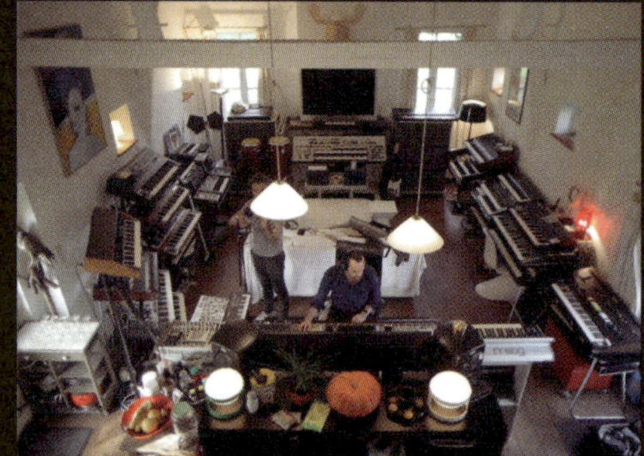
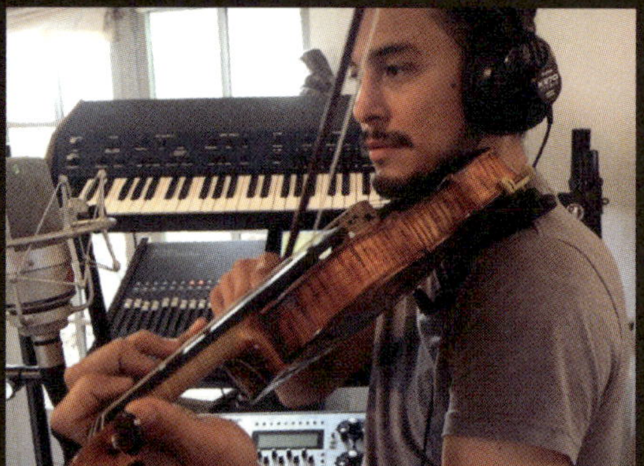
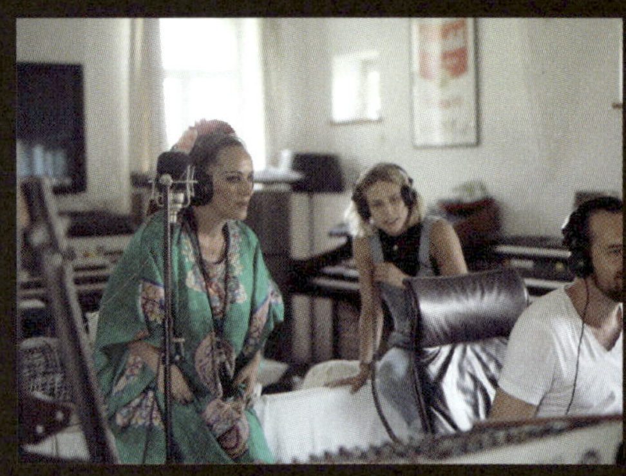
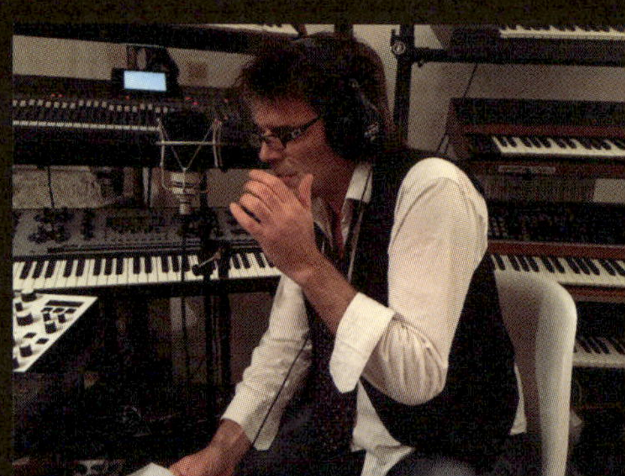
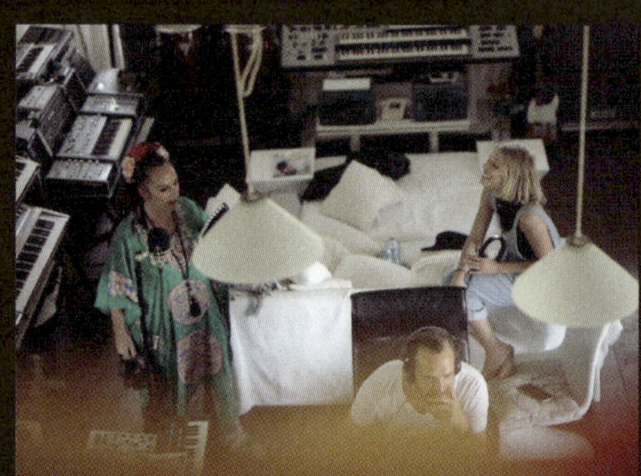

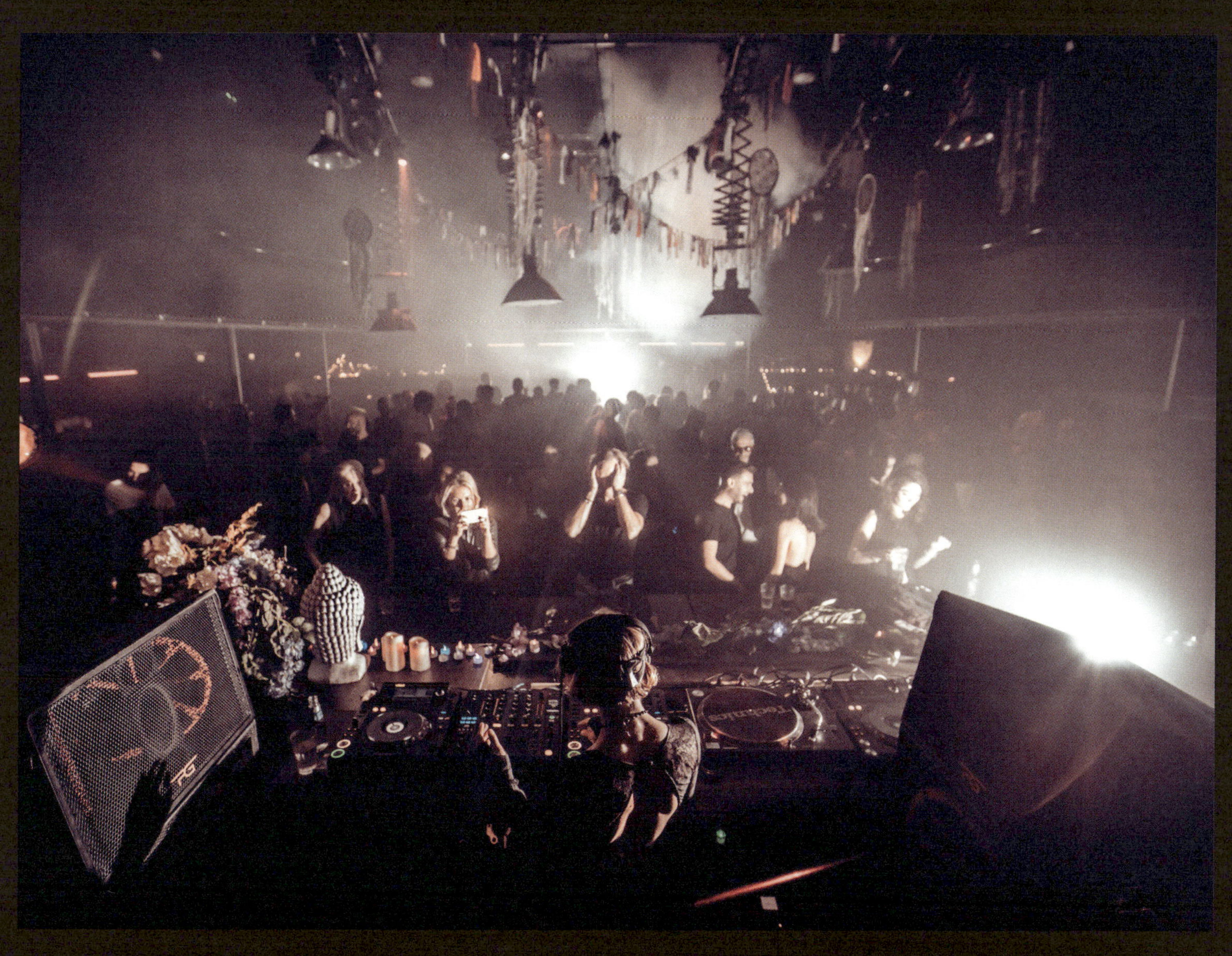

 6. DAOUD

A Journey with Charlotte

Water and wind, sand and snow, roads and stars:
on a trip with Charlotte De Cock means to find
yourself amidst the grand plains of nature,
of life, of existence, whether it concerns
the oceans, deserts and wildernesses, rocky
mountains, frozen snowscapes, endless roads, the
sweltering firmament, the sky at night. Always,
she brings / leads you in / to the middle of an
overwhelming land-/sea-/skyscape … where man is
nothing and nature is everything.

And yet, in these overwhelming surroundings, as
a star entering the stage, little Charlotte, with
her lithe, mercurial body, masters the scene, as
if these immense, ancient surroundings have been
waiting an eternity for her to appear.
She is not being crushed or swallowed, reduced
to nothing by these immensities, and maybe that
is because she doesn't intrude, or wants to
conquer them, but enters them cautiously and
respectfully, as a cat, letting nature come to
her, enter her.

As I mentioned already, Charlotte constantly
portrays herself, picturing the world around her
through these portraits; even her depictions
of objects, landscapes, seascapes, still lives,
or other people are, in a way, projected self-
portraits. Reflections of her inner world
projected on, or summarized in those pictures.
And sometimes, she reduces her presence in
certain tableaux to a part of the environment,
especially if she wants to make a statement,
usually of an environmental nature, even when
the focus is one particular element: Charlotte.

Thus she plays a kind of ping pong with herself
and the environment, and with the spectator:
ping-pong-pang! In that kind of triangle one
never knows if the next move is to the right
or the left, putting one on the wrong track,
something painters love to do. To accomplish
this she constantly photographs her subjects,
returning to locations she visited years before,
armed with camera and pictures, making pictures
of pictures, confronting the subject with its
past, playing ping pong with time.

Charlotte De Cock paints as a fighter, fighting
openly, honest and straightforward, contrary to
the way she approaches her subjects, surrendering
herself completely, trying to identify herself
with them, absorbing them or letting herself
being absorbed, especially in her trips to the
Southwest of the USA. (LÉON LEMAHIEU)

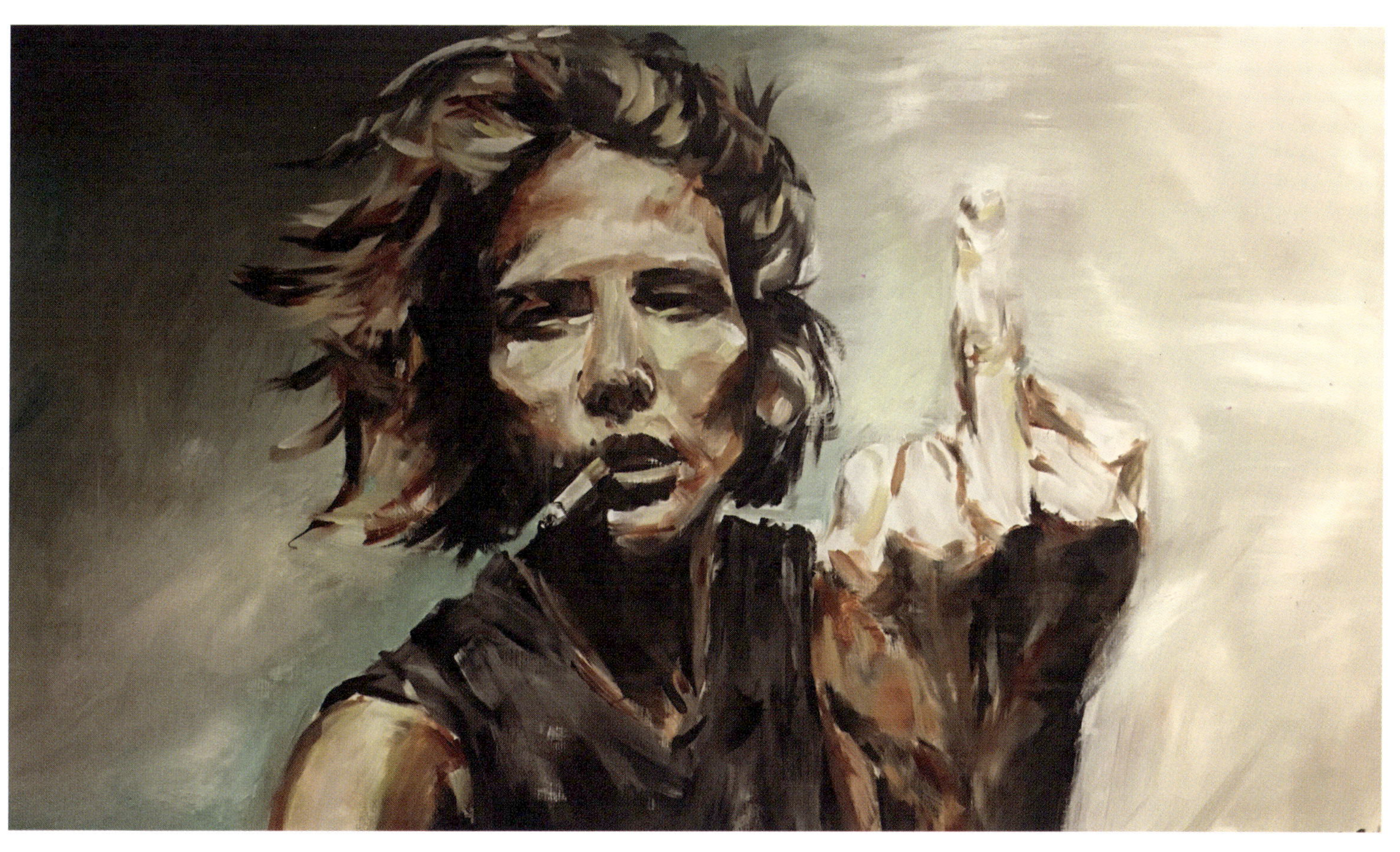

Bela Lugosi's Dead,
A Journey with Charlotte series,
acrylic on canvas, 200 x 120 cm, 2017

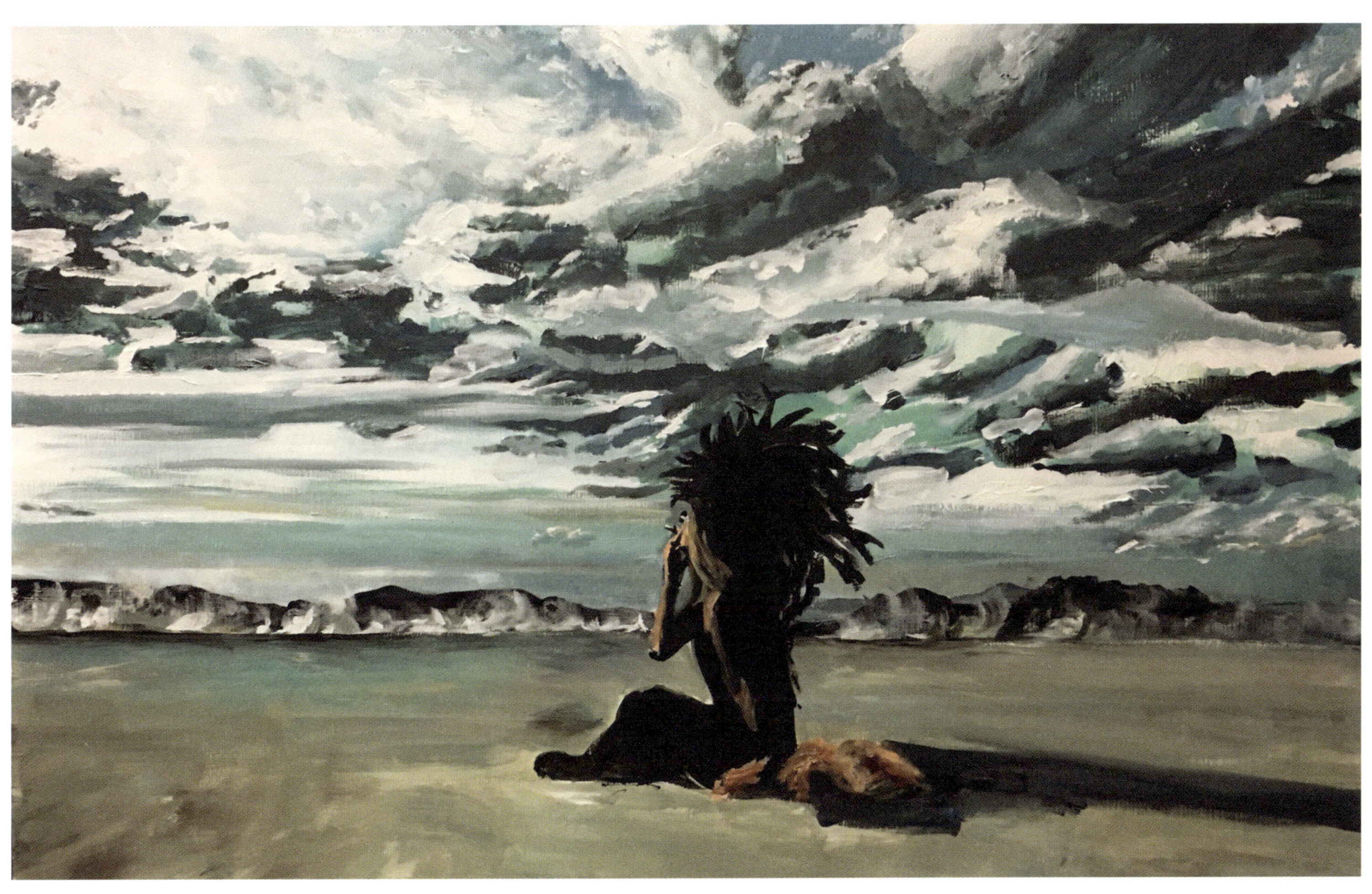

Desert Raven,
A Journey with Charlotte series,
acrylic on canvas, 150 x 100 cm, 2017

7. A JOURNEY WITH CHARLOTTE

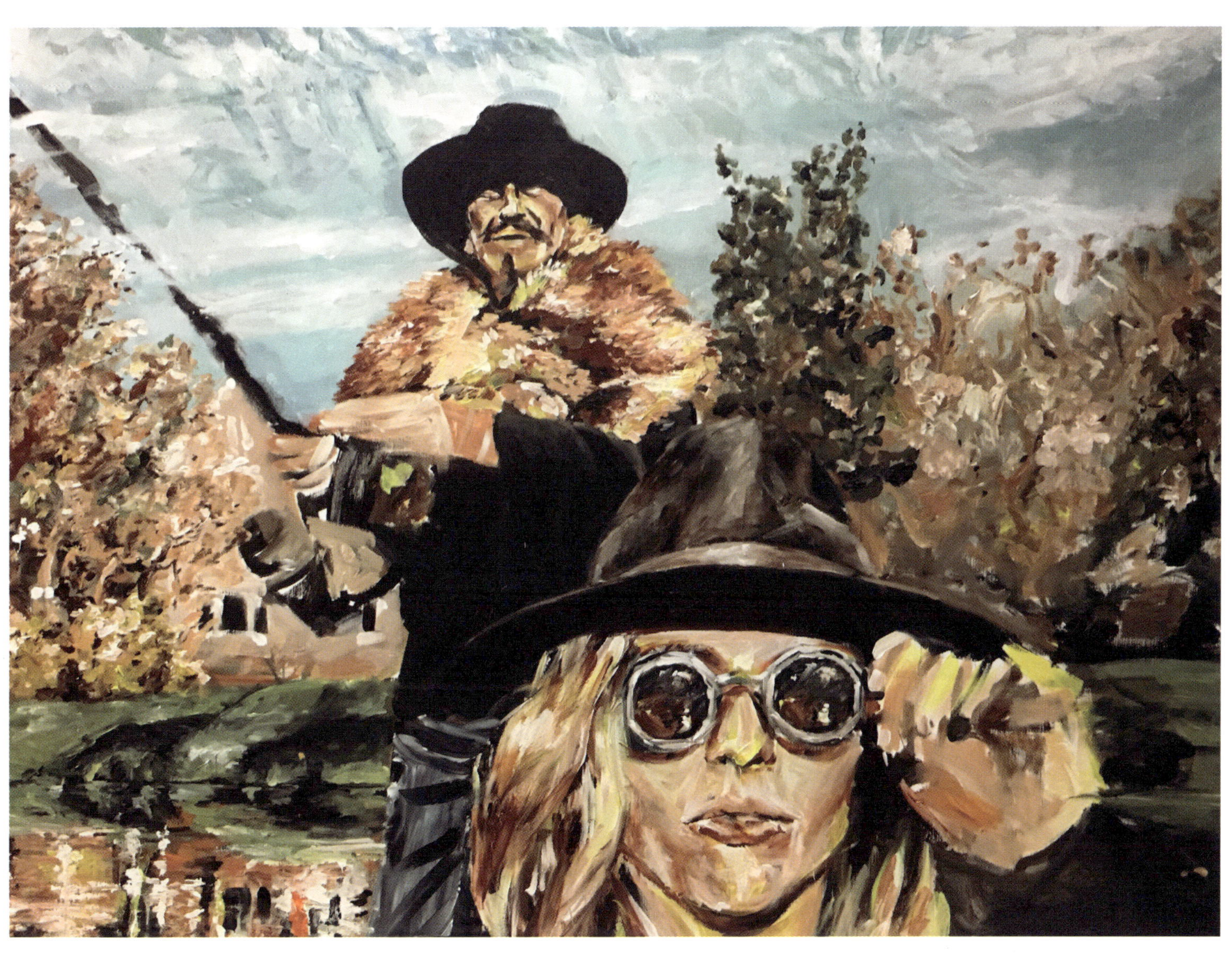

A Forest,
A Journey with Charlotte series,
acrylic on canvas, 250 x 150 cm, 2017

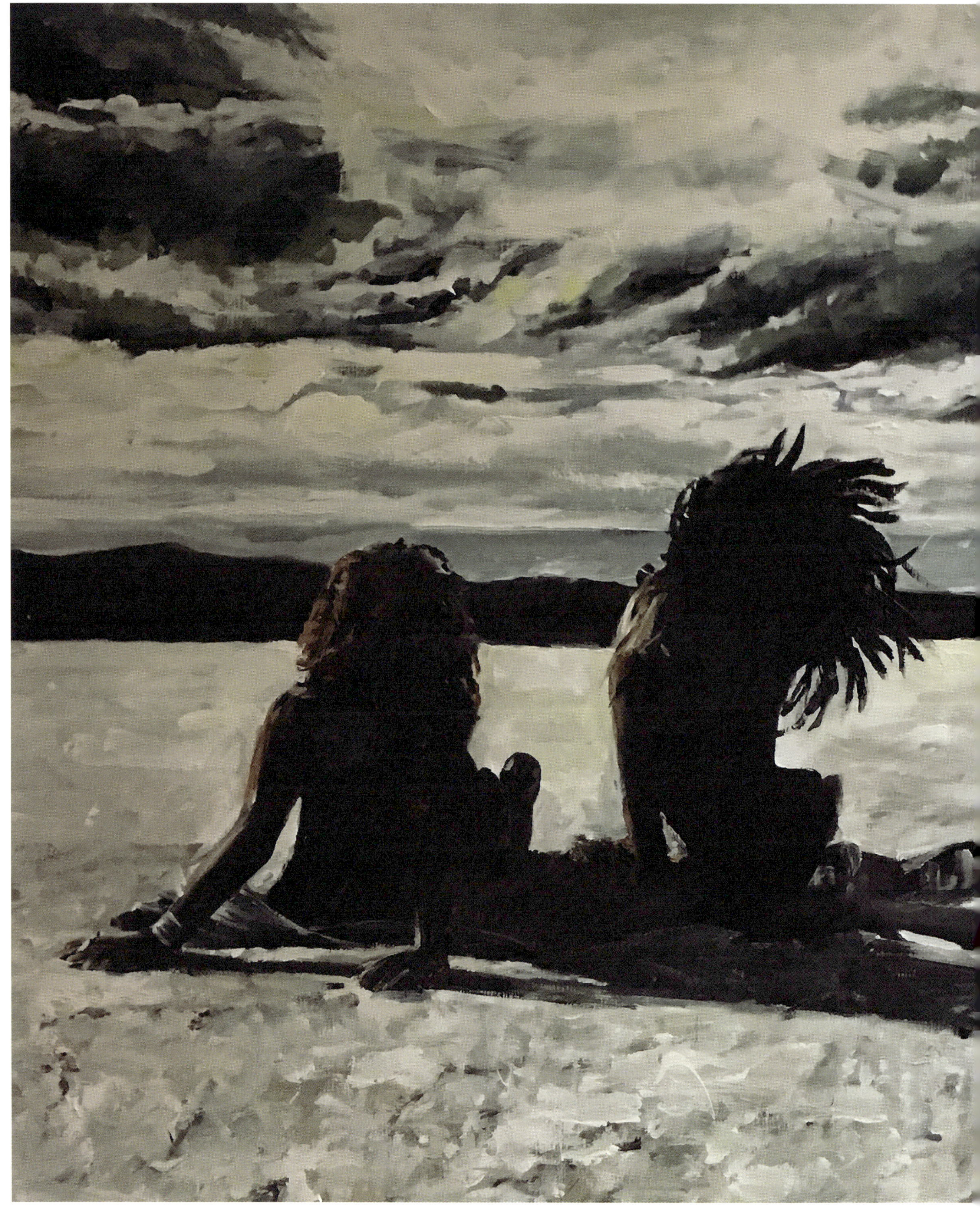

7. A JOURNEY WITH CHARLOTTE

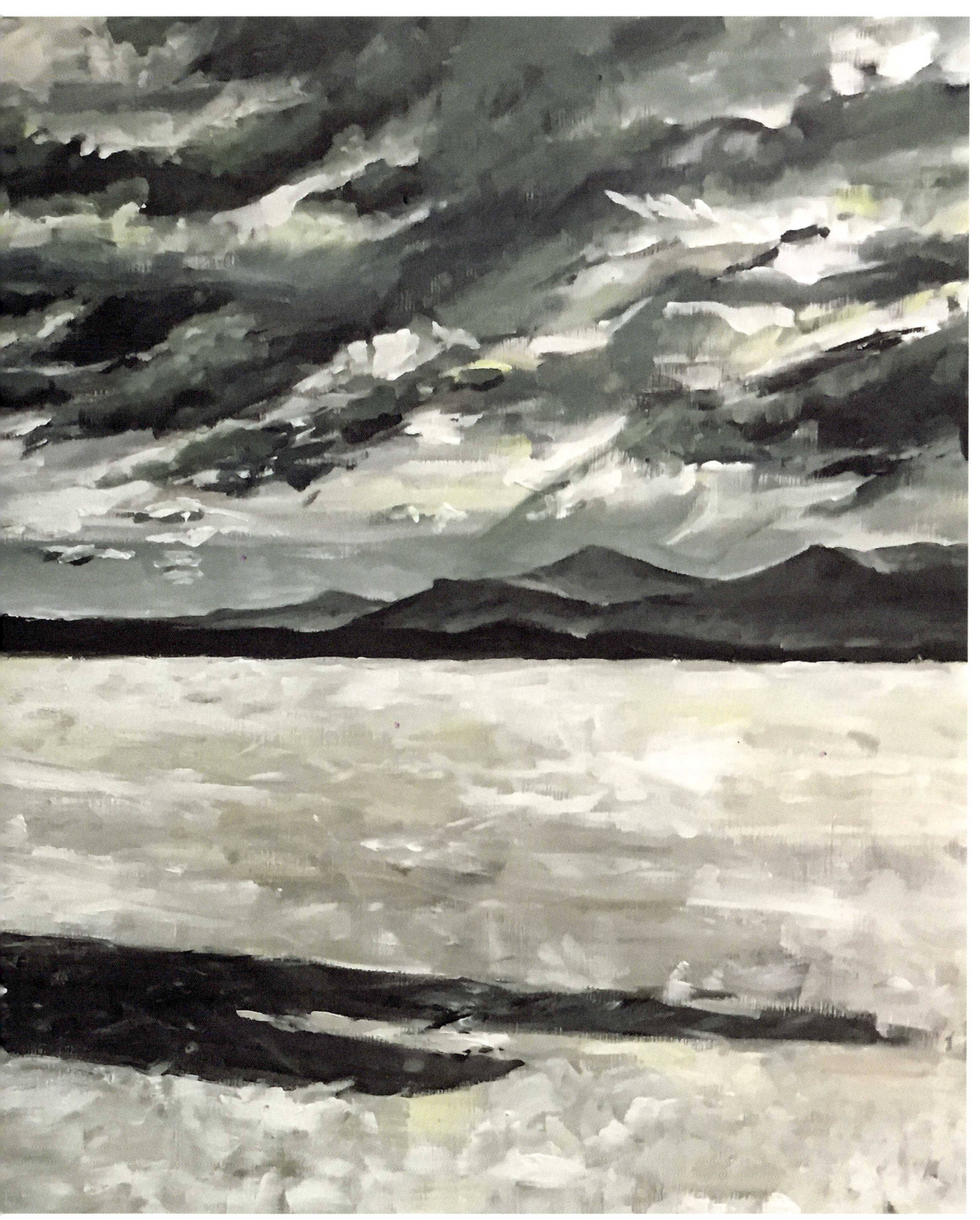

Shine on You Crazy Diamond,
A Journey with Charlotte series,
acrylic on canvas, 200 x 120 cm, 2017

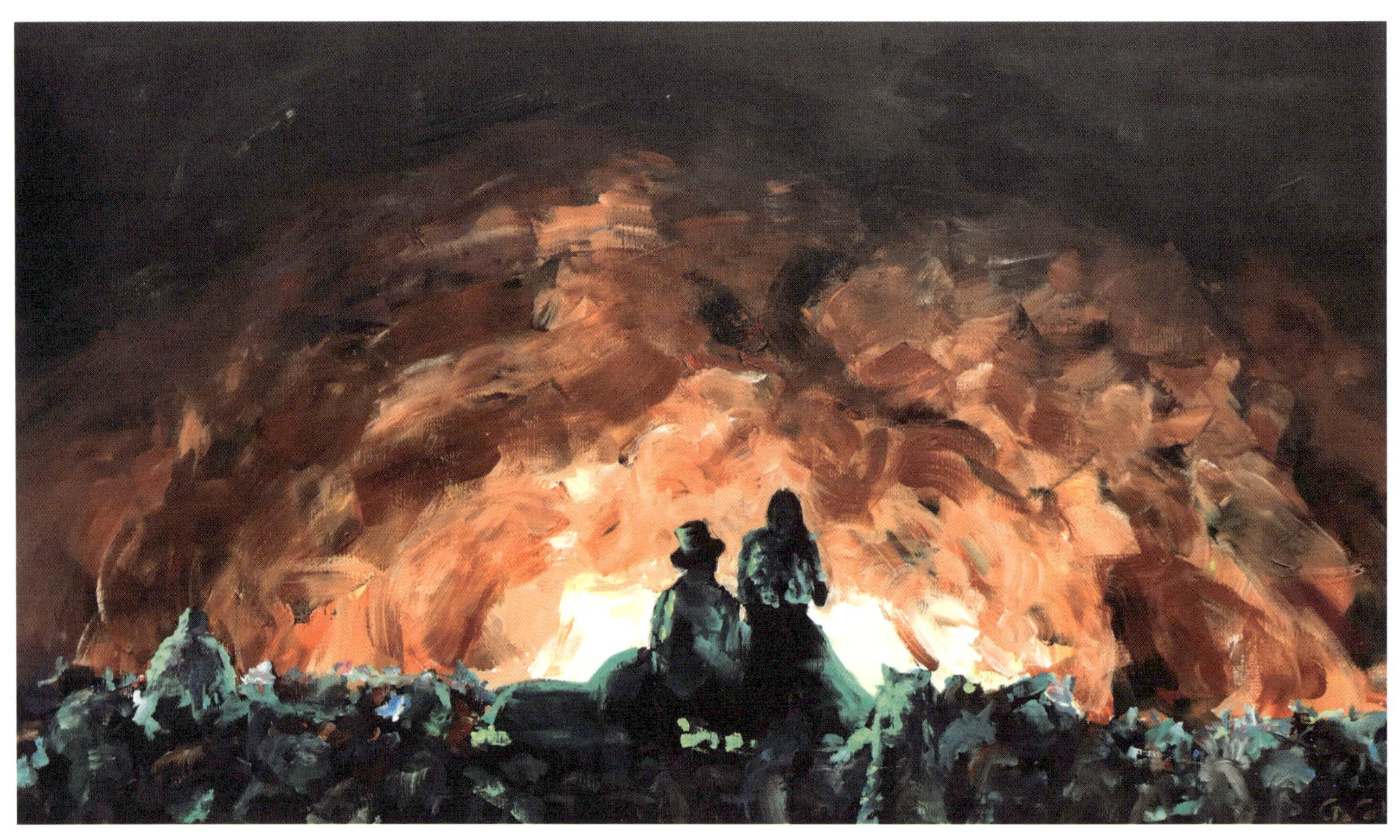

7. A JOURNEY WITH CHARLOTTE

Blue Moon,
A Journey with Charlotte series,
acrylic on canvas, 200 x 120 cm, 2017

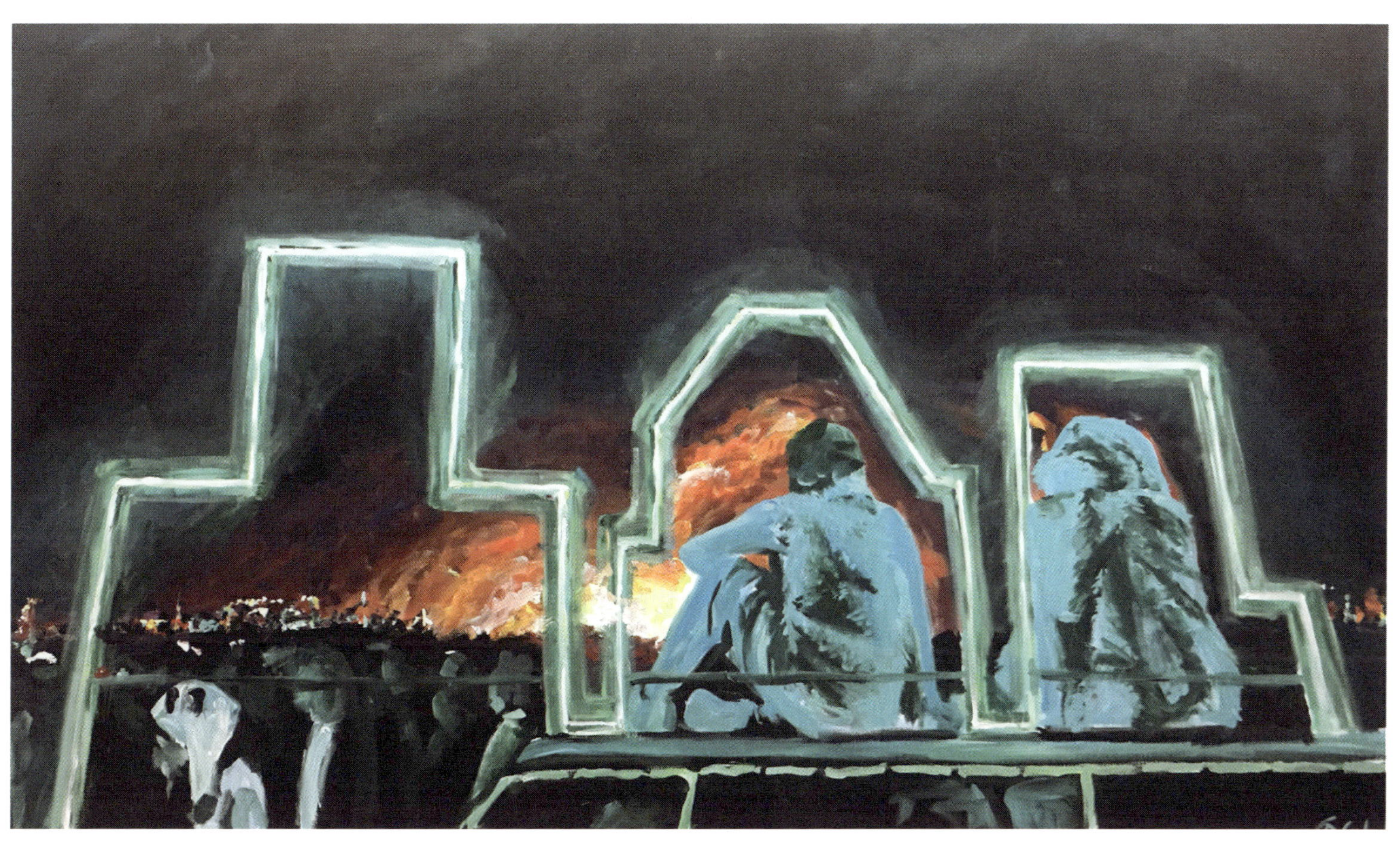

This Must Be the Place,
A Journey with Charlotte series,
acrylic on canvas, 250 x 150 cm, 2017

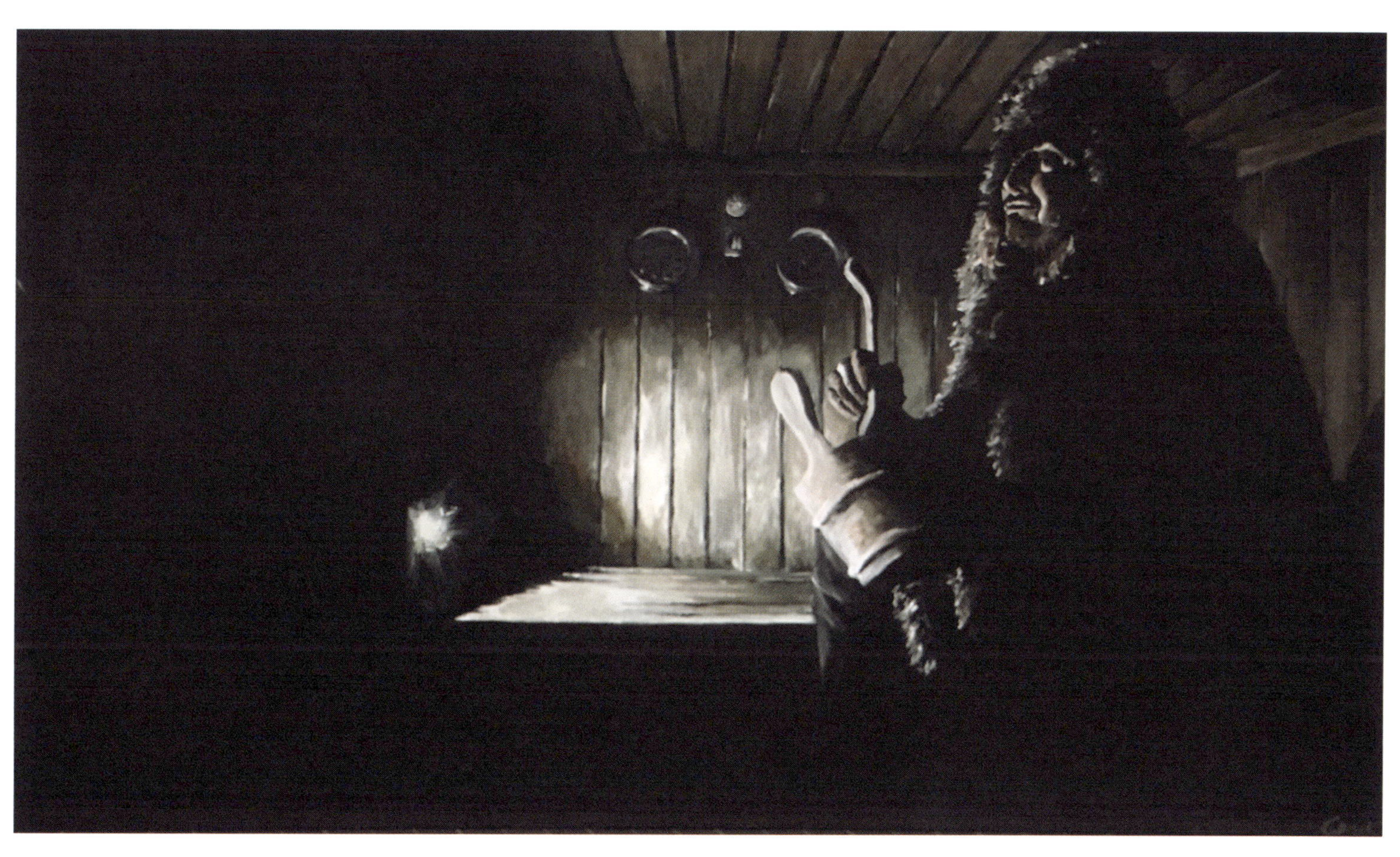

I Can't Live in a Living Room,
A Journey with Charlotte series,
acrylic on canvas, 250 x 150 cm, 2017

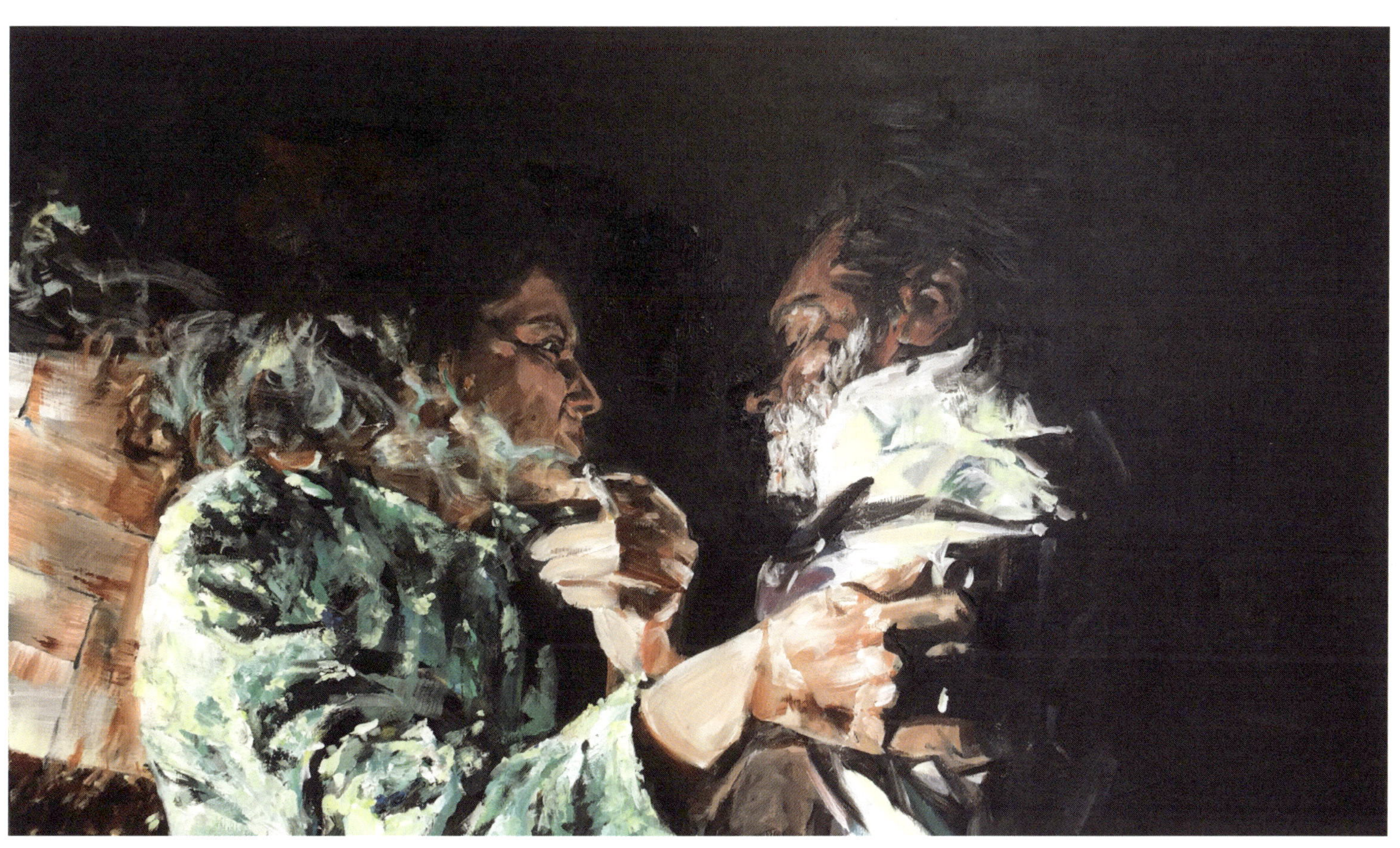

Friend, A Journey with Charlotte series,
acrylic on canvas, 200 x 120 cm, 2017

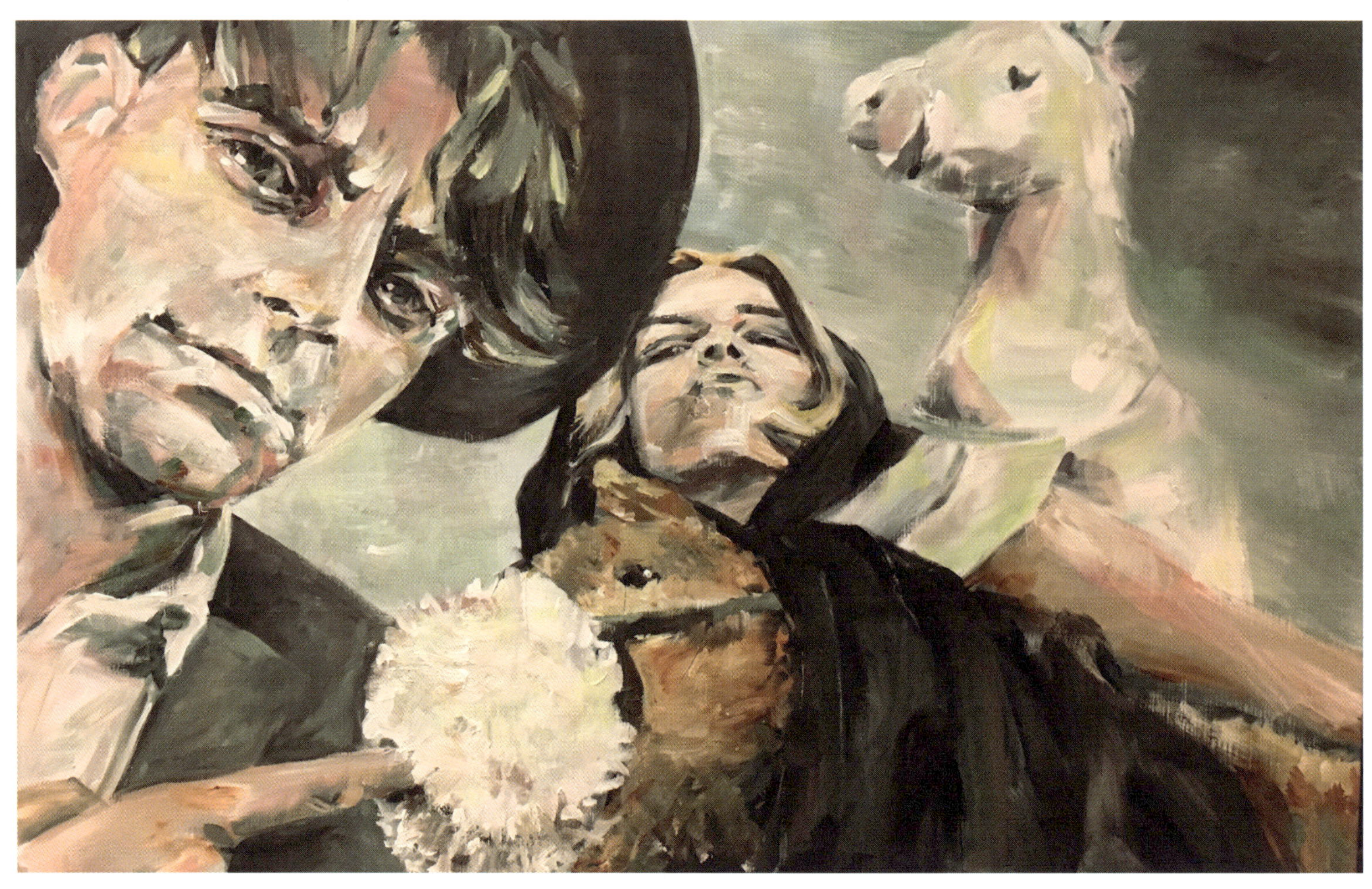

Goodbye Horses (I),
A Journey with Charlotte series,
acrylic on canvas, 150 x 100 cm, 2017

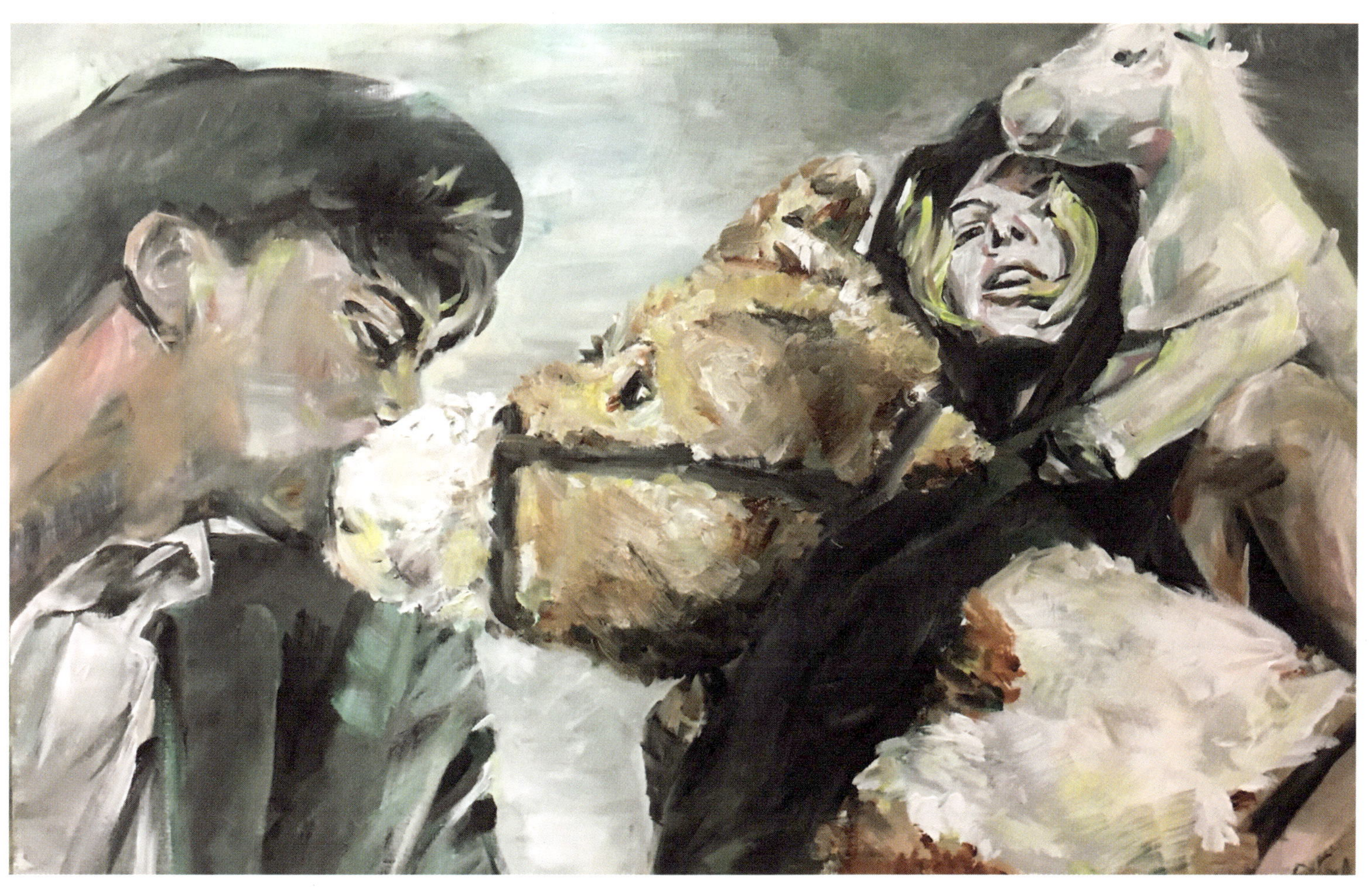

Goodbye Horses (II),
A Journey with Charlotte series,
acrylic on canvas, 150 x 100 cm, 2017

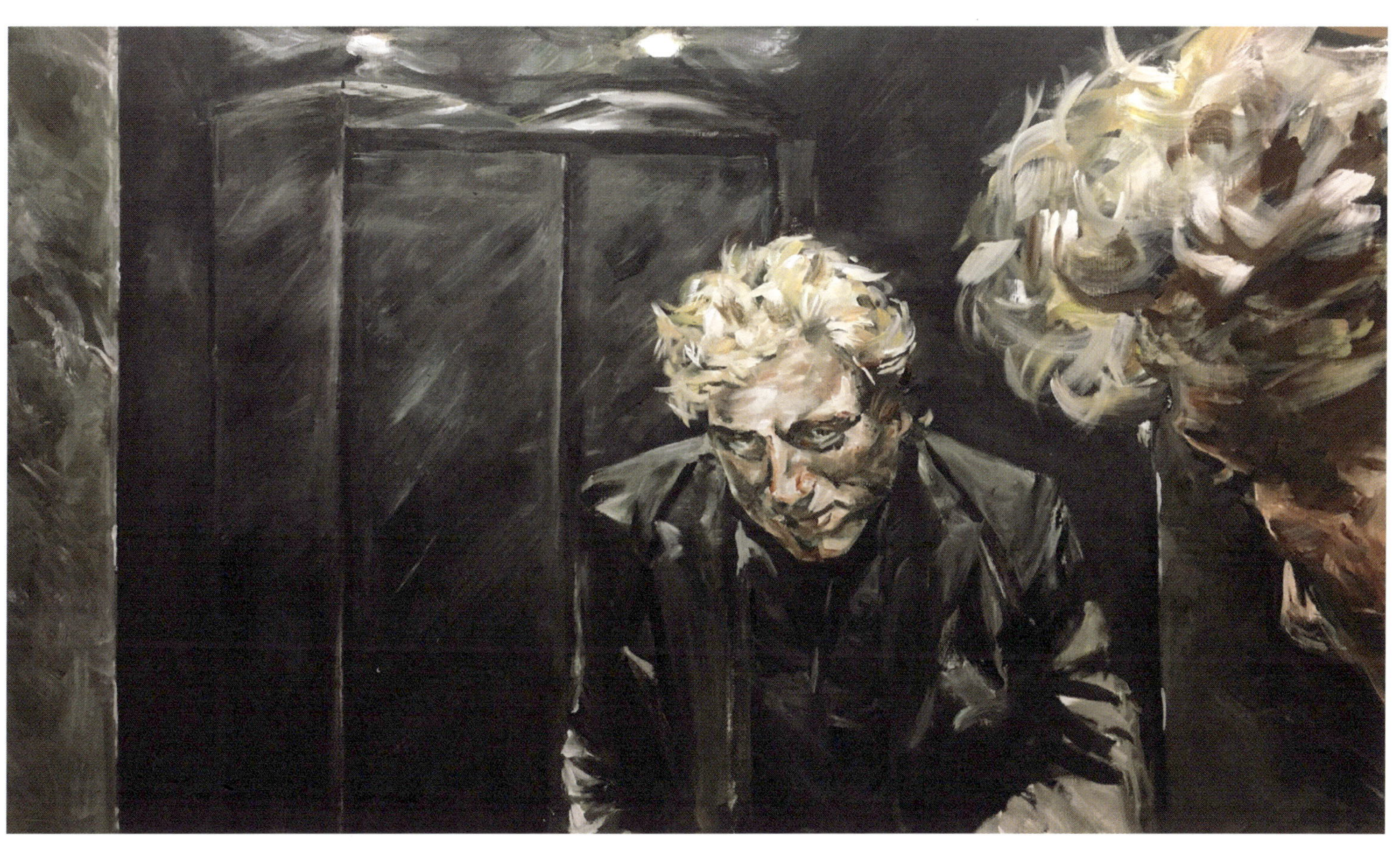

Set the Controls for the Heart of the Sun,
A Journey with Charlotte series,
250 x 150 cm, 2017

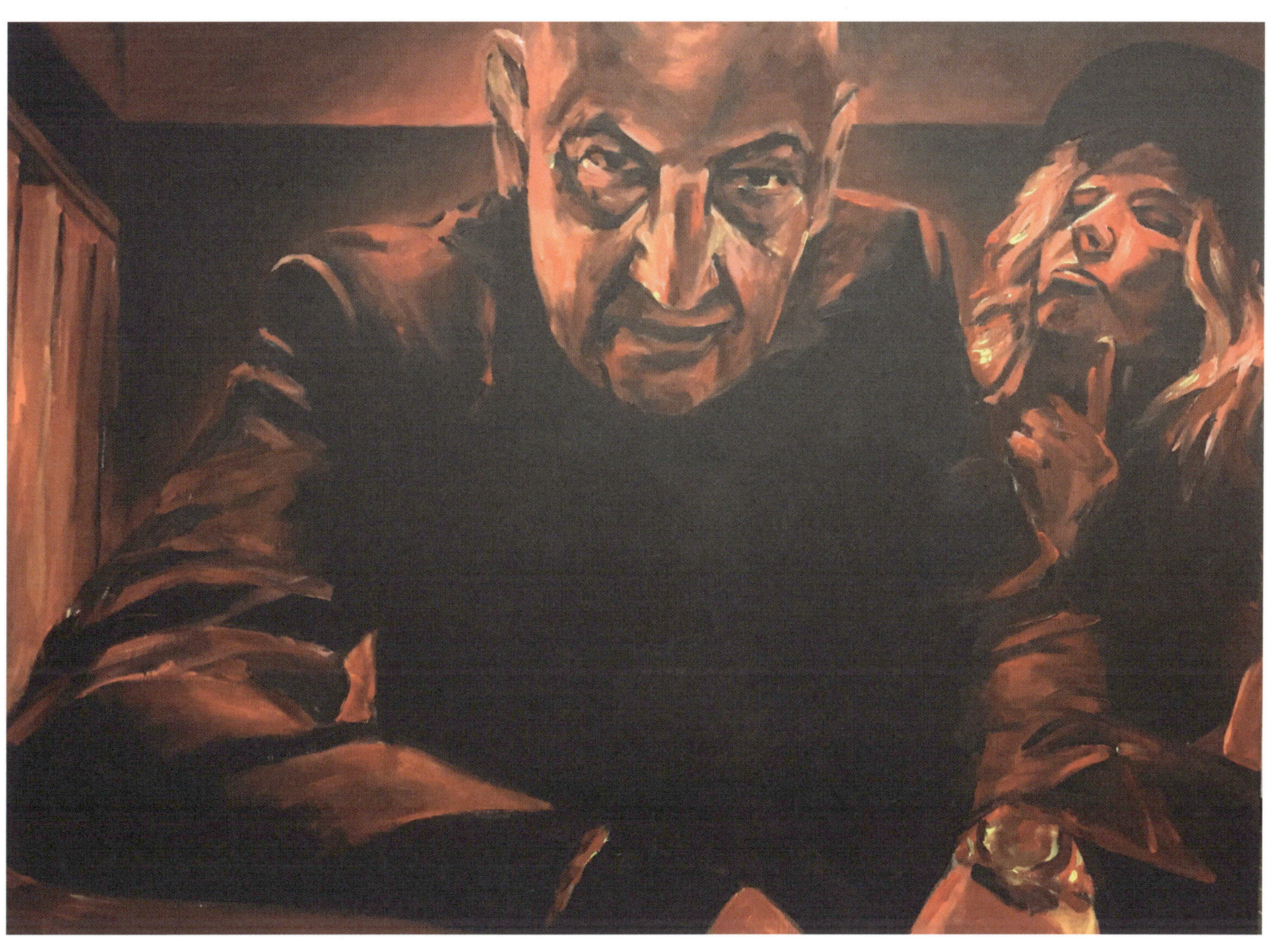

Los niños del parque,
A Journey with Charlotte series,
200 x 150 cm, 2017

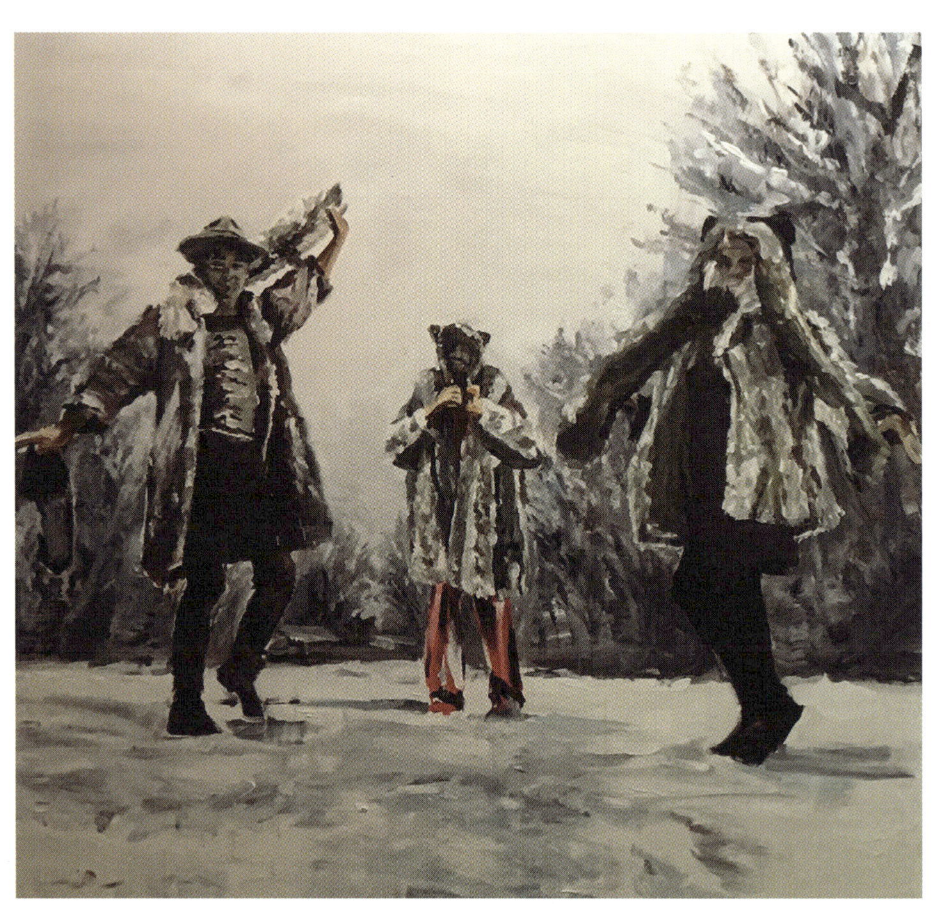

Street Hassle Pt. I,
A Journey with Charlotte series,
150 x 150 cm, 2017

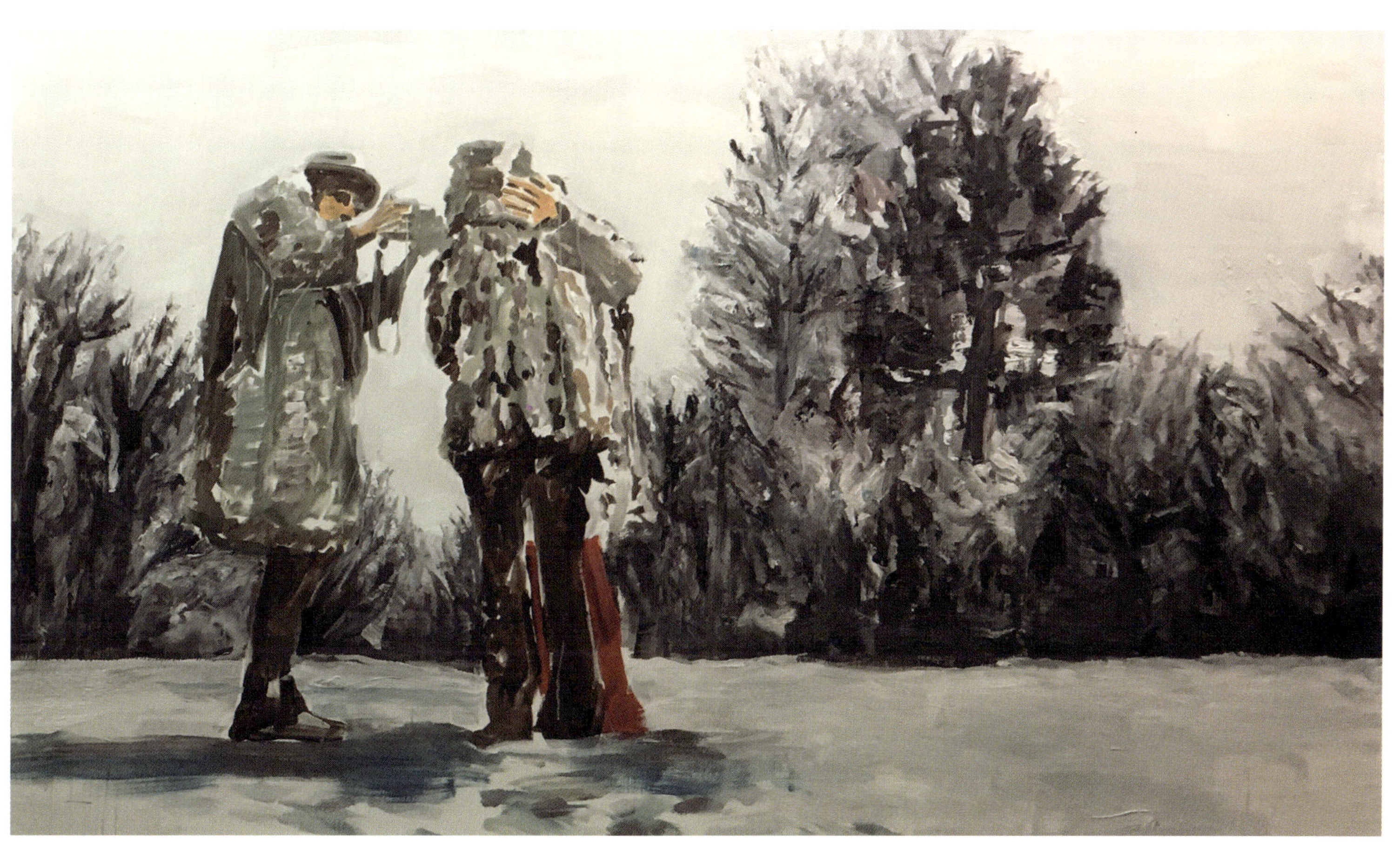

Street Hassle Pt. II,
A Journey with Charlotte series,
250 x 150 cm, 2017

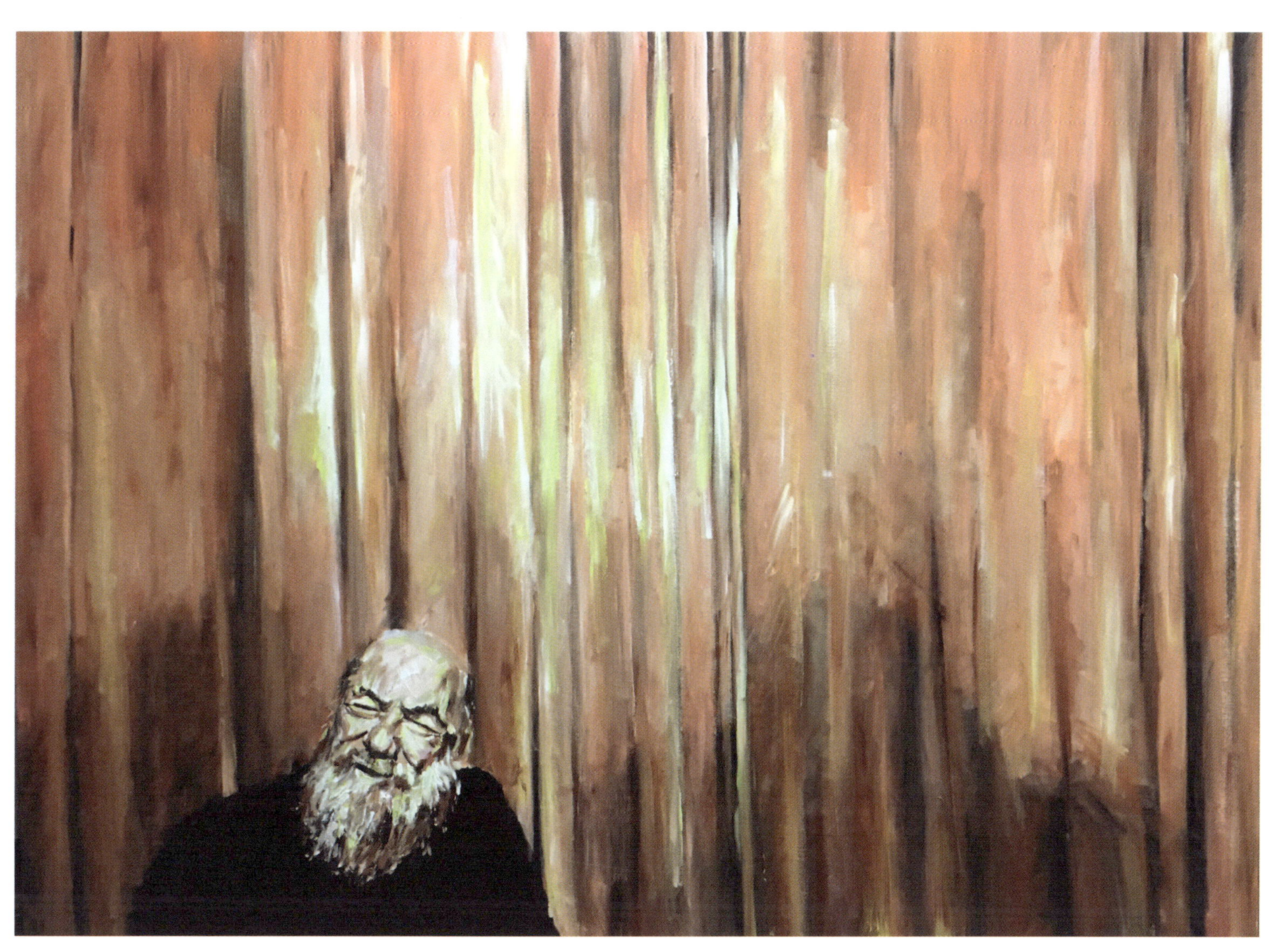

Mellow Yellow,
A Journey with Charlotte series,
200 x 150 cm, 2017

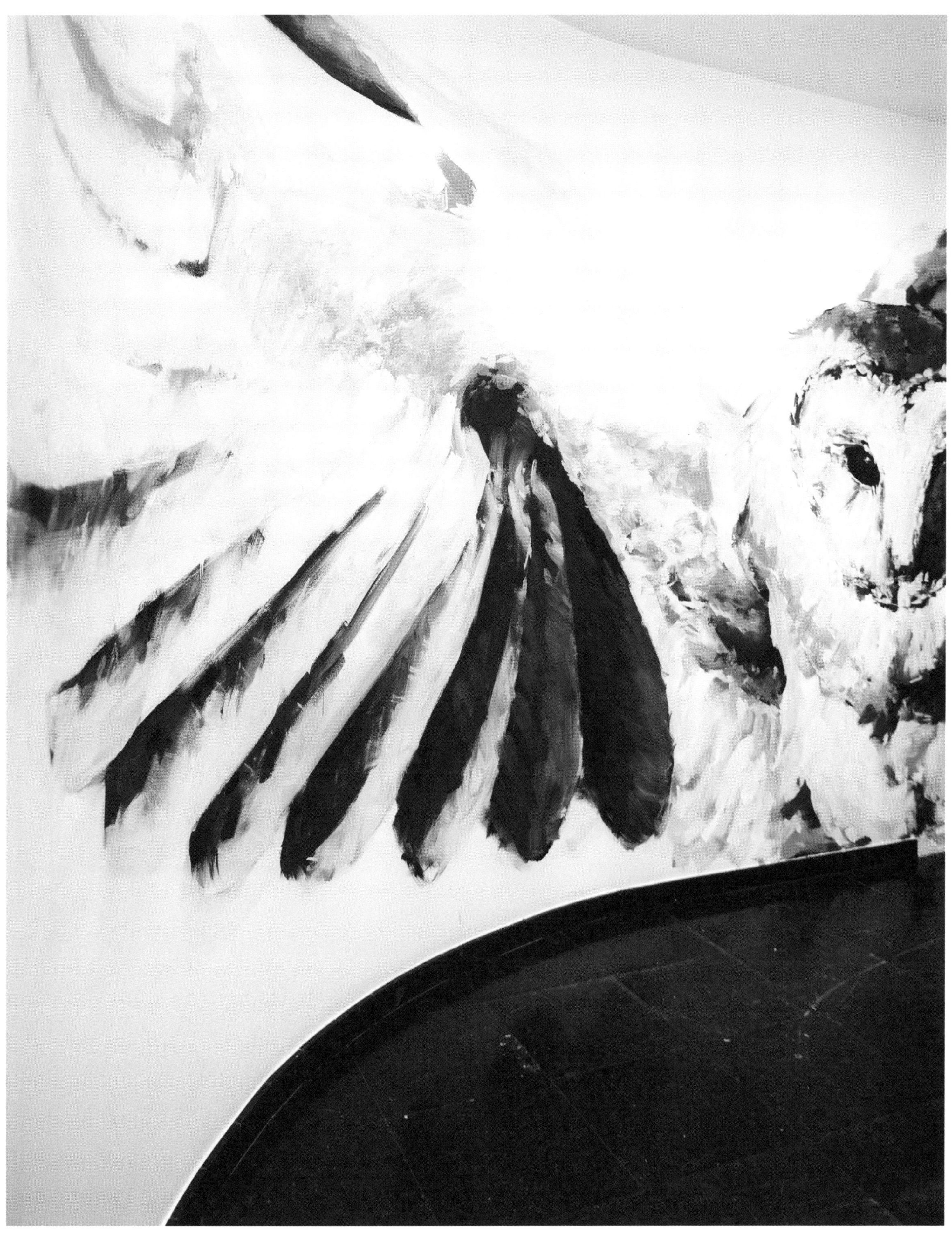

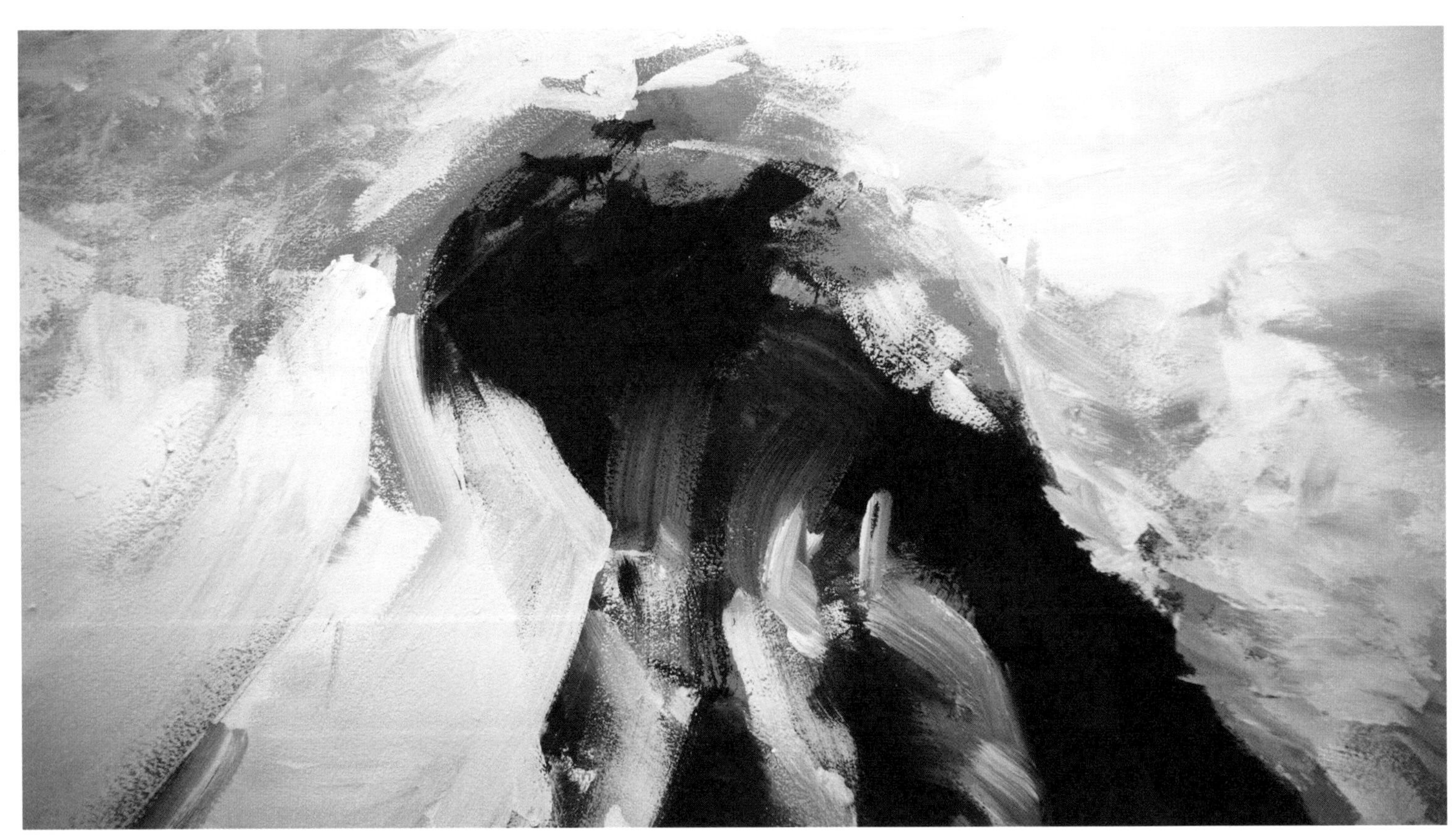

MURALS

Howl (detail), mural (private collection),
300 x 400 cm, 2017, © Kris Lathouwers

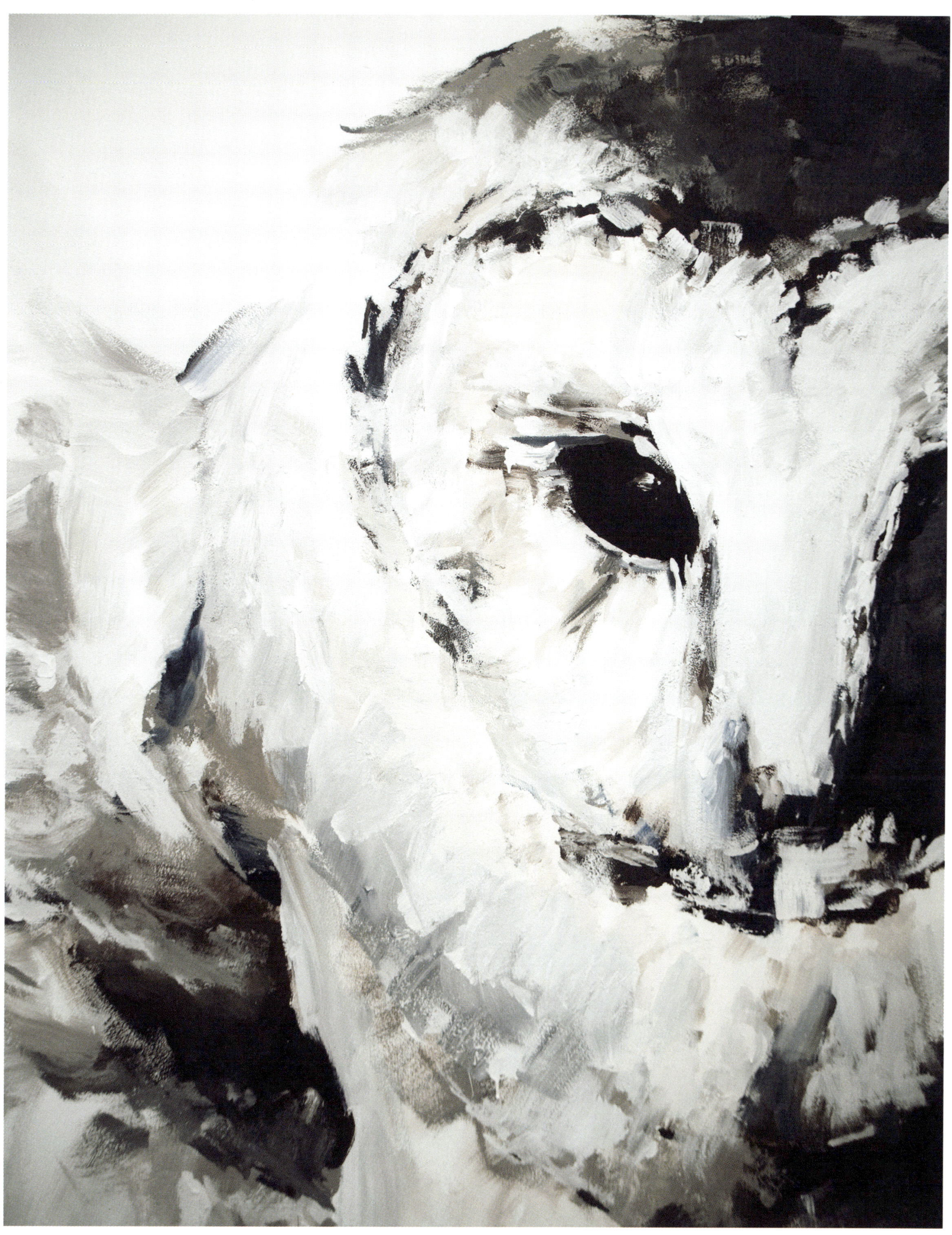

Epilogue

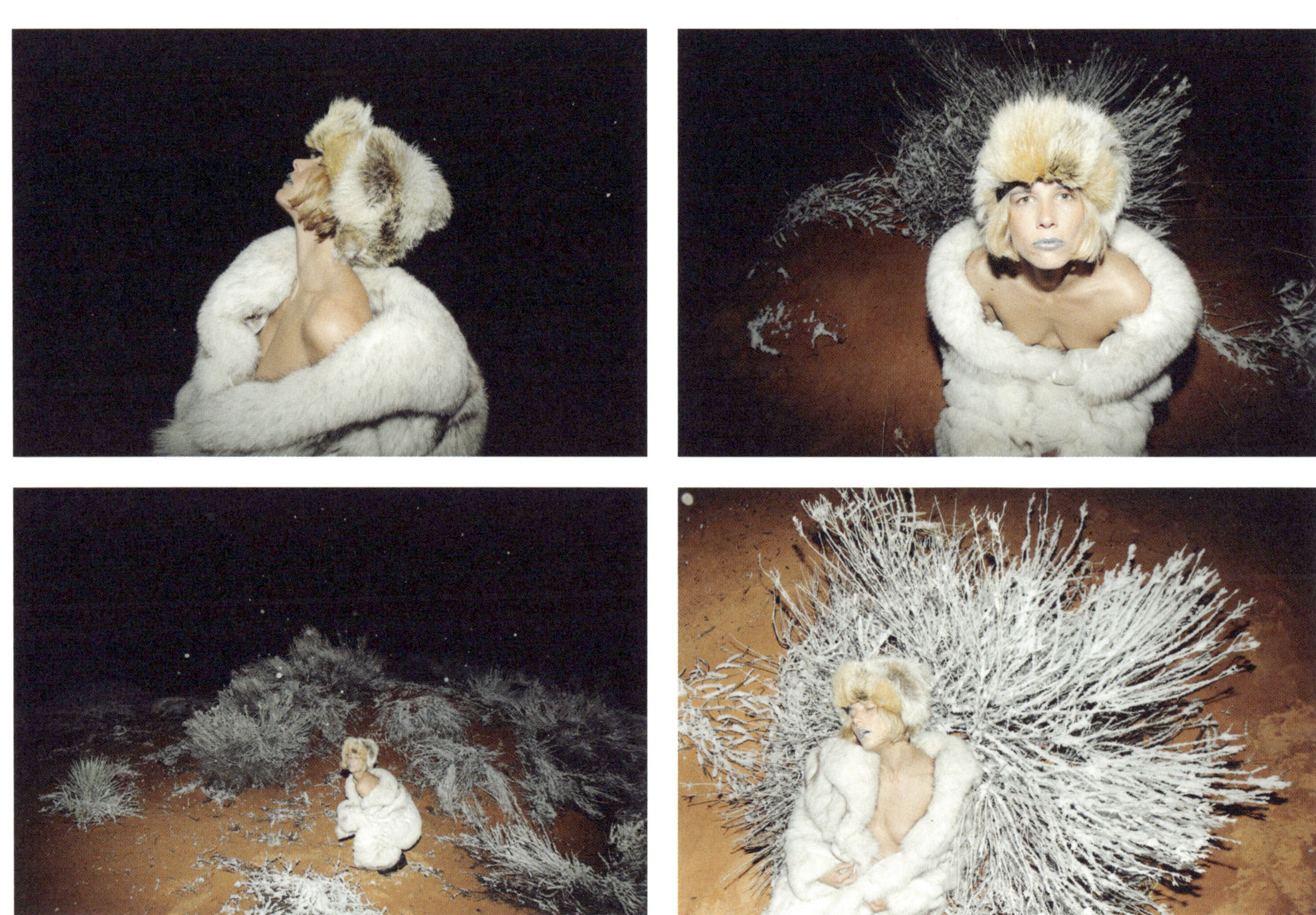

Colophon

www.charlottedecock.be

Texts
Stefan Ashkenazy
Léon Lemahieu
Patrick Kreydt
Charlotte De Cock

Photography
Kris Lathouwers
Mike Steegmans
ARTICLE 17
Sara De Graeve
Kemizz
OOGILLES
Allison Rachel Johnston
Jan Steylemans
Charlotte De Cock
Alessandra Ruyten

Copy-editing
Robert Fulton

Book Design
Jelle Maréchal/Mirror Mirror

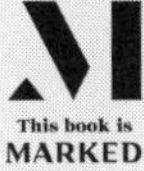

www.marked-books.com
MARKED is an initiative by Lannoo Publishers.

Sign up for our MARKED newsletter with news about
new and forthcoming publications on art, interior
design, food & travel, photography and fashion as
well as exclusive offers and events.

If you have any questions or comments about the
material in this book, please do not hesitate to
contact our editorial team: markedteam@lannoo.com

www.lannoo.com
© Lannoo Publishers, Tielt, 2018
D/2018/45/30 - NUR 642/646
ISBN: 9789401449434

#AREYOUMARKED

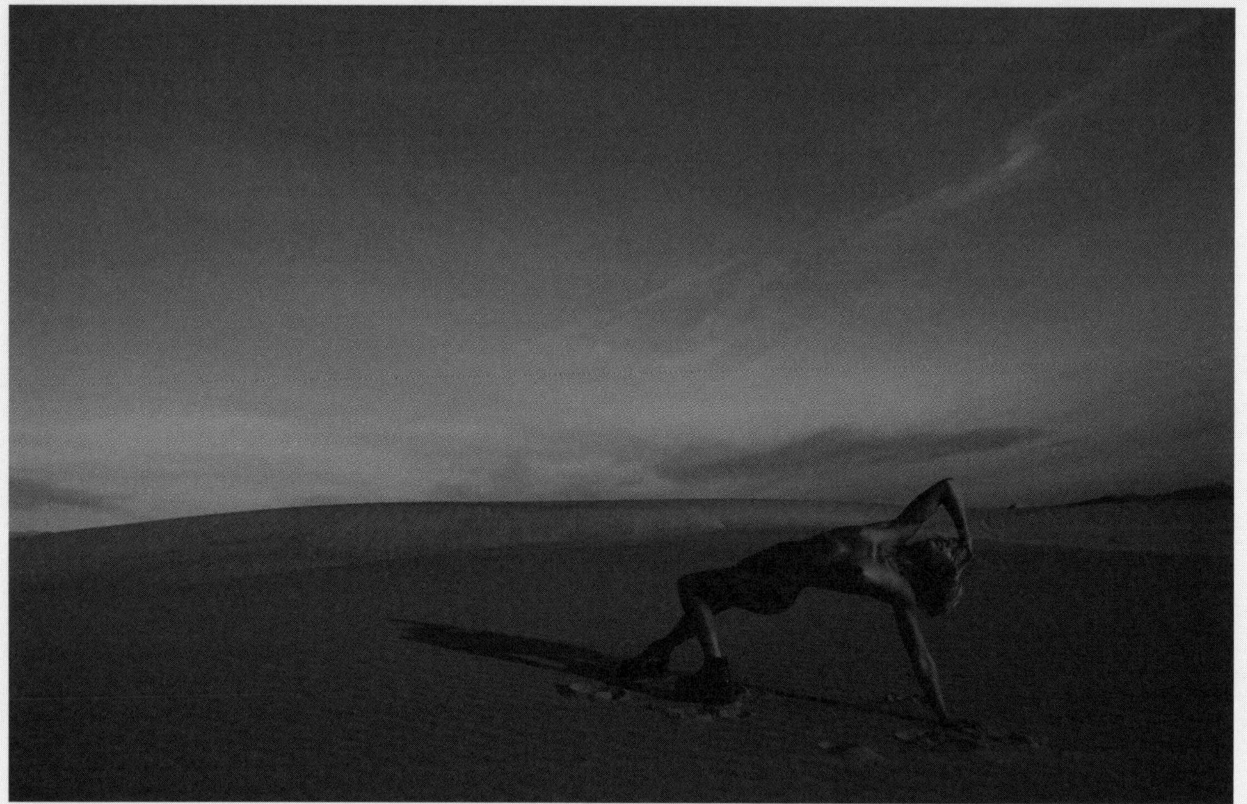

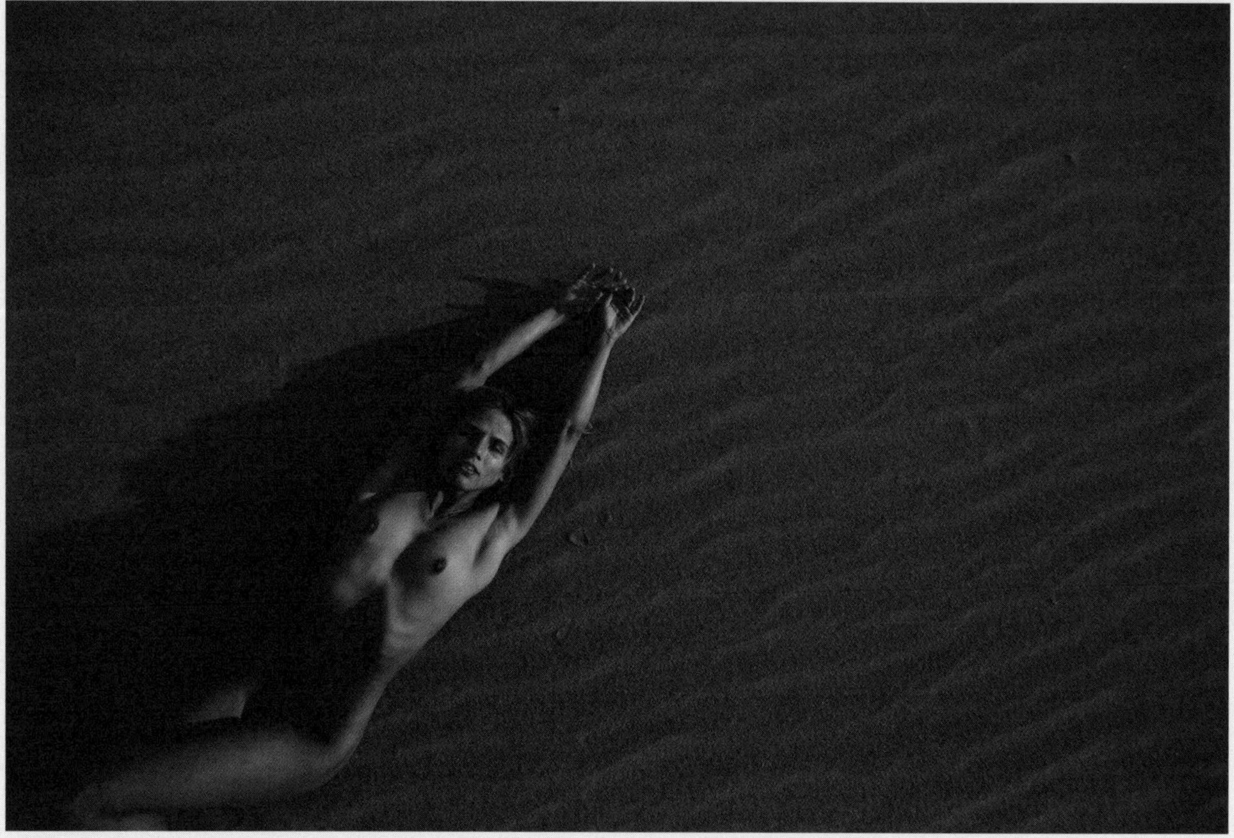

© Kris Lathouwers

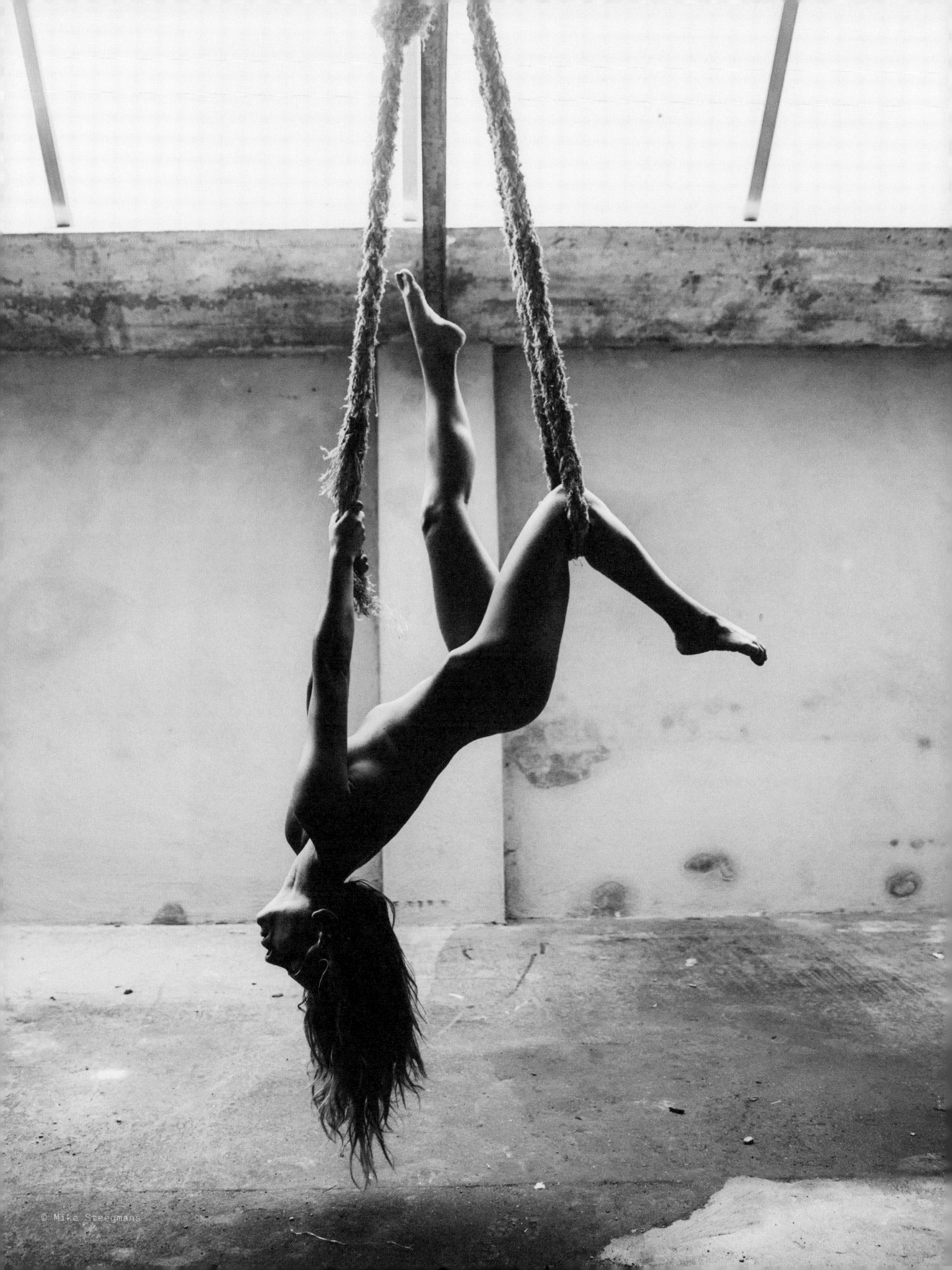
© Mike Steegmans

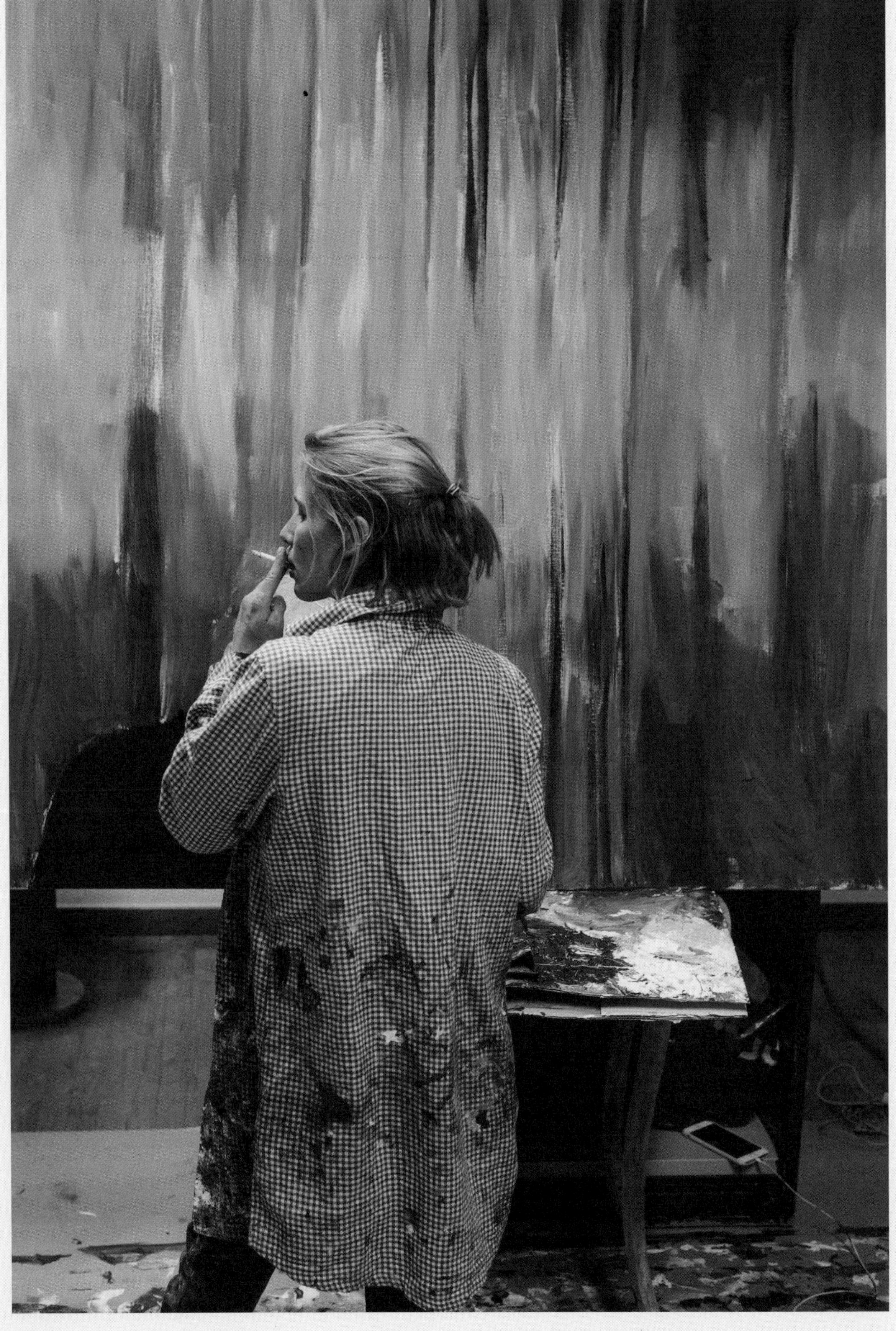

© Kris Lathouwers

    EPILOGUE

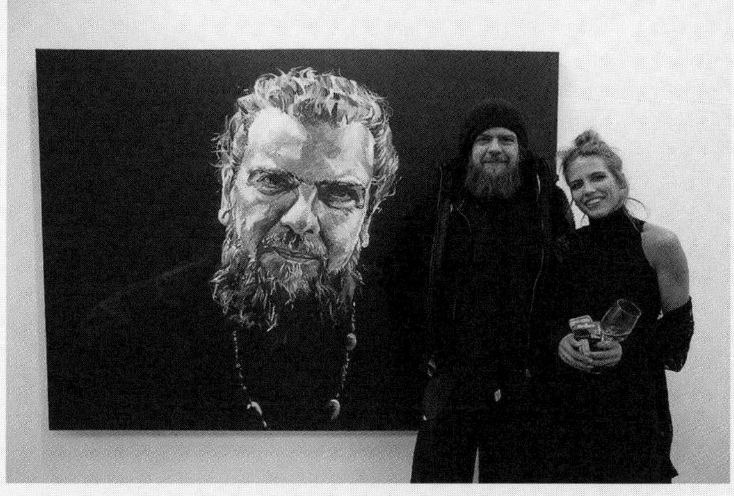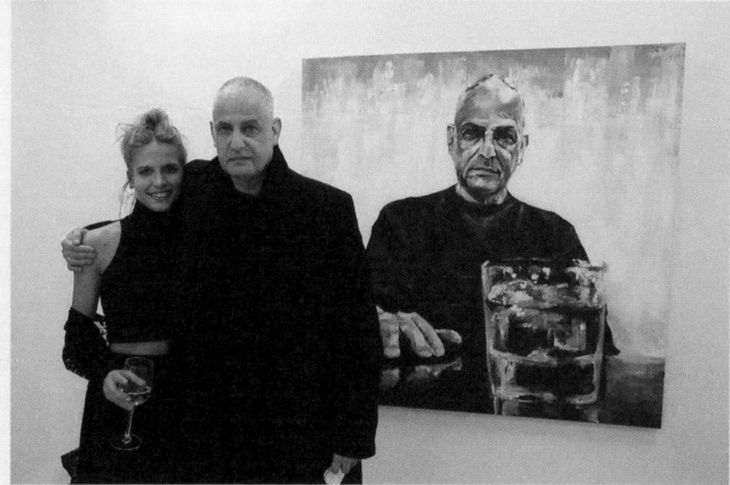

© Allison Rachel Johnstone

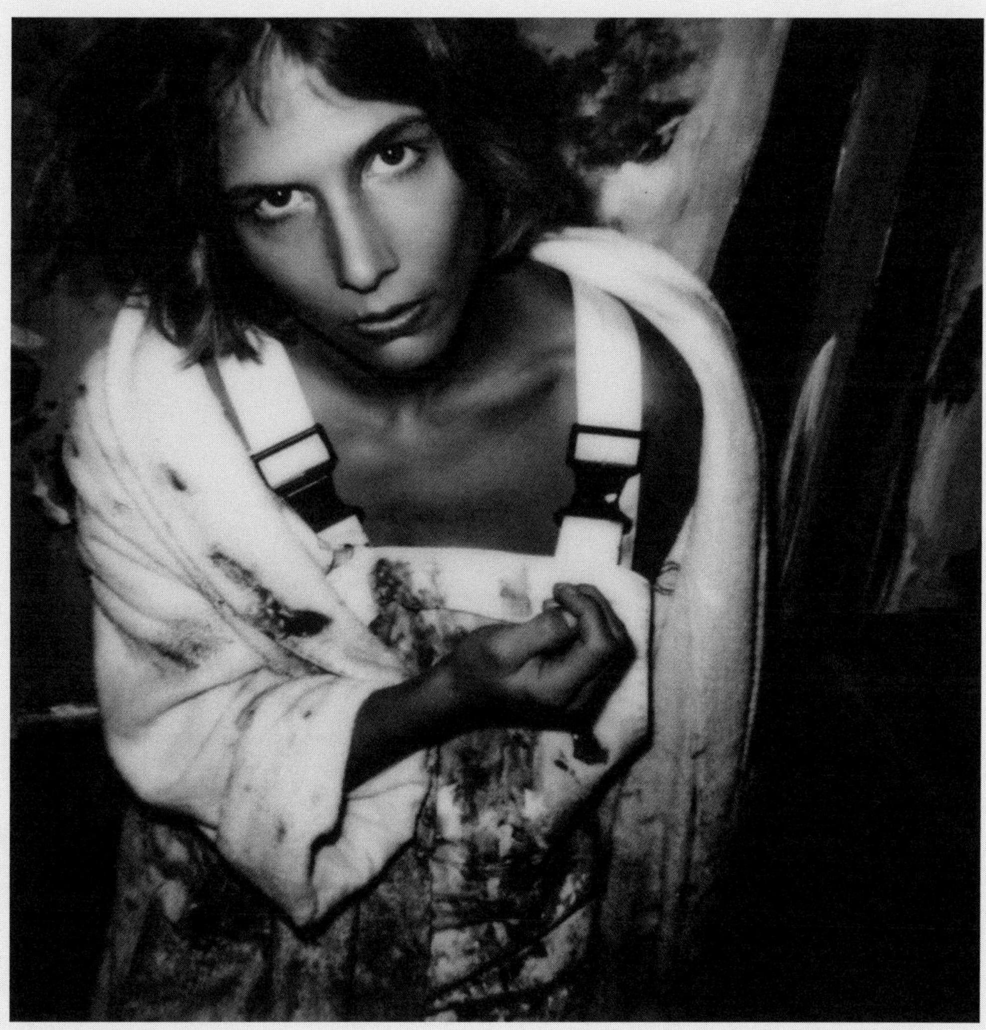

© Alessandra Ruyten

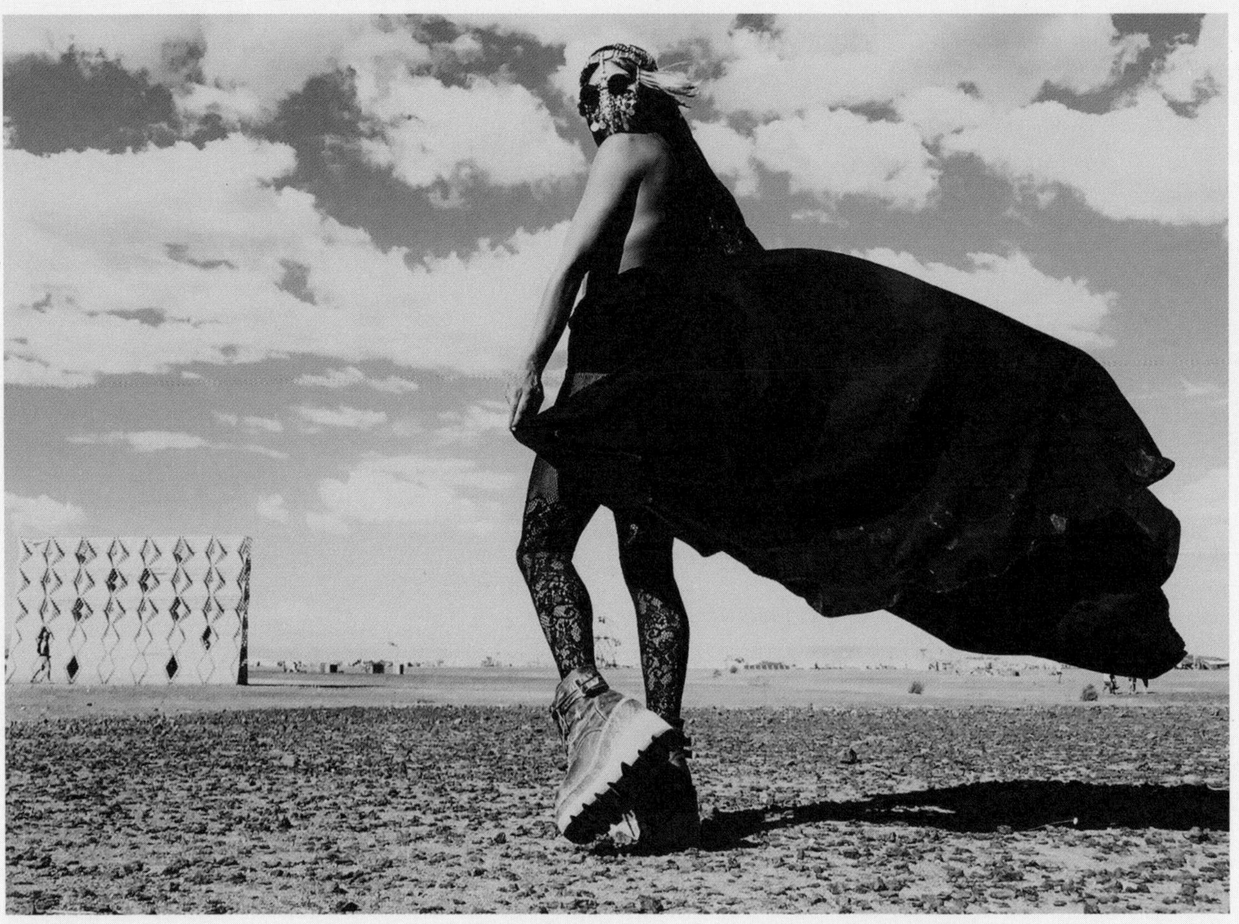

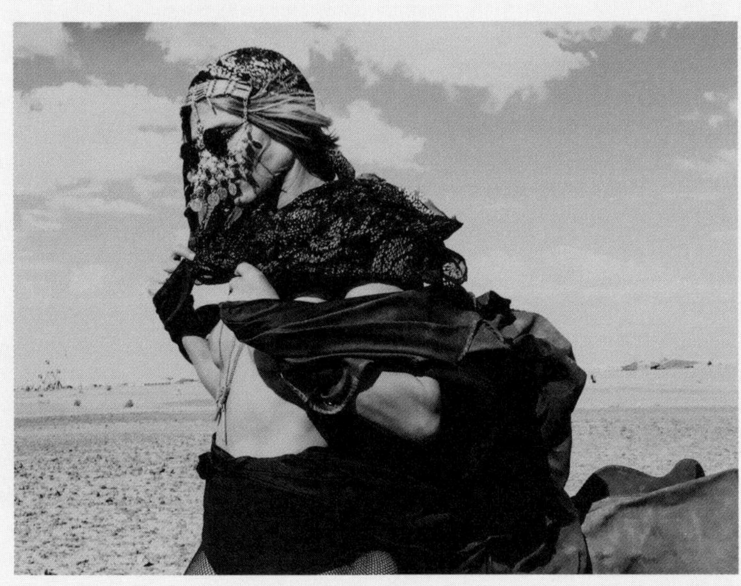

 EPILOGUE

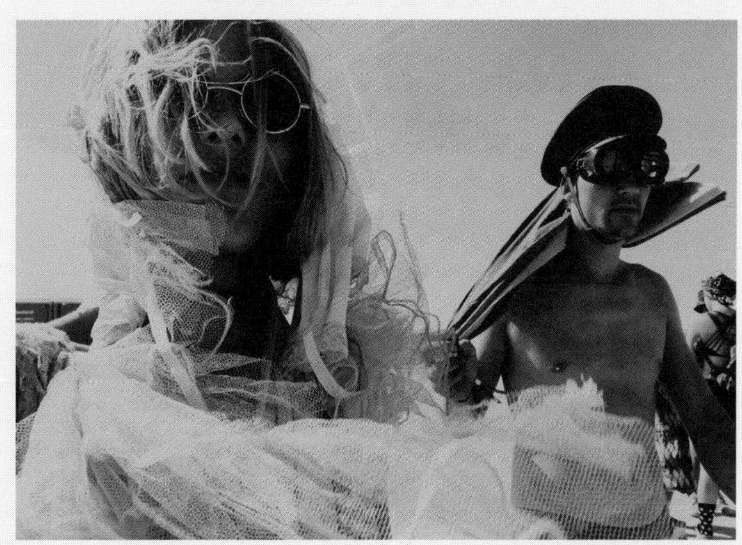

© Charlotte De Cock

© Kris Lathouwers

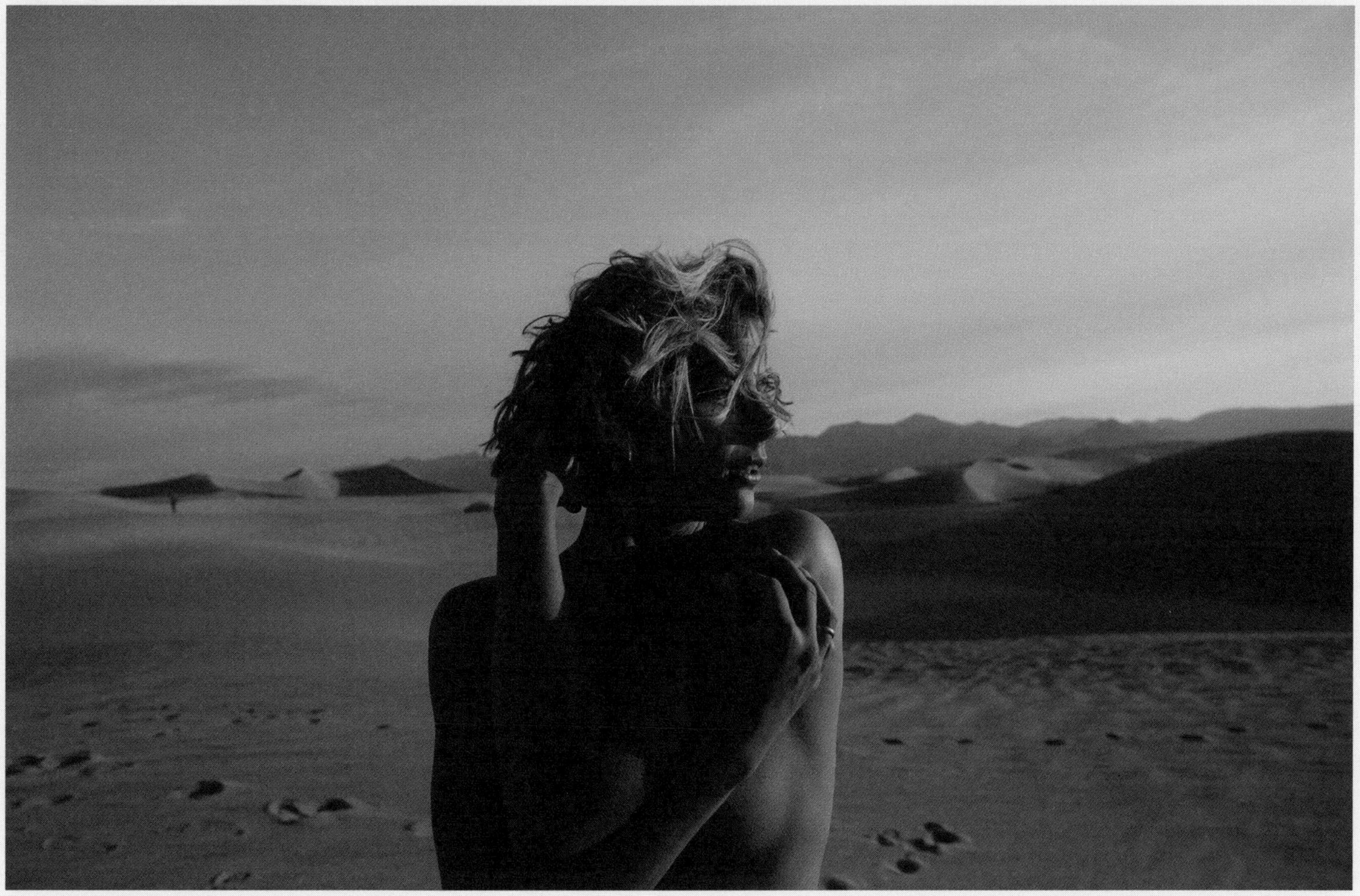

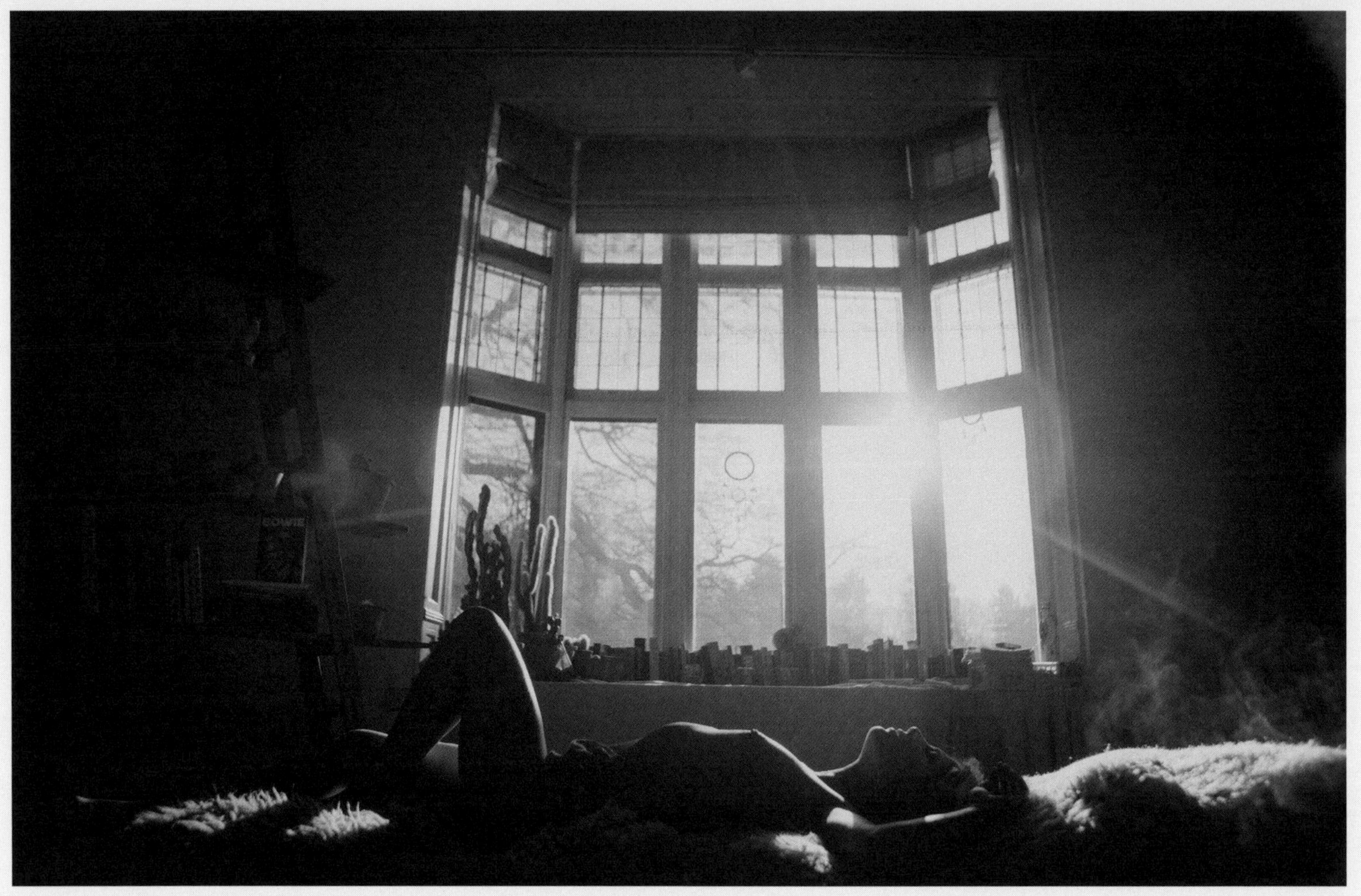

© Kris Lathouwers